CONTEMPORARY CERAMICS

CONTEMPORARY CERAMICS

EMMANUEL COOPER

With 611 color illustrations

Thames & Hudson

For David

page 2: Bertozzi & Casoni, *Intervallo*, 2008, 38 × 36 × 50 cm (15 × 14 × 19½ in.)
Glazed ceramic. Courtesy Sperone Westwater Gallery, New York

First published in 2009 in hardcover in the United States of America by Thames & Hudson Inc.,
500 Fifth Avenue, New York, New York 10110

thamesandhudsonusa.com

Library of Congress Catalog Card Number 2008912007

ISBN 978-0-500-51487-0

Printed and bound in China by SNP Leefung Printers Ltd

CONTENTS

INTRODUCTION

This book presents some 600 objects that reflect the energy, vitality, skill and innovation of contemporary artists working with clay today. Many use traditional techniques and processes, others explore new technologies using familiar materials. The artists – using the term in its broadest sense to include potters, ceramists, sculptors, designer-makers and designer-producers – come from many countries around the world, though the selection is not intended in any sense to be representative other than to reflect the range of current practice. Ceramics encompass a diverse range of possibilities, which extend from functional/useful pieces that continue a long tradition and often make historical references to works that have no concern with function but with what Howard Risatti calls 'critical objects of craft'.[1] Individually, the objects illustrated address universal and relevant cultural, social, personal and even political issues.

A few years ago *Contemporary Ceramics* would have presented a very different picture. There would, for example, have been little evidence of installation work or of collaboration between ceramists and industry. The huge diversity of current work with clay presented in this book serves as an indicator of profound change within this area of visual art practice, ranging as it does from potters making pots to sculptors modelling figures, all of whom choose to work with clay because it is the medium that is intrinsic to their ideas. Much of the work illustrated suggests the breaking down of the groupings of conceptual and figurative art, traditional craft and innovative design, which continue to fragment the world of aesthetic and functional objects.

RETHINKING CLAY

Grayson Perry's success in winning the Turner Prize in 2003 marked a seismic shift in the perception of ceramics, particularly in the world

REBECCA WARREN
Pony, 2003, h 94 cm (37 in.)
Reinforced clay, acrylic paint and plinth

of fine art, and its reverberations were felt around the globe. With the pot having found a place within such a high-profile event, ceramics – or even pottery – could not again be easily relegated to a more modest status, but the success was hard won. As Perry wryly remarked, coming out as a potter was far more challenging than coming out as a transvestite. While the international success of one potter does not make a summer, Perry's award of the most prestigious prize in the art world is part of a loosening of attitudes to craft that has found echoes in many countries.

The reasons for the loosening of these attitudes are complex but relevant. The decline of the grip of modernism on the wider art world allowed for a more pluralistic view, with artists generally feeling increasingly able to look at other materials, to investigate other ways of working. The rise of the so-called Pattern and Decoration Movement in painting encouraged a wider vocabulary of forms, surfaces and techniques, particularly from the world of decorative artists, which had previously been seen as beyond the pale. Tentatively, painters and sculptors began to make furniture, ceramics and embroidery and show them within fine-art contexts. The line that was once finely drawn between the fine and applied arts started to blur, though change was slow. Some of this change is evident in national and international exhibitions. In addition to Perry, UK artist Rebecca Warren was a Turner Prize nominee for her figurative work with clay. Ceramics have also made appearances at the Venice Biennale. The work of Chinese artist Liu Jianhua was featured in 2003, Jennifer Allora and Guillermo Calzadilla's hippopotamus in unfired clay found a place in 2005 and Bertozzi & Casoni in 2007.

Contemporary ceramic work includes divergent areas as artists are lured by the plastic and tactile qualities of the material itself, for,

unlike most other areas of creative activity, artists who work with clay have been largely defined by their chosen medium. At art school, for instance, students who study ceramics work in one of the few subject areas referenced to the material. By contrast, fine artists, sculptors, designers and photographers are defined by their activities and concepts and approach their creative work free to choose the processes, techniques and materials that seem most appropriate. The focus on material has had the effect of opening ceramics to a wide range of expressions, which may include considerations of function, engineering and construction, design and aesthetics, all of which call on different languages but have the material – clay – in common.

Each of these areas has its own relationship with history and tradition, to which practitioners may respond or ignore. Whether artists choose to address or cast aside the long and evocative traditions of clay is up to the individual, but it is a history redolent with powerful metaphorical and pictorial references, for of all the materials used by artists none is as potent as clay in conjuring up myth and legend. This, according to the gods, is the ubiquitous material from which we are all made.

JENNIFER ALLORA AND
GUILLERMO CALZADILLA
Hope Hippo, 2005,
approx. 488 × 183 × 152 cm
(192 × 72 × 60 in.)
Mud, whistle, daily newspaper,
live performer

Prometheus is said to have taken mud from the river bed and stolen fire from the hearth of Zeus to animate the messy creature that he modelled.

In Egyptian legend the God Khum is depicted as creating man on the potter's wheel. In the Bible God is the creator, the ultimate maker, 'Yet, O Lord, you are our Father. We are the clay, you are the potter; we are all the work of your hand' (Isaiah, 64:8). In the Qu'ran God is described as making the human form from aged clay, while references to clay in the *Rubaiyat of Omar Khayyam* pose such eternal questions as, 'Who is the potter, pray, and who the pot?' The metaphor of the pot as man and the potter as God occurs in much literature, while the shaping of a vessel on the wheel has taken on many meanings, the spinning form often seen to suggest the rotating earth itself. The concept of clay – the 'human clay' to use W. H. Auden's evocative praise – readily serves as a metaphor for the human vessel and continues to inform much current work.[2]

This book deals with objects – vessels, urns, tableware, installations and both abstract and figurative sculpture – all of which reflect current practice within ceramics, offering analysis as well as image. Rather than adopt a chronological approach, or one based on particular geographical areas, the book is organized by themes around a broad topic. In deciding on the presentation of the work I have drawn on the ideas of the philosopher Gilles Deleuze and the psychoanalyst Félix Guattari and their concept of the rhizome. This rejects hierarchical organization in favour of 'rhizomatic' growth, a term that suggests multiple nodes of activity indicating a mapping rather than a tracing, multiple options rather than any single direction. According to Deleuze, 'the map fosters connections between fields and is open and connectable in all its dimensions.'[3]

Yet, however broad or concise the analysis, it gives rise to the problem of 'placing' much of the work, which could sit within several groupings. I have chosen the ones that seems most appropriate but many could easily sit elsewhere. In addition, some artists produce more than one type of work that may, for instance, include functional form and sculptural objects. For this reason some artists appear in more than one chapter.

Most of the work illustrated has been produced within the last few years. The opening chapter is devoted to a discussion of tableware, or domestic ware as it is often called. It considers what inspires potters to continue to produce such work and discusses the ideas that inform it. The chapter also questions why, at a time when industrial production has become more diverse and engaging, potters still feel the need to continue making functional pots. It also looks at the broad range of influences, be it metal work, traditional slip-decorating techniques, the elegance of Song porcelain or the drama of *anagama* and salt-glaze stoneware firings. While many ceramists acknowledge tradition, all create work that is fresh, vibrant and modern. The chapter concludes that handmade tableware continues to offer a satisfying product for both the maker and the user.[4]

The chapter on decorative wares – objects that are based around the idea of the vessel but which do not address use in a direct way – debates the humanist qualities of clay. It discusses why such work, with its allusions to familiar, everyday forms, constitute the majority of ceramics made. It also looks at the range of ideas that lies behind the forms and asks why such work is often seen as 'self-explanatory', requiring little or no discussion, even suggesting that critical writing about ceramics hinders the enjoyment of the qualities of the piece.

LUCIE RIE
Breakfast Service, c. 1955
Stoneware, tin glaze and
manganese pigment

The chapter argues that, far from being 'self-explanatory', the work is part of a thoughtful language that involves technical, social and aesthetic considerations.

The third chapter looks at the way clay is used as a sculptural medium, at individual objects that use the qualities of the material as an essential part of the expressive qualities of the work. It includes figurative work as well as more abstract forms, placing it within a wider sculptural context. It considers the wide range of ideas that inform the work, whether they are political, environmental, autobiographical or social and discusses the sorts of issues raised that can be physical and sensual as well as intellectual or even confrontational.

The fourth chapter focuses on the way some artists working with clay have moved towards installation as a way of exploring ideas freed from the notion of product or production, aspects often seen as an intrinsic part of ceramics. The chapter steers a path through the different approaches, be they site-specific, site-sensitive, interventions or multi-media environments.

The fifth chapter focus on the often highly creative work produced by creative partnerships between the ceramic industry and individual ceramic artists/designers. Partly as a way of identifying new markets and partly because of the ceramist's understanding of the material, industry has commissioned and/or worked with potters and designers to produce inventive, often unconventional objects that combine function with sculptural qualities. While the groupings within the five chapters are a useful means of addressing current concerns, this structure is not intended to be definitive as, in many cases, objects could be readily placed in a variety of contexts. A reference section lists the biographical details of featured artists and contains a commentary either in the form of an 'artist's statement' or critical comment.

Part of the 'coming of age' of ceramics, challenging the perception that clay = craft, has seen the beginnings of a critical language for looking at and analysing ceramic objects; this critical language provides ways to explore the various 'meanings' ceramics embody and, possibly, to identify their historical and modern contexts. This critical language may call on aspects of literature, philosophy, politics, aesthetics and tradition to broaden and deepen our understanding of the qualities of modern work. Books on the history of ceramics, individual monographs, biographies of major ceramists, magazines and journals have all added different elements to this writing.

This book offers an in-depth introduction to a wide-ranging and diverse area of creative activity. It is copiously referenced with text that identifies the range of ideas and philosophies that inspired – and continue to inspire – ceramists. It also looks at the broader concerns around perceptions of ceramics today. In its comprehensive, international coverage the book affirms ceramics as a major contributor to the visual arts with work that is accessible, aesthetically expressive and visually engaging.

1 Howard Risatti, *A Theory of Craft: Function and Aesthetic Expression*, University of North Carolina Press, Chapel Hill, 2007, p. 302.
2 The phrase occurs in W. H. Auden's long poem *Letter to Lord Byron* which reads, 'To me Art's subject is the human clay'.
3 Quoted in Clarrie Wallis, 'Abstract Machines', in *Nick Evans: Abstract Machines*, Tate St Ives, 2007, p. 13.
4 This point is elegantly and passionately expressed in *NeoCraft: Modernity and the Crafts*, Sandra Alfoldy (ed.), The Nova Scotia College of Art and Design Press, Halifax, 2007, by Alfoldy who writes, 'The crafts can stand as oppositional forces against global homogenization, capitalism, and mass production: they are deeply satisfying to makers; they forge intimate connections with; they are essential to tourist economies and generate governmental support for creative industries users and consumers; they are tools used to define national and personal identities.'

CHAPTER ONE

BEYOND UTILITY

The Useful Pot

preceding pages: **NATASHA DAINTRY**
Small Ocean, 2007, 225 small pots,
approx. 110 × 100 cm (43¼ × 39¼ in.)
Porcelain, thrown, palest to deepest
acid yellow glazes

below: **JEONG YONG HAN**
Bowl, 2007
Porcelain, reduction-fired

right: **CLIVE BOWEN**
Three Tall Jugs, 2006,
41 × 20 cm (16 × 7¾ in.)
Red earthenware, thrown, poured
black and white slip with green
trailing, wood-fired. Green slip, finger
combed; black and gold with white
slip trailing

opposite: **JOHN LEACH**
Muchelney Kitchenware, 2007
Stoneware, wood-fired, from the
catalogue range

*Handmade tableware objects are like the Trojan Horse. Making
tableware is a way of smuggling 'dangerous' objects into people's lives
without them noticing. They seem initially as unthreatening, familiar
objects which one can get close to, hold and handle, yet they are
dangerous because they can affect people and change them in ways
they are unaware of and cannot control.*

Edmund de Waal

THE ABSURD

Whichever way it is looked at, there is something decidedly paradoxical
about studio potters making tableware in the twenty-first century,
appearing to compete against the ceramic industry, which, after years of
stagnation, has begun to revolutionize itself in terms of style and variety.
It was a paradox recognized by the potter Hans Coper, who, in a letter
about his work sent to the Victoria and Albert Museum in London forty
years ago, wrote eloquently about the situation in which he saw himself.
'Practising a craft with ambiguous reference to function one has occasionally to face absurdity. More than anything, like a demented piano
tuner, one is trying to approximate phantom pitch. One is apt to take
refuge in principles which crumble.'

Despite the difficulties of
making useful pots, after a falling
off in interest by studio potters in
the 1990s, there are signs that
producing such work is seen as
viable and attractive, and the
ceramists are prepared to face
accusations of the absurd. By continuing to make useful or functional
pots, studio potters are following in the footsteps of their artisan fore-
bears who, for several hundred years, produced pots that were made
not because the potter wanted to make them but because they fulfilled
a need, their purpose and intention recognized by the communities
within which they worked. But, as Gaston Bachelard points out, 'Man
is a creation of desire, not a creation of need',[1] times change, things nor
people remain the same.

After the onset of the industrial production of useful pots, the
role of the artisan potter began to fade away; because they worked
by hand they were unable to compete in terms of price or efficiency.
With the advent of studio potters – or to use Bernard Leach's term
'artist potters' – the skills and techniques of artisan potters were
appropriated, and far from attempting to compete with industry,
they realized that they, like all artists, worked because of their own
need for creative expression. This presented them with the challenge
of creating work that people desired rather than needed.

STATUS

The utopian ideal of combining function with sculpture, elevating
everyday objects to the status of art, has a long and noble history,
whether in Ancient Greece or Dynastic China. Today, the situation
around the world is different: the role of the potter more ambiguous
and less fixed, concerned with creating rather than meeting need and
therefore seen as a luxury and indulgence. Nevertheless, potters who
make functional ware want it to speak directly; as the Canadian potter
Bruce Cochrane says, his intention is 'to make pottery that continues

to engage the user, to intrigue and satisfy with repeated exposure, and to provide a sense of the making and a connection to the maker'.[2]

Successful tableware made by studio potters does far more than serve as containers for keeping food off the table. Not only is it likely to be a thing of beauty in its own right, but also, more importantly, it carries the personality of the maker, something that, however well made, an industrially produced pot can never do. The handmade pot is perceived as carrying the potter's 'thumb print', a romantic but evocative association that transmits a powerful sense of the maker's life. Many ceramists today find such an association makes them uneasy for, while accepting the qualities of the handmade as a crucial part of their work, they do not want it to look consciously crafted, rustic in style or in any sense consciously contrived.[3]

Discussions of contemporary craft tend to shy away from issues such as function as seemingly too outdated, preferring to regard handmade objects intended for use as having social, aesthetic or even poetic significance. As any maker of tableware will assert, the potential to produce beautifully conceived, well-made and thoughtful ware is just as possible with their work as it is for decorative or sculptural pieces; functional pots, they argue, can be quietly or loudly expressive and as meaningful as other art forms.

ARTISAN/ARTIST

In reality, as stated earlier, what studio potters can never do is vie with factory-made objects. When Pierre-Aimé Normandeau was appointed as the first ceramics teacher in Quebec at the Ecole des beaux-arts in Montreal, spearheading the pottery revival, he was adamant that there was an essential difference between studio and factory production. 'The one cardinal rule', he cautioned, 'is not to try to compete with machine-made ware'.[4] Putting his advice into action he proposed an artistic rather than an artisan approach, advocating that students use the wheel thoughtfully rather than aiming for speed.

While, in terms of pure function, handmade tableware appears to offer a meaningful alternative to industrially manufactured ware, it can rarely rival it in price – potters would need to produce hundreds of thousands of pieces to even begin to be competitive. Nor could such production compete in terms of efficiency. Industrially produced pots are uniform and consistent in shape, size, weight, finish and surface quality; they are usually, but not always, light in weight. Such qualities may simplify marketing but, despite the recent upsurge in imaginative design, they do little to lessen the impersonal aspects of the work.[5]

In the late 1980s and 1990s a new generation of potters, who found the romantic idyll of the country potter not only too restrictive but also physically demanding with little financial reward, sought to broaden Leach's ideas as a way of exploring more expressive work and of reaching new markets. Some, such as Janice Tchalenko, rejected the established orthodoxy about earth tones, brightening and enlivening her pots by introducing a range of blues, yellows and red glazes trailed onto her tableware in intriguing patterns. She also collaborated with industry to produce colourful pots in quantity. Generally there was a move towards more adventurous decoration, fiercely rejecting Adolf Loos's strictures on the horrors of unnecessary ornament by moving towards bright, colourful pots

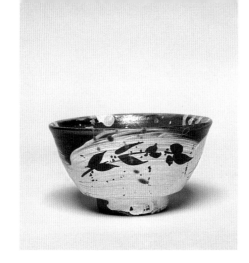

right: JIM MALONE
Bowl, 2007, dia 17.5 cm (6¾ in.)
Stoneware, thrown, brushed slip,
iron painting

far right: WALTER KEELER
Green Cut Branch Teapot, 2005,
h 26 cm (10¼ in.)
Earthenware, thrown, extruded,
press-moulded, modelled

with brushed, painted or sprayed decoration, some of which explored the use of transfer or decal patterns. Technological advances resulted in high temperature reds and yellows, which further stimulated more daring responses.

The potter Clive Bowen, a highly respected maker of wood-fired earthenware in the UK, acknowledged the value of making tableware in quantity when he wrote, 'It is only through making constantly, repetitively, that I can achieve the fluency to make the sort of pieces I want. I think this is the only way my work can ever stand up against the pots made by unknown craftsmen of the past. I see them as "the competition", the yardstick against which my pots will be judged.'[6] Annie Hewett, Catherine Vanier, Paul Young and Nick Chapman offer their own interpretations of slip-decorated earthenware, giving the pieces fresh friendly qualities. In their slipware Michael and Victoria Eden take this concept further by contrasting areas of colour and unglazed clay body to introduce illusionistic elements of thrown forms. Walter Keeler, followed by Jane Hamlyn and others, investigated the rich surface textures of salt-glaze stoneware, while Keeler later looked to wares produced in Stoke-on-Trent in the eighteenth century as a way of looking at shape, decoration and colour.

Linda Christianson, Malcolm Davis, Mark Shapiro and Jack Troy are among the potters who use salt, soda and wood-firing to reveal the structure of the pots. Potters such as Lisa Hammond, working primarily on the wheel, continue to refine and hone ideas around tableware in soda firings, while William Plumptre uses decoration to heighten awareness of the form. The pots, inevitably, are seen to carry much of the character of the maker. With sensitivity

and restraint, their work combines the finest qualities of the hand-made, which owe little to fashion or modish production.

Equally alluring are the salt-kissed jugs and serving bowls made by potters such as Jeremy Steward, Rob Bernard and Jim Malone, all of whom fire in a wood-burning kiln, the rich orange brown colours radiating reassuring warmth. The richly speckled surfaces achieved by Yo Thom combine sophistication with simplicity. The seductive, swirling lines and glowing colours achieved by Ruthanne Tudball in her thrown and manipulated jugs, dishes and teapots capture a sense of movement and repose. Aware of the long tradition of potter in the country, makers in Korea such as Seung-Ki Min, Cheon-Soo Lee, Sang-Wook Huh and Eun-Bum Lee have simplified and abstracted shape and surface while remaining within an identifiable tradition. Chris Keenan, a city potter, approaches making tableware from a different point of view. His finely thrown porcelain in dark, mysterious *temmokus* and green blues are both urban and urbane, so much about the hand of the potter as the eye of the designer.

Broadly, the work illustrated in this chapter appears able to do the task for which it was intended, much of it used as part of an act, whether of pouring, drinking, serving or storing. While, by their very nature, pots can be used whenever food is consumed, the heart of the work shown lies in the home, the personal sphere where we create/shape our own nest. The pots we choose reflect individual taste and changing needs.

Occasionally the preference is for a minimalist porcelain cup and saucer with the opportunity to savour the depth of the glaze and its honed-down beauty as in the work of makers Young-Ho Lee and Jeong Yong Han, both of whom make sensitive use of the qualities

far left: **ELISA HELLAND-HANSEN**
Pitchers, 2006, h 15 cm (5¾ in.) and 11 cm (4¼ in.)
Stoneware, wood-fired, cone 11

left: **THOMAS AITKEN**
Mixing/Low Serving Bowls, 2007
Top left set, large mixing bowl, h 13.5 cm (5¼ in.),
w 26.5 cm (10½ in.); medium mixing bowl, h 11.2
cm (4½ in.), w 20 cm (7¾ in.); small mixing bowl,
h 9 cm (3½ in.), w 13. 5 cm (5¼ in.); bottom right
set, large low serving bowl, h 9 cm (3½ in.), w 26.5
cm (10½ in.); medium low serving bowl, h 7 cm
(2¾ in.), w 21 cm (8½ in.); small low serving bowl,
h 5 cm (2 in.), w 14 cm (5½ in.)

of their chosen material, porcelain. At other times we want a sense of adventure, such as when selecting a lively, decorated earthenware cooking pot like those by Niek Hoogland and Josie Walter, both of whom make pieces redolent with ceramic history; Jane Sawyer and Dylan Bowen also work in earthenware but adopt a freer, more painterly approach. Alternatively, when serving tea we may feel the need for quieter, more intimate shapes such as the porcelain tray with four cups by Elisa Helland-Hansen or the homely feel created by Kaye Pemberton. All heighten our awareness of the qualities of everyday objects. Other potters, deterred by Leach's advocacy of Eastern forms, prefer to look to more European models, though influences from Japan are often evident. Tea bowls or *unomis* continue to challenge potters, taking an iconic form but giving it a modern feel, with some potters such as Phil Rogers preferring to remain within established tradition.

PATTERN AND COLOUR

While the colour or decoration of tableware will have little effect on its ability to fulfil the purpose for which it was made, such qualities do have a profound effect on our reading of them. A yellow teapot is likely to be just as practical if glazed brown, but the two will carry different messages. Commenting on his painting *The Night Café* of 1888, Vincent van Gogh wrote to his brother saying that he had 'tried to express the terrible passion of humanity by means of red and green', seeing the colours as able to signify powerful feelings and emotions. Neither pattern nor colour will directly influence the physical function of an object, which suggests that its purpose is expressive and subjective,

and quite outside any consideration of Immanuel Kant's assertion that functional objects are assessed as 'right or consistent'.

The use of pattern and colour, such as in the lidded pots and dishes by Gail Kendall, Sandy Brown and Linda Sikora break away from the tradition of studio ceramics with more quiet, muted colours, hues that have a close association with the natural shades of rocks, pebbles and stones, so allying them with nature. For many years these were the easiest colours to obtain, especially at high temperatures, in contrast to low temperature where a wide range of colours were available. The advent of more sophisticated stains has opened up fresh fields of exploration by making available colours such as reds, yellows and oranges that can be successfully fired to high temperature. This enables potters to use strong colour on tougher, more hard-wearing bodies such as porcelain and stoneware.

The effect of using bright colour on tableware has a profoundly expressive effect, possibly adding humour and wit as well as a modern, contemporary feel. Janet DeBoos throws pots in porcelain and decorates them with cheerful, abstract patterns that boldly explore shape and decoration. These are in great contrast to her bone china teasets produced in China by industrial methods for semi mass production, which have a purity and simplicity that celebrates the chosen material. Equally effective is the thrown stoneware by Zeita Scott and Thomas Aitken, both of whom feel uninhibited in their use of colour. Their functional bowls, dishes and trays are transformed by large areas of saturated colour that owe much to the colour field painting of such artists as Barnett Newman and Ellsworth Kelly. Likewise, the neat, repetitive porcelain pots by Natasha Daintry handle rich colour with authority and sensitivity. By contrast, the square

right: **ANDREW WICKS**
Sotto Espresso Cup and Saucer/Egg Cup and Cover,
2007, h 9.5 cm (3¾ in.)
Slip-cast semi-porcelain

below: **PRUE VENABLES**
Black Oval Bowl and Pierced Ladle, 2007,
bowl, h 18 × w 27 × l 33 cm (7 × 10½ × 13 in.);
ladle, pierced h 11 × w 6 × l 38 cm
(4¼ × 2¼ × 15 in.)
Porcelain

porcelain bowls produced by Ane-Katrine von Bülow make use of the basic forms to explore how the application of repeating geometrical patterns can energize and enliven the shape.

AN ESSENTIAL STILLNESS

Partly in response to the growth of interest in pattern and decoration, partly to the vigorous concern with 'process', be it salt, soda or wood-firing, and partly in response to the availability of more plastic and workable bodies, some potters prefer to focus on the simplicity and strength of form. A flame-burning kiln, for instance, that gives a reduction atmosphere can produce sensual, cool pale blues and greens, particularly on porcelain. Such work borrows from the purity of porcelain from Song Dynasty China. Others prefer the more neutral soft whites and creams obtained in an electric kiln, finding them to be more in keeping with a modernist aesthetic.

Writing about her pots, Prue Venables says, 'A search for simplicity and quietness, an essential stillness, motivates my work. The making of functional pots, the exploration of objects to be held and used, alongside a search for new and innovative forms, provides a lifetime of challenge and excitement.'[7] Venables's sensual, handmade tableware is minimal, spare and elegant, the forms gently eased and shaped into ovals to take them away from the strict symmetry of the wheel. Every detail of the pieces is considered, the weight, balance, angle, thickness of lip, all of which contribute to a refined and defined minimalism in which every detail is significant.

Other potters who favour cleanly thrown and turned shapes uncluttered with detail and with decoration kept to a minimum, with pale blue or creamy white glazes, include Karen Downing, Takeshi Yasuda, Matthew Blakely, Antje Ernestus and Fritz Rossmann. Kirsten Coelho, who is also intrigued by an 'essential stillness', gives her forms a slightly more robust quality, choosing to highlight rims and ridges with thin lines of iron oxide that run off the edges adding an element of movement to the formality of the forms. By contrast, potters such as Heather Mae Erickson, Sun Kim and Carina Ciscato work with shapes that are almost paper thin. Ciscato cuts or manipulates her thrown forms into curving, flowing shapes that are crisp, precise and controlled. The slip-cast forms produced by Andrew Wicks make thoughtful use of the process to give clean, attractive forms that are eminently usable, an impression that is also reflected in his thrown forms. Equally honed down are Louisa Taylor's thrown stacking teapots and bowls. Through the minimal use of colour to heighten the form, Taylor produces shapes that are both functional and elegant.

An element of freedom is introduced by Jonathan Keep, whose use of blue and white achieve a classic simplicity, while Martin Lungley produces bowls and teasets that have some of the qualities reminiscent of landscape. More spiky, assertive shapes are produced by Sonia Lewis. Appearance offers an initial attraction, but it is only when pieces are handled that enjoyment is fully realized. In this sense who could resist the cool, pale blue porcelain dishes and mugs made by Joanna Howells with the unctuous glaze forming sensuous beads of colour on the side, or the magnificent champagne set of one hundred flutes produced by Piet Stockmans?

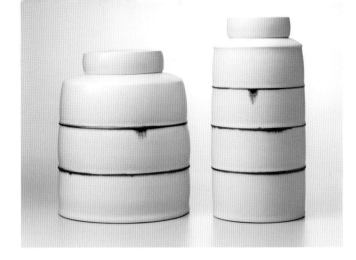

left: **KIRSTEN COELHO**
Two Ginger Jars, 2007, left, h 20.5 × dia 15.5 cm
(8 × 6 in.); right, h 24 × dia 11 cm (9½ × 4¼ in.)
Porcelain, matt white glaze and banded iron oxide

below: **LOUISA TAYLOR**
Stacking Bowls, 2008, dia 18 cm (7 in.)
Porcelain, thrown

THE HAND-BUILT

While the wheel has remained supreme for many potters, a method of producing pots quickly and efficiently, paradoxically, some potters prefer to hand build tableware, choosing to aim for a particular handmade quality rather than compete with the symmetry of wheel-thrown forms. Hylton Nel hand builds dishes, plates and bowls, freely press-moulding them without seeking to disguise the way they are made or to achieve a 'perfect' effect. The form of his dishes celebrates handmadeness, a quality reflected in the making and in the decoration with painted enamel designs that are witty jokes or light-hearted floral or human representations. Sometimes these are overtly sexual, but always with humour, the assured line decoration delightfully combining the quality of the handmade with a sophisticated understanding of the process of making and the purpose for which the pieces are intended.

Using a combination of hand building and throwing, Bernadette Curran creates colourful, lively forms that are both witty and useful. She enlivens the thrown and modelled forms with dashes of bright greens, yellows, reds or blues, creating work that is sophisticated and naïve.

Hand building without the use of moulds is the method used by potters such as Petra Reynolds and Kaori Tatebayashi. Reynolds shapes her cups, casseroles, plates and jugs from thin slabs of clay that are gently teased into functional and pleasingly quirky forms. The wood-fired salt-glaze firing to which they are subjected subtly brings out the fine detail of the making. For Tatebayashi, it is the more intimate methods of coiling and pinching that she prefers. The rounded cups are softly modelled, their delicate form heightened by soft, silky matt glazes.

INTERNATIONALISM

Potters in countries around the world have developed their own styles and approaches to tableware that have often reflected regional as well as personal tastes. In 2007 the Gardiner Museum in Toronto put together the exhibition *On the Table: 100 Years of Functional Ceramics in Canada*[8], a show that included both industrially made ware (hence its covering 100 years) as well as studio pottery, which traced the development of tableware manufacture in Canada. It toured throughout Canada in 2007 and was seen as an important recognition of the creative achievement of everyday pots.

In 2005 the Crafts Council in London mounted the exhibition *Table Manners: International Contemporary Ceramics*[9] which looked at the range, diversity and skill of work made by 18 potters working in ten different countries. The exhibition asserted the creative energy and stylistic diversity of the handmade and functional at a time when attention is often directed to more obviously expressive and art-orientated objects. More recently, Marek Cecula curated *Object Factory: The Art of Industrial Ceramics* at the Gardiner Museum that focused on the imaginative way industry has approached the exploration of innovative design.[10]

Today, many international exhibitions, whether in Korea, Vallauris or Faenza, have a section devoted to functional work, recognition that just as, for example, painters and sculptors continue to come up with fresh insights and perspectives as they

KAORI TATEBAYASHI
Kage Plate and Cup, 2004, plate, 23 × 23 × 3 cm
(9 × 9 × 1 in.), cup, 12 × 12 × 5 cm (4¼ × 4¼ × 2 in.)
Stoneware, hand-built

question and interrogate the figure, so makers, designer-makers and designer-producers respond with vigour and enthusiasm to changing needs and new opportunities around tableware. The resulting work offers the pleasure of close intimacy with the handmade object, satisfying haptic and numinous needs.

THE SEMIOTICS OF THE EVERYDAY

Two everyday items – the mug and the teapot – are recurring forms throughout the world, yet each is distinctive and different although they both share a common concern. The mug, long a key signifier of the work of the tableware potter, might appear to have exhausted all the forms, variations and patterns possible yet new shapes and designs continue to appear. In many households and offices the mug has replaced the cup and saucer, and is likely to have been chosen with care by its owner. Many kitchens boast a collection of mugs, proudly displayed and selected for use according to size, mood, time of day and any association of who made it or how it was acquired.[11]

While mugs can be an impulse buy – a modest investment in the handmade – a teapot demands more serious thought for not only may it require more of a financial commitment, but it may also be seen to carry more metaphysical connotations. Out of all the objects made by potters, the teapot is generally regarded as posing the biggest challenge in demanding not only a high level of making skills, but also the understanding of an engineer in assembling the four basic parts – body, spout, handle and knob – for the pot to carry out its allotted task efficiently. It also requires the eye of a designer to create a form that will be good to look at and pleasant to use.

Whether fitted with a side- or a kettle-type handle, teapots emblemize a welcome refreshing drink, for some a central part of the daily ritual, for others an object to be used only on special occasions.

Teapots also offer a diverse commentary on the history and culture of ceramics. First developed in China, teapots began to be made in the West when tea was imported in large quantities in the eighteenth century. Generally seen as status symbols, artists often depicted wealthy families taking tea, the Chinese utensils proudly on display. At first, keen to emulate the refinement of the oriental wares, potters copied the shape of Chinese wares but gradually they evolved their own distinctive designs. Nevertheless, forms retain aspects of oriental design, whether in the use of a footring or in the overhead or kettle handle such as in a piece by Svend Bayer. In comparison to ware made today, early teapots were modest in size, reflecting the high price and status of tea. Today, they can range from exquisite rounded pale blue porcelain forms to the more earthy stoneware, colourful earthenware or decorated stoneware. The lace-like forms by Julie Shepherd take the idea of the teapot and teacup to its extremes, recognizable but not usable.

THE AESTHETICS OF FUNCTION

Writing about his work in 2006, the UK potter Julian Stair discussed what was involved in appraising an apparently simple and everyday object such as a cup and saucer, two interrelated but separate forms. This, he said, includes discussion of 'surface treatment, ergonomics, tactile characteristics, kinesthetic appreciation, architectural site specificity, relationship to other objects, issues of human scale,

HYLTON NEL
'Tell us the truth Mr President', from set of
seven plates, 2007, dia 26 cm (10¼ in.) each
Glazed ceramic

perceptions of heat and cold, conveyance of taste and smell and, of course, aesthetic discernment'.[12] Even this comprehensive list omits any consideration of how well the object functions.

Two examples that come to mind in terms of resolution, although very different in their historical and stylistic references, fulfil their purpose in similar ways. One is the robust thrown stoneware teacups and saucers by Debbie Joy. The saucer is distorted to add an element of surprise, which may also enable it to be picked up more easily. In keeping with the free feel of the throwing, the cups are only half dipped in glaze, leaving the lower part of the body to respond to the reduction firing. As a result, it is richly speckled with iron spots, which contrast well with the smooth glaze. The whole piece has a relaxed, almost casual feel that makes imaginative use of the material, the firing, the making process and the glaze. Contrast these with the cups and saucers made in porcelain by Rupert Spira. The cups are elegant, straight-sided cylinders about 7 cm (2¾ in.) in height, sitting in a gently rounded saucer some 14 cm (5½ in.) in diameter. A soft lemon-yellow on the inside contrasts with a white opaque glaze with tiny iron speckles on the outside. The objects are sophisticated, cool, modern in feel and inviting to use. Both are cups and saucers with very different aesthetic qualities. The thrown and gently manipulated cups by Marie Torbensdatter Hermann are equally seductive in their simplicity.

The pieces by Joy and Spira exist in a long continuum, which includes recognized use and historical precedents. Both potters have responded with modern interpretations of forms that have existed in the West since the early decades of the eighteenth century. Teacups and saucers are surrounded by a range of involved social rituals about the taking of tea and coffee that entails a complex etiquette of manners. Today, such objects may be found on the draining board, in the kitchen, on the tea or coffee tray waiting for use, on display in a cabinet as valued objects to be admired rather than used, or in a museum showcase. Any assessment of the status of these objects will involve consideration of their aesthetic qualities as well as the renown of the maker and perceived financial value.

1 Gaston Bachelard, translated by Alan C. M. Ross, *The Psychoanalysis of Fire*, Routledge and Kegan Paul, London 1964, first published 1938.
2 Quoted in Sandra Alfoldy, 'The Function of Ceramics', in *On the Table: 100 Years of Functional Ceramics in Canada*, Sandra Alfoldy and Rachel Gotlieb (eds), exhibition catalogue, Gardiner Museum, Toronto, Canada, 15 February–22 April 2007.
3 For a discussion of the 'practical' and 'poetic' functions of objects see Edward Lebow, 'The Aesthetics of Function', in Garth Clark (ed.), *Ceramic Millennium: Critical Writings on Ceramic History, Theory, and Art*, The Nova Scotia College of Art and Design Press, Halifax, 2006, pp. 362–72.
4 Rachel Gotlieb, 'Craft, Design, and Industry: Parallels and Paradoxes in Canadian Ceramics', op. cit., 2007.
5 William Morris wrote much about the destructive lifestyle of commerce which he saw as destroying pride in work, reduced the materials used to the blandest and most expedient and divided making into specialisms, so none of the workers identified with the goods they produced.
6 Quoted in Jane Hamlyn, *Making Sense: Crafts in Context*, exhibition catalogue, Exeter City Museums and Art Gallery, 1995.
7 Quoted in 'Prue Venables', Grace Cochrane (ed.), *Smart Works: Design and the Handmade*, Powerhouse Publishing, Sydney, Australia, 2007, p. 110.
8 Sandra Alfoldy and Rachel Gotlieb (eds), op. cit.
9 *Table Manners: International Contemporary Ceramics*, Emmanuel Cooper (curator), Crafts Council, London, 2005, plus national tour until 2007.
10 *Object Factory: The Art of Industrial Ceramics*, Marek Cecula (curator), Gardiner Museum, Toronto, 2007.
11 The majority of the 80-odd mugs on show in *Table Manners: International Contemporary Ceramics* were purchased direct from potters at craft fairs.
12 Julian Stair, 'The Body as a Core Element in Ceramics', in *Keramik Magazin* (English edition), vol. 28, no. 3, June/July 2006.

above: JULIAN STAIR
Teapot and Two Cups, 2007, h 36 cm (14 in.)
Stoneware and porcelain; thrown and constructed

right: JULIAN STAIR
Teapot and Three Cups, 2007, h 36 cm (14 in.)
Stoneware and porcelain; thrown and constructed
porcelain oval teapot with wisteria handle, thrown
cups on a hand-built square red stoneware ground

above, left: **ANDREW WICKS**
Sotto, 2007, h 4–11 cm (1½–4¼ in.)
Slip-cast semi-porcelain breakfast range designed in
1997, still in production

above, right: **ANDREW WICKS**
Bloom Jugs, 2007, h 7.5–19.5 cm (3–7½ in.)
Slip-cast semi-porcelain with applied porcelain sprigs

above, left: **NICK CHAPMAN**
Jewellery Box, 2006, h 8 cm (3¼ in.)
Earthenware, silver bird on lid

above, right: **SVEND BAYER**
Two-pint Teapot, 2006, h 19 cm (7½ in.)
Stoneware, *shino* glaze, brass handle

above: **PAUL YOUNG**
Charger, 2005, dia 42 cm (16.5 in.)
Earthenware, thrown, slip-trailed decoration

right: **WILLIAM PLUMPTRE**
Plate, 2006, w 24 cm (9½ in.)
Stoneware, press-moulded, inlaid slip, clear
wood-ash glaze

above: **LINDA CHRISTIANSON**
Baking Dish, 2008, h 15 cm (5¾ in.)
Stoneware, wood-fired

right: **LINDA CHRISTIANSON**
Black Striped Ewer, 2007,
15 × 9 × 11.5 cm (6 × 3½ × 4½ in.)
Stoneware, wood-fired

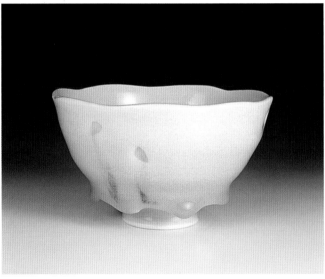

top: **MATTHEW BLAKELY**
Tilted Oil/Soy Bottles, 2007, h 16 cm (6¼ in.)
Porcelain, fluid blue, green and yellow glazes with *temmoku* splashes; copper red glaze

above, left: **MATTHEW BLAKELY**
Small Wavy Bowl, 2007, h 7.5 cm (3 in.)
Southern Ice Porcelain with fluid blue glaze and *temmoku* splashes

above, right: **MATTHEW BLAKELY**
Tilted Teapot, 2007, h 17 cm (6¾ in.)
Thrown and altered porcelain, fluid blue celadon glaze with *temmoku* dribbles

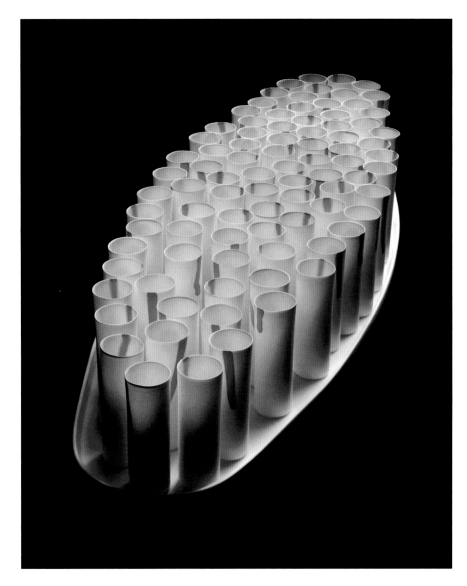

above, left: **PIET STOCKMANS**
Champagne for a Full House, 2001, h 12.5 cm (5 in.)
Porcelain

above, right: **CARINA CISCATO**
Series of Pocket Pots, 2007, tallest 20 cm (8 in.)
Porcelain, thrown, altered and assembled

above: **KIRSTEN COELHO**
Tea Can and Two Cups, 2007,
tea can, h 22 × dia 9.5 cm (8½ × 3¾ in.);
left-hand cup, h 8.5 × dia 8.5 cm (3¾ × 3¾ in.);
right-hand cup, h 9.5 × dia 8.5 cm (8½ × 3¾ in.)
Porcelain, matt white glaze, banded iron oxide

left: **KIRSTEN COELHO**
Cup and Saucers, 2006, cup, 7 × 9 cm
(2¾ × 3½ in.); saucer, 3 × 15 cm (1 × 6 in.)
Porcelain, satin glaze, banded iron oxide

top: **CHRIS KEENAN**
Celadon Teapot, Cups, Wooden Tray, 2007,
h 18 cm (7 in.)
Limoges porcelain, thrown

above: **CHRIS KEENAN**
Six Beakers, 2007, h 10 cm (4 in.)
Limoges porcelain, thrown

opposite: **MARIE TORBENSDATTER HERMANN**
'A joyful gathering of a defenseless legion', 2007,
h 6–12 cm (2¼–4¾ in.), d 30 cm (11¾ in.), 6 cm
(2¼ in.) each; w 210 cm (82½ in.)
175 porcelain vessels , thrown , white glazed,
grey and yellow, fired in oxidation, 1260°C

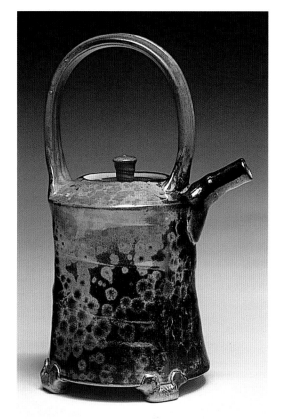

left: **GAIL KENDALL**
Dish, 2008, dia 25 cm (10 in.)
Decorated with slip and commercial underglazes,
glazed with coloured transparent/clear glazes

below: **GAIL KENDALL**
Tureen, 2007, dia 35.5 cm (14 in.)
Terracotta, hand built, slipware, decorated with
slip and commercial underglazes and glazed with
coloured transparent/clear glazes

opposite, left: **MALCOLM DAVIS**
Tall Teapot, 2007, h 18 cm (7 in.)
Grolleg porcelain, wheel-thrown, carbon-trap *shino*
formula, fired in a gas (propane) kiln in heavy reduction

opposite, top right: **LISA HAMMOND**
Square Lidded Jar, 2007, 17 × 15 cm (6¾ × 5¾ in.)
Stoneware, *shino* glaze, salt-fired

opposite, bottom right: **MALCOLM DAVIS**
Teabowl Duo, 2007, approx. h 9 dia × 8 cm (3½ × 3¼ in.)
Grolleg porcelain, wheel-thrown, with a carbon-trap *shino*
formula, fired in a gas (propane) kiln in heavy reduction

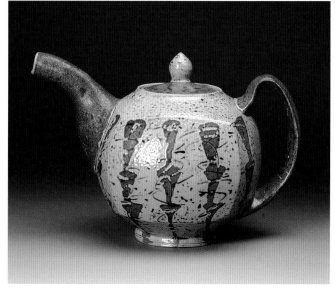

top: **MARTIN LUNGLEY**
Tea Set, 2005, h 12 cm (4¾ in.)
Porcelain, thrown, iron glaze

above, left: **ANNIE HEWETT**
Vase/Vessel with Lug Handles, 2008
White earthenware with a yellow slipped interior; the decoration
is drawn and scratched through the slip into the white

above, right: **MARK SHAPIRO**
Teapot with Spout, 2007, 15 × 20 × 15 cm (6 × 8 × 6 in.)
Stoneware

ZEITA SCOTT
The Shuffle Range, 2006, round platters, 36 × 6 cm
(14 × 2¼ in.), small dishes, 6 × 6 cm (2¼ × 2¼ in.)
and 5 × 3 cm (2 × 1 in.)
Spanish black earthenware with stained
porcelain slips and transparent glaze

above: **LINDA SIKORA**
Teapot with Bail Handle, 2005, h 14 cm (5.5 in.)
Porcelain, wood/oil/salt-firing, polychrome glaze

right: **LINDA SIKORA**
Tea for Twenty (Two Teapots, Twenty Cups), 2006,
teapot, h 18 cm (7 in.); cup, 8 cm (3 in.)
Porcelainous stoneware, wood/oil/salt-firing,
polychrome glaze

above: **YO THOM**
Soya Sauce Bottles, 2004,
h 9 cm (3½ in.)
Stoneware, gas-fired, carbon-trap
shino glaze

top left: **JACK TROY**
Capacious Jar, 2007,
30.5 × 35.5 × 23 cm (12 × 14 × 9 in.)
Porcelain with granitic and siliceous
inclusions, natural ash glaze

top right: **YO THOM**
Guinomi, 2006, h 5 cm (2 in.)
Stoneware, gas-fired with *shino* glaze

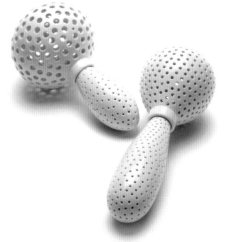

above: **PRUE VENABLES**
Teaset, 2003, h 20 cm (8 in.) max.
Hand-thrown Limoges porcelain

right: **PRUE VENABLES**
Pair of Rattles – Judaica for Jewish Museum,
Melbourne, 2007, h 22 × w 14 × d 14 cm
(8¼ × 5½ × 5½ in.), h 28 × w 10 × d 10 cm
(11 × 4 × 4 in.)
Porcelain

above: **JOSIE WALTER**
Three Jugs, 2007, h 10 cm (4 in.)
Chocolate black/red clay, slip decoration,
once fired, cone 03

right: **THOMAS AITKEN**
Dinnerware, 2007, back, from left to right, pasta
plate, h 3.7 × w 26. 5 cm (1½ × 10½ in.); lunch
plate, h 2. 5 × w 27 cm (1 × 10½ in.); dinner plate,
h 2. 8 × w 29.5 cm (1 × 11½ in.); front, from left
to right, coffee mug, h 10 × w 8.5 cm (4 × 3½ in.);
salad plate, h 2. 3 × w 21 cm (1 × 8¼ in.); side plate,
h 1.9 × w 16. 7 cm (¾ × 6½ in.); dessert bowl,
h 7 × w 13.5 cm (2¾ × 5¼ in.); soup/cereal bowl,
h 7.5 × w 15. 5 cm (3 × 6 in.)

right: **KAREN DOWNING**
Large Stack, 2006, dia 33 cm (13 in.)
Porcelain, thrown

below: **KAREN DOWNING**
Four Bowls on Plates, 2006, 9 × 20 cm (3½ × 8 in.)
Porcelain, thrown

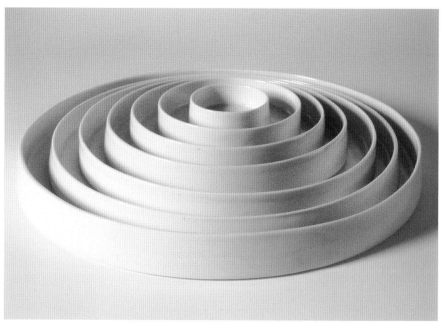

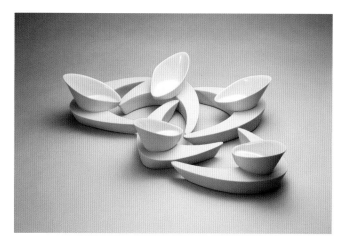

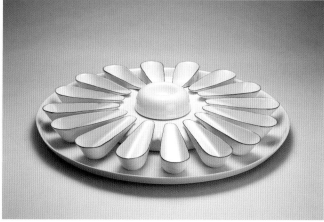

above, left: **HEATHER MAE ERICKSON**
Dessert Compotes, 2007, 10 × 18 × 19 cm (3.75 × 7 × 7.5 in.)
Porcelain, slip-cast from carved plaster models, cone 6 oxidized

above, right: **HEATHER MAE ERICKSON**
Appetizer Platter with Spoons, 2007,
4 × 44 × 44 cm (1¾ × 17½ × 17½ in.)
Porcelain, slip-cast from carved plaster models, cone 6 oxidized

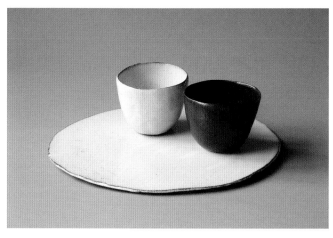

top: **SUE PARASKEVA**
Tableware, 2008, dinner plate 27.5 cm (11 in.)
Porcelain, thrown

above, left: **KAORI TATEBAYASHI**
Kohiki Tray and Cups, 2008, tray, 35 × 26 (13¾ × 10¼ in.),
cup, 8 × 8 × 7 cm (3¼ × 3¼ × 2¾ in.)
Stoneware, hand-built

above, right: **MICHAEL EDEN**
Double-round Rolling Bowl, 2004, dia 32 cm (12½ in.)
Red earthenware, thrown, slip, decorated with coloured glazes

top left: **PHIL ROGERS**
Yunomi, 2008, h 10 cm (4 in.)
Stoneware, thrown, ash and Kington stone glaze,
impressed decoration, wood-fired

above, left: **PETRA REYNOLDS**
Teapot, 2007, h 20 cm (8 in.)
Stoneware, wood-fired

above, right: **CLIVE BOWEN**
Lidded Store Jar, 2006, 36.5 × 26 cm (14¼ × 10¼ in.)
Red earthenware, thrown, green slip and ochre
trailing, wood-fired

top left: **JACK TROY**
Teabowl, 2007, 9 × 10 × 9 cm (3.5 × 4 × 3.5 in.)
Porcelain with feldspathic inclusions, *shino*-lined, natural ash glaze

above, left: **RUTHANNE TUDBALL**
Ginger Jar, 2007, h 30 × dia 20 cm (11¾ × 7¾ in.)
Stoneware, thrown, faceted, soda-fired

above, right: **RUTHANNE TUDBALL**
Oval Teapot on Three Feet, 2007,
h 21 × 17 cm (8¼ × 6¼ in.)
Stoneware, thrown, faceted, soda-fired faceted

above, left: **HYLTON NEL**
Seated Figure (Salt Holder), 2007, h 15 cm (5¾ in.)
Glazed ceramic

above, right: **HYLTON NEL**
Monster Lion, 2004, w 31 cm (12 in.)
Glazed ceramic

right: **HYLTON NEL**
'Champagne for my real friends',
from a set of 15 plates, 2007, dia 27 cm (10½ in.)
Glazed ceramic

above, left: **CATHERINE VANIER**
Square Dish, 2007, 25 cm (10 in.)
Earthenware, slips, glaze

above, right: **NIEK HOOGLAND**
Oval Lidded Pot, 2006, h 17 cm (6¾ in.)
Slipware

right: **BERNADETTE CURRAN**
Night and Day, Tumblers, 2007,
15 × 7.5 × 7.5 cm (6 × 3 × 3 in.)
Porcelain, thrown and modelled, cone 6

above: **SUN KIM**
Two Cups and Saucers, 2007,
h 11 × w 16 cm (4¼ × 6¼ in.)
Porcelain, wheel-thrown and altered,
functional wares

right: **SUN KIM**
Vase, 2008,
h 13 × w 22 × l 25 cm (5 × 8⅝ × 9¾ in.)
Porcelain, wheel-thrown and altered

left: **WALTER KEELER**
Green Cut Branch Teapot, 2005, h 26 cm (10¼ in.)
Earthenware, thrown, extruded, press-moulded,
modelled

below: **WALTER KEELER**
Angular Teapot, 2006, h 23 cm (9 in.)
Stoneware, thrown and altered with extruded
handle, salt-glaze

top left: **NATASHA DAINTRY**
Ziggurat, 2007, 6.5 × 7.2 cm (2½ × 2¾ in.)
Porcelain, thrown, deep orange, dirty yellow and
violet-grey glaze, three separate pieces, stacked

top right: **RUPERT SPIRA**
Teapot and Four Bowls, Yellow and White, 2007,
h 15 cm × dia 13 cm (5¾ × 5 in.)
Stoneware, thrown and turned, reduction-fired

above: **FRITZ ROSSMANN**
Plates and Bowls, 2006, 50 cm (19½ in.) max.
Thrown, porcelain and stoneware

above: **JONATHAN KEEP**
Oval Salad Bowl, 2008, 34 × 28 × 20 cm
(13¼ × 11 × 7¾ in.)
Thrown altered Keuper red clay,
porcelain cream slip and painted oxide

right: **JONATHAN KEEP**
Tableware, 2008, dinner plate, 26 × 3 cm
(10¼ × 1 in.); side plate, 19.5 × 2.5 cm (7¾ × 1 in.);
coffee cup, 15 × 8 cm (5¾ × 3 in.)
Semi-porcelain creamware, thrown and
manipulated, painted oxide

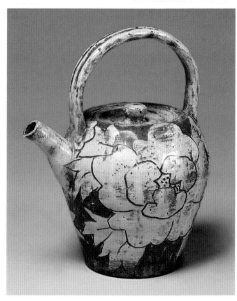

above: **SANDY BROWN**
Plate, 2007, dia 20 cm (7¾ in.)
Stoneware, thrown, with pink,
manganese trailing, copper green

above, right: **SANDY BROWN**
Teapot, 2007
Stoneware, thrown, with pink,
manganese trailing, copper green

right: **SANG-WOOK HUH**
Teapot, 2007, h approx. 18 cm (7 in.)
Stoneware, white slip, decoration, wood-fired

opposite, top: **JANE SAWYER**
Teapot and Cups, 2003, teapot, 18 × dia 16 cm
(7 × 6¼ in.); cups, 8 × 9 cm (3 × 3½ in.)
Red earthenware, cream slip, transparent
leadless glaze

opposite, bottom left: **DEBBIE JOY**
Cappuccino Cups, 2007, h 8.5 cm (3¼ in.)
Stoneware, thrown, reduction-fired

opposite, bottom right: **ROB BERNARD**
Platter, 2007, h 3 × w 38 cm (1 × 15 in.)
Stoneware, thrown, carved, wood-fired

above: **KAYE PEMBERTON**
Tuesday Morning Solitude, 2007,
teapot, h 12 cm (4¾ in.)
Porcelain with murini motifs

right: **JANET DEBOOS**
*After Kanazawa, 'Solitary Pleasures' Series,
Teaset, Tray,* 2006, h 13 cm (5 in.)
Thrown Australian porcelain, decals,
overglaze enamels

JULIE SHEPHERD
Emperor's New Teaset, 2005, teapot,
h 15 × w 24 × dia 15 cm (6 × 9½ × 6 in.);
cup, h 6 × dia 10 cm (2¼ × 4 in.); plate,
h 3 × w 15 × dia 15 cm (1 × 6 × 6 in.)
Porcelain

YOUNG-HO LEE
Tableware, 2007
Porcelain, reduction-fired

top: **EUN-BUM LEE**
Tableware, 2007
Porcelain, celadon glaze, reduction-fired

above: **LOUISA TAYLOR**
Stack of Three Cups, Sugar Pot and Jug, 2008,
dia 15 cm (6 in.)
Porcelain, thrown

above: **ELISA HELLAND-HANSEN**
Four Black and White Beakers, Tray, 2007,
8 × 9 cm (3 × 3½ in.)
Porcelain with black slip, reduction-fired, cone 10

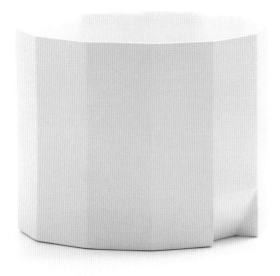

above, left: **JEONG YONG HAN**
Vessel, 2007, h 15 cm (6 in.)
Porcelain, reduction-fired

above, right: **JEONG YONG HAN**
Two Vessels, 2007, h 14 cm (5½ in.)
Porcelain, reduction-fired

right: **SONIA LEWIS**
Conversation Piece, 2004, h 20.5 cm (8 in.) max.
Porcelain, ying-ching glaze

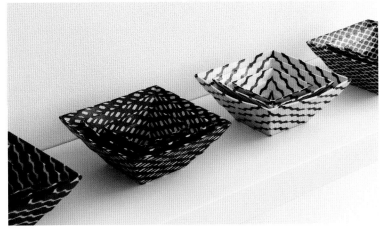

above: **JOANNA HOWELLS**
Joanna-paks, 2007, h 20 cm (7¾ in.)
Southern Ice Porcelain, thrown
and textured with slip

right: **ANE-KATRINE VON BULOW**
Three Square in One, 2005,
w 16.5 cm (6½ in.) max.
Double-cast in porcelain

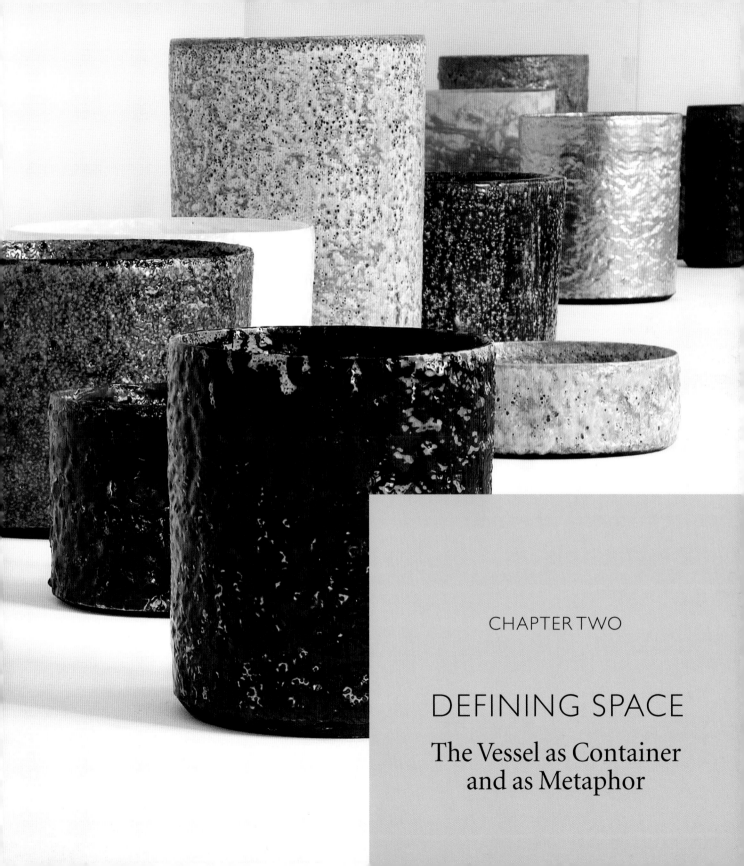

CHAPTER TWO

DEFINING SPACE

The Vessel as Container
and as Metaphor

preceding pages: **MORTEN LØBNER ESPERSEN**
Installation View at Galleri Nørby, 2006
Stoneware and earthenware

below: **STEVE HARRISON**
Simplicity, Bowl, 2007, 12 × 11.5 × 7.5 cm (4¾ × 4½ × 3 in.)
Thrown, ash glaze over carbon

right: **GARETH MASON**
Jar, Appended Iron Stone Series, 2007, h 66 cm (26 in.)
Stoneware and porcelain, thrown, altered, vitreous slips, glaze, mineral, oxide, iron stone, reduction-fired

far right: **UWE LÖLLMANN**
Vessel, 2007, h 52 cm (20½ in.)
Stoneware, thrown, reduction-fired

The French social theorist Jean Baudrillard argues that when an object is divested of its function, 'its destiny is to be collected.'[1]

The dynamics of the vessel, in all its potency, are the starting point for the work discussed in this chapter. One of the reasons the vessel remains such a powerful genre, even when no longer specifically addressing function, is its often overwhelming sense of intimacy, even, on occasions, offering a 'hands on' experience. Technically, the forms may range from those thrown on the wheel to those made in moulds either by pouring in liquid clay slip or by pressing in plastic clay. Shapes may also be constructed by a variety of hand-building processes; these include pinching or squeezing clay into a vessel form with the hand, coiling – where long thin sausages of clay are joined together to form walls – and slab building where flat slabs of clay are assembled to create the vessel.

Whichever technique is used, it will impose particular qualities on the finished object. Thrown pots, for example, will tend to be round and symmetrical while other processes produce objects that can be rounded, angular or asymmetrical. Moulds enable identical objects to be produced in quantity. Firing techniques may include bonfire or sawdust firing or more elaborate kilns, fired by electricity, gas or oil. More dramatic firings involve the use of wood or the long slow firing of an *anagama*, a type of Japanese kiln adapted for use in the West in which pots are subjected to heat, flame and wood ash for several days. The pieces finally emerge bearing the marks and encrustations of ash resulting from the firing process.

The magnificent thrown stoneware bottles by Svend Bayer, the patterning on the porcelain bowls by, for instance, Jack Doherty and those by Steve Harrison, which carry the flashing of flame on the clay are testament to the processes of making and firing. The excitement of a long, slow firing is beautifully captured in the bottles and bowls by Uwe Löllmann, where the ash-type glaze dramatically animates the toasted surface. All are vivid reminders of the processes of their production and their association with the fundamentals of ceramics – clay and fire.

Whatever the techniques or processes used, all seek to make work that addresses both the space within – the emptiness – and the space around; the internal space and its relationship to the space it inhabits. At their strongest, vessels are objects that are likely to have a deep resonance with the past that may be combined with a sense of identification with the present, although this may be deeply buried or encoded within the form. Most, though not all, are objects that invite touch or caress to establish personal, direct contact.

With the freedom of post-modernism, many artists who work with clay feel able to call on a variety of relevant historical styles or processes to decorate their work using a combination of techniques and, where appropriate, to look for minimal surface treatment in the search for expressive form. In scale, much of the work relates in some way to the domestic environment, and may even play around with the concept of the domestic. Some, for example, use the jug forms, as in the work of Alison Britton, taking up familiar concerns of giving and plenty. While paying little heed to the notion of function, such

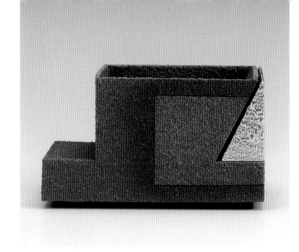

far left: **RON NAGLE**
Pinto Squire, 2005,
5.5 × 9.5 × 6 cm (2¼ × 3¾ × 2½ in.)
Ceramic, glazed

left: **TINA VLASSOPULOS**
Moebius, 2004, h 38 cm (15 in.)
Hand-built form, burnished, fired, 920°C

work does address what can be termed 'symbolic function'. For Hwang Jeng-daw and Richard Notkin the teapot is the starting point for fantasy pieces, de-constructing the form and reassembling it as a series of oddly placed components. For Notkin the form is also an object that can carry social, political and environmental issues. Ron Nagle uses the cup as a starting point for endless subtle variations on the theme of the container and the handle in objects that are sculptural and carefully considered.

VESSEL/POT/CONTAINER

Within studio ceramic convention, objects defined as vessels are usually seen to have a distant, if sometimes faint, relationship to use. Yet, however loose this connection, it is a vital link to the broadly perceived but significant association of clay with its humanist history. Contemporary vessel makers who have appropriated territory for their own purposes, while retaining references to the container, may make a work that takes on more metaphorical or symbolic qualities – the vessel as signifier, container of meaning and of ideas. Such work occupies territory between the pot and the object, asserting its independence and authority with expressive forms that have freed themselves from any explicit function, but which engage the eye and head through material, idea and shape. Tina Vlassopulos's carefully hand-built forms are containers in a literal sense but the rococo lines and the sumptuous curves defy any simple definition in terms of use but take us into new worlds in which meaning is fluid and open. The vessel-like structures created by artists such as Barbro Åberg are powerfully referenced to containers but fulfil few of the usual criteria.

ORGANIC ABSTRACTIONS

The idea that form can occur or develop gradually, without being forced or contrived, is one of the major approaches adapted by ceramists. Some artists seek to unite form and surface decoration to create a harmonious whole in which each informs the other in some way. Such a quality informs the tall vessels of, among others, Pippin Drysdale. Standing some 36 cm (14 in.) high, her pieces not only demonstrate the ability of the thrower to control such a monumental form given that it would have been a further ten centimetres tall when newly made before shrinking when it dried, but also to produce a refined, crisply defined piece. Drysdale's tall bowl forms are enhanced by fine linear decoration that gently flows round the shape. A similar sense of gentle but purposeful growth is suggested by Jennifer Lee's coil-built bowls, which make effective use of the colours of rocks and earth to evoke an intriguing geology, and by the poised calm of the thrown and coil-built forms of Alev Siesbye. The sense of order that surrounds Lee's forms is twisted and turned inside out in Anne-Marie Laureys's convoluted bowl forms. With references to both nature and the human form, Laureys takes the bowl into darker, more introverted areas.

While Drysdale's bowls soar upwards, the full rounded bottle forms of Gareth Mason appear to act like a balloon in holding and setting up a tension between the inner and outer space that gives the pieces arresting interest. Close examination reveals the bottles to be thrown in two or more parts and joined together with no real attempt to conceal the join but incorporating this into the structure of the pot. A series of uniting throwing lines add a further sense of strength to the shape.

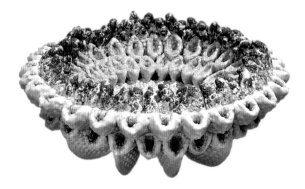

Like many artists working today, Mason draws ideas from other cultures, in particular those of the Far East, making use of the processes of throwing and reduction-fired stoneware and porcelain to explore the qualities of the material and techniques. Yet, far from seeking to replicate in any sense the great classic exemplars, he pushes at the limits of form and firing, taking us to the edge in terms of process and ideas. These, too, are rooted in contemporary ideas, and in the way we deal with the past and the present.

There is a similar sense of tension in the process of throwing taken to its extreme in the thrown bowl by Rupert Spira. Here the clay has been stretched, pulled and pushed to create a quiveringly subtle form reminiscent of landscape that appears to stand serene, perfectly balanced as it seems to sway, poised on its narrow foot. A close look reveals the surface to be covered with fine text, lines of script in which individual words rather than sentences or even phrases can be deciphered. The messages here are deeply encoded, we may or may not discover their meaning. In contrast, Ivar Mackay reinterprets classic forms within a more conventional idiom while keeping them alive and vibrant.

The sense of abstracted landscape that informs the work of such artists as Spira is taken in different directions by others. David Garland's bowls and vases, or those by Tanya Gomez and Kyra Cane use the rounded wheel-thrown forms as part of a response to landscape, the decoration adding a further layer of meaning to this. For Angela Mellor the form and decoration are intimately combined. She makes use of the translucency of the finely potted porcelain to create bowl forms with undulating rims, which, like tree-lined horizons, seem to move and shimmer. However, for Jean-François Fouilhoux it is the

qualities of porcelain that are the vehicle for his ideas. He appears literally to carve the body into rock-like structures, their craggy qualities softened by a soft, retiring pale blue-green celadon glaze.

The sense of the organic evident in work by Mellor and Fouilhoux is interpreted differently by makers such as Kato Yasukage and Susan Collett who evoke the essence of natural form, be it coral, gourd or shell through carefully abstracted form and surface. The natural world for Kate Malone is one to be examined and celebrated. For her the vessel becomes a vehicle for systematically applied sprigging, in some pieces appearing to make use of Fibernarche notation, while in others she creates still-life compositions in which foliage takes on rich, patterned quality. Bonnie Seeman and Ying-Yueh Chuang create exotic and colourful responses to nature, which have a thrilling, hot house quality, whose fantastic and intricate forms take on a surreal sense of the real.

PATTERN AND DECORATION

The Pattern and Decoration (P & D) Movement that arose in the mid-1970s in the US was partly in response to what was seen as the lack of adventure in the restrained and austere minimalism generally in vogue. These artists filled and crowded their paintings with colour and pattern to create a riot of ordered excess. The movement also led to a wider vocabulary of forms, surfaces and techniques that were previously seen as not appropriate.[2] Within ceramics, practitioners have reacted to the quiet, withdrawn refinement of 'the new white', with its pale creams, whites and soft blues that arose in the 1990s, with work that is, by contrast, exuberant, busy and often colourful,

opposite, left: **YING-YUEH CHUANG**
Plant-Creature, 2003, 11.5 × 30.5 × 30.5 cm
(4½ × 12 × 12 in.); Ceramic, multi-fired

opposite, right: **EMMANUEL COOPER**
Two Jug Forms, 2008, h 15 cm (6 in.); Black stoneware,
thrown, assembled, enamel lustre, 1250°C

left: **MATTHIAS OSTERMANN**
Les Demoiselles (Mahogany Base), 2004, w 42 cm
(16½ in.); Earthenware, thrown and altered

below: **ABHAY PANDIT**
Seascape, Platter, 2004, dia 51 cm (20 in.)
Stoneware, wire-cut

sometimes with a sense of rococo-like extravagance. Unlike the minimalists, P & D artists investigate all the processes of surface decoration available in ceramics and, if appropriate, apply them on their work. The bold surface treatment by artists such as Steve Irvine celebrates both the form and the ability to make bold, assertive marks that are in harmony with the shape.

For some it is the idea of clay as a canvas that is the starting point for their work, clearly making a close link with painting. The dishes by artists such as Gunhild Rudjord, Ralph Bacerra, Abhay Pandit and B. R. Pandit use the qualities of glaze and stain to animate the surface while retaining the clay-like qualities of the process. Others, such as the forms by Zahara Harel, Matthias Ostermann, Stephen Bowers and Karen Atherley use the flat surfaces as a canvas to draw on the form, twisting and arranging the figures and designs to fit the particular shape with Picasso-like abandon. Pattern and form are also beautifully integrated in the work produced by potters at Ardmore Ceramics, which combine indigenous design with rich colour. For Anne Kraus, everyday vessels such as cups and saucers and teapots are vehicles for philosophic observations expressed through careful pictorial imagery and text. By contrast, the dishes built by Lidia Bosevski have an organic quality, some recalling the purposeful structures of a bird's nest. The rich, terracotta colour reinforces this impression.

Clay lends itself to many sorts of graphic qualities that enrich and enhance the surface. Linear decoration applied on dry or semi-matt surfaces can be used to divide up the space, moving the eye around the form as one area of colour balances another. The bottle and bowl forms by Sam Hall and Yuk Kan Yeung, for example, create particular types of surface that lend themselves to the use of colour

and texture. Some, such as the hand-built vessels by Hall covered with areas of pigment and a variety of marks, recall the graffiti of well-worn walls.

The relationship between form and surface treatment is an important consideration for all ceramists, but none more so than for those who are particularly concerned with pattern and colour as a major ingredient of their work. The pattern skilfully used by Tor Alex Erichsen completely covers the surface, with the size of the patterning subtly adjusted to the form of bottle as it swells and expands from its foot. Erichsen's classic combination of black and white gives equal weight to each colour, creating a harmonious composition flowing round and engulfing the pot. The colourful patterned bowls by artists such as Janice Tchalenko and Ashley Howard integrate form and decoration with beguiling ease. Tchalenko's bold patterning echoes the shape of the bowl, while Howard makes use of enamels to create surfaces that positively radiate colour, the addition of gold lustre further enhancing the design.

Sensitive use of colour and pattern are combined with complex cultural references in the work of Robin Best, who makes creative use of computer-aided design. Best, following a stay in China, started to employ familiar patterning of blue and white, reconfigured to disrupt any easy or straightforward meaning. Sin-Ying Ho calls on her own Asian-Chinese background to explore cross-cultural themes in work that might combine classical Chinese forms with motifs

drawn from East and West. In keeping with her questioning approach, Sin-Ying Ho makes use of computer-generated designs as well as more conventional forms of decoration.

Photography and ceramics are skilfully brought together by Alice Mara. Using either industrially produced blanks or forms she has made, she applies a decal (or transfer), prepared from photographs she has taken, to the glazed surface. These are related to the shape of the dish, so a square form might carry an image of a metal sink or the front of a washing machine, while a round dish pictures a room. The integration of colour, pattern and form is taken to its ultimate conclusion in the work of Sasha Wardell, David Pottinger and Dorothy Feibleman, all of whom have devised ingenious ways of integrating form, colour and pattern. Feibleman's delicately potted porcelain bowls have the colour literally embedded in them to make full use of the translucency of the material. The effect is one of great delicacy and softness. Colour also plays an intrinsic part in the vessel forms of Kathryn Hearn. Using many layers of different-coloured slips to cast vessel forms, she works back the surface to reveal the layering in a process that ingeniously unites form and surface.

Conventionally, potters working at high temperature have tended to opt for earthy creams, greys, soft blues and lovat greens, colours in keeping with the landscape that encourage contemplation and retreat. Technical developments within the ceramics industry have resulted in a range of high-temperature colours that have opened up new possibilities so that post-modernist ideas have begun to challenge this hegemony. Artists such as Morten Løbner Espersen, Toshiko Takaezu and Emmanuel Cooper make use of the availability of the new colours and textures, partly as a statement about feeling and emotion and partly to explore the new range of pigments as a way of challenging assumptions about ceramics. The forms used tend to be classically simple – cylinders, funnel-like bowls or rounded bottles – that serve as carriers for the colour and texture. Colour here can be opulent, deep and resonant, and at its most effective integrated into the fabric of the vessel. In its absence of restraint it challenges notions of good taste while defining a broader, more inclusive aesthetic.

AESTHETIC PRIMITIVISM

The search for what might be called 'real' pottery, that is one perceived to be deeply rooted in tradition and so having both a fundamental relationship with the past while also being relevant to today, has been the concern of potters keen to explore the qualities of clay and fire as they interact at high temperature. Just as in the early decades of the twentieth century painters and sculptors found inspiration in anthropological objects such as the masks produced on the African continent or the stylized approach of objects fashioned in Ancient Egypt, so potters look to both long-established techniques of making and firing and also to an aesthetic that is rooted in such work.

In Japan Ken Matsuzaki is one of several potters who have looked critically at the history of his own country, including the decorative qualities of Oribe wares and the effects of long, slow firings. He incorporates both aspects in his forms that include hand-built bottles. Potters in other countries have also responded, but as observers appropriating and adapting the techniques and firing processes to produce their own work. Makers such as Betsy Williams, Janet Mansfield and Phil Rogers produce work that skilfully amalgamates an awareness of form and firing.

Charles Bound and Nic Collins, who specialize in *anagama* firing, produce work that is taken to the edge of destruction in terms of form and surface. Their monumental dishes and vessels, with their textured surface, pierced holes and warmly mottled oranges and browns proclaim their origins within the long, slow kiln firing, yet succeed in retaining their powerful sense of form. The hand-built forms by Martin McWilliam use the gritty qualities of the clay, the patterning effect of the firing and the optical effect of forms that are flattened but appear three dimensional, while artists such as Christine Fabre are concerned with both organic form and also the effects of smoke firing.

In comparison to the technically sophisticated firings developed in countries in the Far East, traditional potters in other countries used simpler processes to fire their work, which also brought it into direct contact with the flames and smoke, some even avoiding the use of the kiln altogether. In parts of Africa and in Mexico, Central and South America, for example, bonfire firings, rapidly carried out, were effective in reaching a sufficiently high temperature to harden the pots so they could be taken into daily use. The fire was slowly built up around the hand-built pots and after the firing the pots were removed from the ashes. The unglazed pots were scared by the smoke and the flame, markings that become a part of the character of the piece. Studio potters such as David Roberts, Simcha Even-Chen and Ashraf Hanna have devised ways of firing to allow for maximum contrast between a dark smoke body and the 'naked' body.

The effect of such firing processes imbues the form with a feel for the primary qualities of clay achieved with quite sophisticated techniques. Ian Garrett and Magdalene Odundo coil build vessels and fire them in complex processes that allow the burnished surface of the vessels to be sensitively smoked to bring out their fullness. In her work Odundo combines her Kenyan/African backgrounds with her art education in Europe. The forms, some symmetrical, some asymmetrical, raise the concept of shifting cultural identities, of ancient processes and techniques as well as the role of the ceramic vessel in the modern world. On them, decoration is kept to a minimum to allow form to be predominant, giving her vessels what has been called a characteristic 'austere beauty and rigour'.

Odundo, along with potters such as Madhvi Subrahmanian, make vessel forms by building up the walls in a slow and laborious coiling and smoothing process, which allows time for the subtleties of the shape to be carefully assessed. For others, throwing is a preferred method, though the effect is crisper and harder. Potters Duncan Ayscough and Duncan Ross throw their vessels, careful to remove any indication of throwing or turning marks so as to produce a perfectly smooth, blemish-free finish. This is a modern version of the technique of using terra sigillata slip, which was brought to perfection by the Ancient Greeks in their Black and Red Figure wares. The black and red terracotta is achieved by the use of specially prepared clay slips and careful control of the firing.

Ceramists working with the vessel today who are aware of their own cultural background often call on the

below: **HALIMA CASSELL**
Solar Flare, 2005, d 30 cm (11¾ in.)
Stoneware, carved and polished, unglazed clay

right: **JOHN HIGGINS**
Vessel, 2007, h 30 × w 25 cm (11¾ × 10 in.)
Grogged clay, slab-formed, oxides, slips,
underglaze colours, 1120°C

forms of traditional work but interpret it in a totally modern way in order to respond to life as they see and experience it. This is certainly the approach followed by Kukuli Velarde, Diego Romero and Virgil Ortiz. The decorated dishes made by Romero highlight the contrast between First American and modern American culture. Using the finely painted decorative style associated with the Mimbres people, the decoration in his rounded bowls addresses current issues within contemporary society. These may be issues around masculinity, sexual desire or awareness of the danger of AIDS/HIV, situations often depicted in graphically explicit designs.

A similar approach is taken by Velarde who adopts traditional forms but subverts them to her own concepts. She is concerned with issues around the manipulation of traditional vessel forms built in the shape of figures or animals, or a combination of both, produced in early Central American societies. These are re-interpreted with a wicked sense of humour, giving them a larger-than-life presence. These engaging, witty forms incorporate such themes as grimacing faces, exaggeratedly large genitalia, humanized animals, same-sex couples, all of which parody traditional work with deceptive ease. The rounded forms by Ortiz are enhanced by designs that cover the entire outer surface, their mix of traditional and modern motifs forming an engrossing commentary on cultural borrowings and assimilation.

ARCHITECTURAL AESTHETICS

The relationship between ceramic form and architecture is one that has long engaged potters. For ceramists working today, the correlation between buildings and vessels may be more encoded, but can be a fascinating aspect of their work. In Masamichi Yoshikawa's porcelain forms, which appear to have been literally carved out of the clay body, the structures have a building-like quality. The use of a pale blue, unctuous glaze that runs to form pearls of intense colour adds softening, seductive qualities. Carving is also an important part of the bowl-like forms by Halima Cassell. Calling on the use of flowing geometrical patterns associated with Islamic architecture, Cassell adapts these to bowl forms, creating objects that take on a stone-like quality, the rhythmic patterns continually moving the eye back to the object itself.

The finely cast porcelain cylinders by Bodil Manz, with their applied decoration tracing divisions and apertures, also evoke building-like structures. But here the buildings are exquisitely delicate, refined and rare. Constructing containers out of flat slabs of clay can take on strong architectural associations, as in the structures created by artists such as Sue Paraskeva and Karin Bablok. Some forms are slightly rounded to evoke a more organic effect that responds to both external and internal space. The coil-built forms created by ceramists such as Kristina Riska, Lut Laleman and Henk Wolvers make use of both light and translucency as integral aspects of their containers, the resulting forms taking on an almost organic feel. Wolvers carefully constructs his cylindrical porcelain forms to recall the strata of rocks or possibly the movement of water, achieving a satisfying and sensitive unity that integrates form and structure. Much the same kind of qualities are

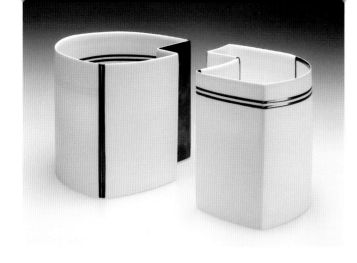

left: **KARIN BABLOK**
Two Vessels, 2007, h approx. 10 cm (4 in.)
Porcelain, thrown, manipulated, black pigment

below: **SARAH-JANE SELWOOD**
Octave Falling – Falling Inversion, 2007,
h 19 × dia 29 cm (7½ × 11¼ in.)
Porcelain, thrown and assembled

evident in the work of Les Blakebrough, whose bottle forms, with their soft, relief surface, embody both simplicity and sophistication.

There is a different sense of the organic in the vessels by Gustavo Pérez. Working with thrown shapes with inlaid colour, he manipulates or carefully cuts the form, the final effect making ingenious use of light and shadow. Such precision, an integral part of his work, is used differently by others. In the assembled bowl forms by Sarah-Jane Selwood, she creates, through meticulous throwing and painstaking cutting and joining, forms that lead the eye in and around the form in a seemingly endless flow. There is a similar sort of concision in the more solid forms built by Wim Borst. Through the use of polished rather than glazed surfaces, Borst creates intriguing arrangements of line, form and structure that make use of the qualities of clay that enable it to be finely worked while constructing forms that take on architectural references. The assemblages put together by John Higgins also have echoes of architectural structures, but here are as concerned with abstract relationships between the different components as the entire structure.

The precise forms constructed by Ken Eastman evoke an air of majesty and restraint, structures that are enigmatic and aloof – part architectural, part landscape and part organic. Both Alison Britton's slab-built containers and Simon Carroll's thrown and manipulated forms are more robust and assertive. Both are as concerned with

inner as outer space, their forms hinting at internal structures. The forms assembled by Britton from soft slabs of clay retain vestigial references to domestic objects, be they jugs, teapots or cups, while the patterned surfaces recall an impression of textile design. The origins of Carroll's assembled structures lie deep in the technology and style of English slipwares, but these have been subjected to a wild and free interpretation that is totally rooted in the twenty-first century. A close look can begin to unravel the sources of the marks and decorative devices, which add to the multi-layered nature of these vessels.

Some of the freedom that Carroll handles with such confidence also informs the slip-decorated dishes and containers produced by Dylan Bowen. His uninhibited use of the conventional technique of slip decoration takes on a Pollock-esque quality in combining freedom and control. Working with thrown plates, dishes and vases, Dillon subverts both technique and the symmetry of the shape. Cutting and carving a basic thrown form can ingeniously combine the organic and architectural. Martin Lungley appears to have literally attacked the thickly thrown bowl to give it a rock-like appearance. Following the glaze firing the shape has been further enhanced with mother-of-pearl lustre, adding a further layer of meaning to an intriguing form.

1 Jean Baudrillard 'The System of Collecting', in Elsner John and Roger Cardinal (eds), *The Cultures of Collecting*, Harvard University Press, Mass., 1994, pp. 7–24.
2 The respected critic/art historian who argued for the acceptance of the Pattern and Decoration movement identified the position of the decorative arts writing, 'decorative art is intellectually empty but it does not have to be stupid'. Quoted by Garth Clark in Yvonne Joris (ed.), *Functional Glamour: Utility in Contemporary American Ceramics*, Museum Het Kruithuis, 's-Hertogenbosch, 1987.

left: **VIRGIL ORTIZ**
Untitled, Plant Tendril Jar, 2006,
h 30.5 × w 25.5 cm (12 × 10 in.)
Native clay, painted red, cream with native clay
slips and black wild spinach, native-fired

above: **VIRGIL ORTIZ**
Untitled, The Face Far, 2005,
h 42 × w 28 cm (16.5 × 11 in.)
Native clay, painted with red, cream native clay
slips and black wild spinach, native-fired

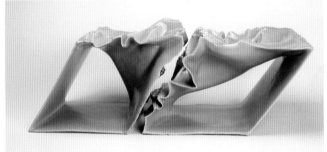

above: **LES BLAKEBROUGH**
Diamonds, 2003, h 18 cm (7 in.)
Southern Ice Porcelain, unglazed, deep-etched, fired to 1300°C reduction

right, top: **JEAN-FRANÇOIS FOUILHOUX**
Dessous, 2008, 34 × 87.5 × 34 cm (13¼ × 34¼ × 13¼ in.)
Porcelain, celadon glaze, reduction-fired

right, bottom: **JEAN-FRANÇOIS FOUILHOUX**
Grâce, 2007, w 43 cm (17 in.)
Porcelain, celadon glaze, reduction-fired

ANNE KRAUS
The Loving Cup, 1989, h 10 × dia 19 cm (4 × 7½ in.)
Whiteware
Legend, cup: I ached to suddenly realize the worlds
that separate us; saucer: I learned to see that when
my sand blew you saw rain falling. And then one
warm evening with my eyes closed I found a river's
edge and heard you call my name.

above, left: **ANNE KRAUS**
Shell Teapot, 1986, h 26 × w 19 cm (10¼ × 7½ in.)
Whiteware
Legend, front: Rick dreamt of a city by the sea. It was the largest city in the area he was
told; reverse: Rick awoke and journeyed on. The desert's edge was two days away.

above, right: **ANNE KRAUS**
Ambition/Patience Vase, 1985,
h 22.75 × w 21.5 cm (9 × 8½ in.)
Whiteware
Legend, front: Goal Ambition; reverse: Your dreams will be realized, but later.

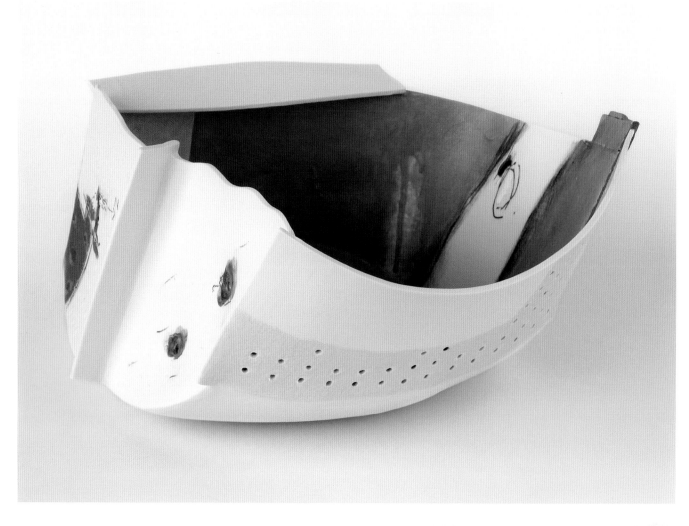

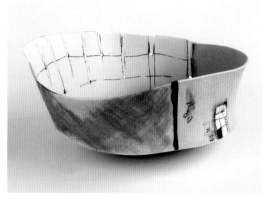

above: **YUK KAN YEUNG**
Float 13, 2007, w 37 cm (14½ in.)
Porcelain, vessel form

right: **YUK KAN YEUNG**
Letters Home, 2007, 14 cm (5½ in.)
Porcelain, vessel form

left: **SVEND BAYER**
Bottle, 2007, h 32 cm (12½ in.)
Stoneware, thrown, reduction-fired in fire box, its side
resting on shells

top: **JACK DOHERTY**
Ribbed Bowl, 2007, 40 × 19 cm (15¾ × 7½ in.)
Porcelain, thrown, altered with a rib when clay is still soft, colour
from a thin wash of a copper slip, soda glazed

above: **DUNCAN AYSCOUGH**
Two Rounded Vessels, 2008, dia 25 cm (10 in.)
White earthenware, terra sigillata, smoke-fired, gold leaf

right: **RICHARD NOTKIN**
All Nations have their Moment of Foolishness, 2004

below: **RICHARD NOTKIN**
Heart Teapot: Hostage/Metamorphosis III, Yixing Series, 2004, 17 × 31 × 15 cm (6½ × 12¼ × 6 in.)
Stoneware, hand-built, lustre

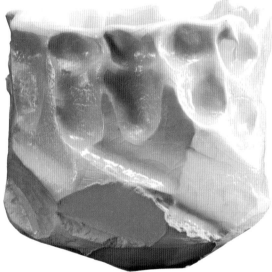

above: **SAM HALL**
Flat Vessel, 2007, h 48 × w 38 cm (19 × 15 in.)
Stoneware, thrown and flattened, earthenware and
porcelain slips, enamels, on-glaze pencil, fired,
1200°C

right, top: **MARTIN LUNGLEY**
Tea Bowl, 2007, h 11 cm (4¼ in.)
Porcelain, thrown and carved, lead glaze, mother-
of-pearl lustre

right, bottom: **KYRA CANE**
Wide Basin, 2007, w 45 cm (17½ in.)
Porcelain, thrown, decorated

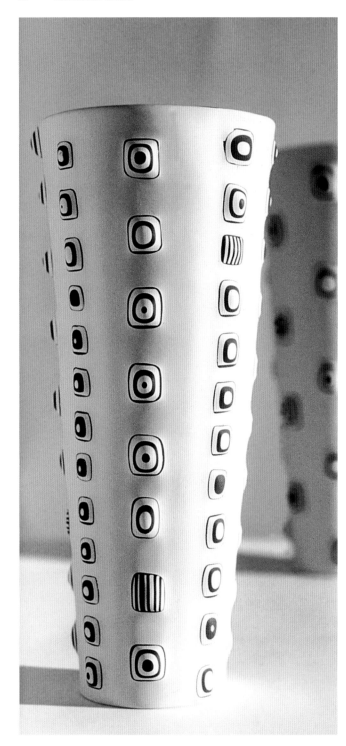

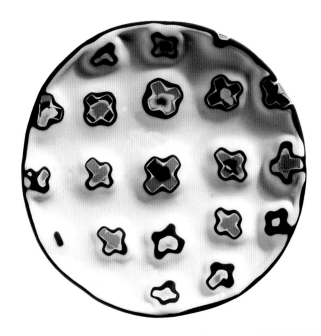

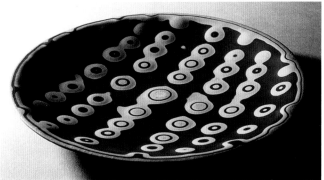

left: **KATHRYN HEARN**
Jasper Squares Vases, 2008, 35 and 30 cm (13¾ and 11¾ in.)
Earthenware, multi layers of coloured slip

top: **KATHRYN HEARN**
Dish, Pink Crosses, 2007, 10 cm (4 in.)
Porcelain, multi layers of coloured slip

above: **KATHRYN HEARN**
Jasper Agua Dish, 2007, 27 cm (10½ in.)
Earthenware, multi layers of coloured slip

right: **DIEGO ROMERO**
Golfer, 2004, dia 26 cm (10¼ in.)
Earthenware, hand-built

below: **DIEGO ROMERO**
Runners, 2006, dia 20 cm (8 in.)
Earthenware, hand-built

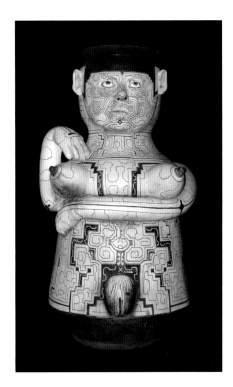

above: **KUKULI VELARDE**
*Chuncha Cretina, Never Know What she is
Thinking. Savage, Simple, Lascivious, Muy
Caliente. Conibo Alto Ucayali, Perú, 1,950, 2006,
h 81 cm (32 in.)*
White clay with stains and wax

right: **KUKULI VELARDE**
*Native Hysteric Macuarra Vulnerable, Defenseless.
A Fascinating Prey. She Gets Scared Easy, Mixteca,
Perú, AD 1250–1500, 2007, h 70 cm (27½ in.)*
Mocha clay with post-fired paint

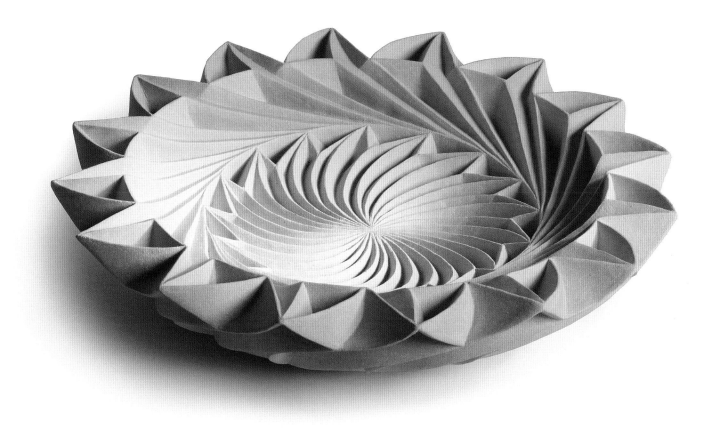

HALIMA CASSELL
R.E.M., 2006, dia 46 cm (18 in.)
Stoneware, carved

opposite, top left: **STEVE HARRISON**
King, Bowl, 2006, 11.7 × 11.4 × 6.3 cm
(4½ × 4½ × 2½ in.)
Thrown, duck egg guan glaze

opposite, middle left: **STEVE HARRISON**
Coura, Bowl, 2006, 12.3 × 12.3 × 6.5 cm
(4¾ × 4¾ × 2½ in.)
Thrown, blue guan glaze

opposite, bottom left: **HWANG JENG-DAW**
Untitled, Tea Bowl, 2008, approx. h 10 cm (4 in.)
Stoneware, thrown and altered, glazed,
fired to cone 9 in reduction

opposite, top right: **HWANG JENG-DAW**
Teapot – Lonely Mouse I, Reverse Side, 2008,
h 16 × w 23 × dia 15 cm (6¼ × 9 × 5¾ in.)
Stoneware, thrown and slab-built, glazed,
fired to cone 9 in reduction and cone 015
lustre firing

opposite, bottom right: **UWE LÖLLMANN**
Vessel, 2007, h 56 cm (22 in.)
Stoneware, thrown, reduction-fired

above, left: **ALISON BRITTON**
Echo, 2007, 40 × 23 × 24 cm (15¾ × 9 × 9½ in.)
Earthenware, slab-built, slip decoration

above, right: **ALISON BRITTON**
Ewer, 2007, 37 × 29 × 19 cm (14½ × 11¼ × 7½ in.)
Earthenware, slab-built, slip decoration

TINA VLASSOPULOS
Fin and Curl, 2007,
h 33.5 cm (13 in.) max.
Hand-built form, burnished
clay, fired, 920˚C

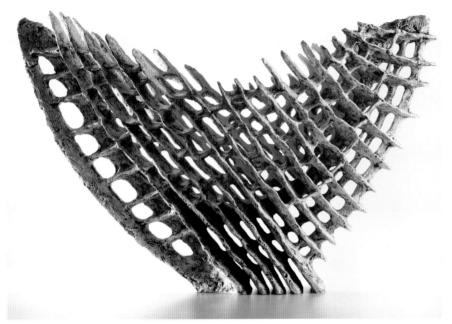

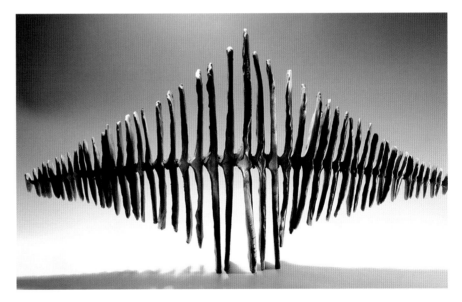

above, left: **BARBRO ÅBERG**
Momentum, 2007, 44 × 67 × 25 cm
(17¼ × 26¼ × 9¾ in.)
Ball clay, volcanic substance perlite and
paper fibres, terra sigillata, stains and oxides,
multi-fired, electric kiln to approx. 1135°C

above, right: **BARBRO ÅBERG**
Black and Blue Vase, 2007, 25 × 34 × 25 cm
(9¾ × 13¼ × 9¾ in.)
Ball clay, volcanic substance perlite and paper
fibres, terra sigillata with stains and oxides,
multi-fired electric kiln to approx. 1135° C

right: **ANTONIA SALMON**
Bridging Form, 2007,
h 34 ×161 cm (13¼ × 24 in.)
White stoneware, terra sigillata, burnished
and smoke-fired

above, left: **CAROL MCNICHOLL**
Shopping, 2007, h 41 × dia 47 cm (16 × 18½ in.)
Slip-cast and assembled components

above, right: **CAROL MCNICHOLL**
Reconstruction in North London, 2007,
h 50 cm (20 in.)
Slip-cast and assembled components

above, left: **PIPPIN DRYSDALE**
Red Dawn Rising – Tanami Traces Series V, 2007,
h 50 × dia 29.5 cm (19½ × 11½ in.)
Porcelain

top right: **PIPPIN DRYSDALE**
Vessels, 2007, heights variable
Porcelain

above, right: **EMMANUEL COOPER**
Bowls, 2008, front bowl, dia 31 cm (12 in.)
Stoneware, thrown and turned, slip, multiple glaze

left: **JENNIFER LEE**
Vessel, 2007, 25 × 24.8 cm (10 × 9¾ in.)
Hand-built coloured stoneware with
grained, speckled traces

below: **ALEV SIESBYE**
Mediterranen Blue Bowl, 2006, h 23.5 cm (9¼ in.), dia top 36.5 cm. (14¼ in.)
Stoneware, hand-built, fired in electric kiln, 1300°C

left: **JENNIFER LEE**
Vessel, 2007, 28.5 × 18.8 cm (11¼ × 7¼ in.)
Hand- built coloured stoneware with
olive, haloed umber band

above: **ALEV SIESBYE**
Matt Grey/Black Bowl, 2008,
h 17 cm (6¾ in.), dia top 28.5 cm (11¼ in.)
Stoneware, hand-built, aluminium coated,
electric kiln, 1300°C

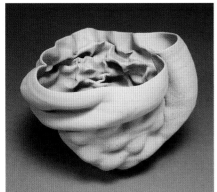

above: **ANNE-MARIE LAUREYS**
Clay-e-motion, Form, 2007,
dia 25 × 33 × 35 cm (10 × 13 × 13¾ in.)
Belgian clay thrown and altered, clay glazes,
1140–1180°C

right: **ANNE-MARIE LAUREYS**
Clay-e-motion, Form, 2006,
21 × 20 × 15 cm (8¼ × 7¾ × 6 in.)
Belgian clay thrown and altered, clay glazes,
1140–1180°C

left: **DAVID GARLAND**
Vase, 2006, h 39 cm (15¼ in.)
Red earthenware clay, thrown, slip

top: **DAVID GARLAND**
Vase, 2006, h 39 cm (15¼ in.)
Red earthenware clay, thrown, slip

above: **DAVID GARLAND**
Bowl Form, 2006, h 27 cm (10½ in.)
Red earthenware, thrown, black and white slips

above: **RUPERT SPIRA**
Open Bowl, 2007, dia 40 cm (15¾ in.)
Stoneware, thrown, incised text
and black pigment over white glaze

right: **TANYA GOMEZ**
Mornington Blue, Bowl, 2007,
11 × 25 cm (4¼ × 9¾ in.)
Porcelain

above, left: **STEVE IRVINE**
Bronze Tradition Vase, 2004, h 30 cm (11¼ in.)
Stoneware, reduction-fired

above, right: **STEVE IRVINE**
Convection Pattern Jar, 2008,
h 53 × w 32 × dia 32 cm (20¾ × 12½ × 12½ in.)
Stoneware, thrown and altered, reduction-fired,
cone 10, glazes, with a post-firing application
of 23K gold leaf

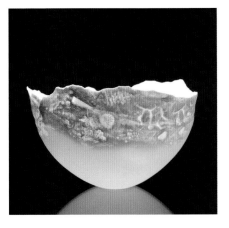

above, left: **SUSAN COLLETT**
Crucible, 2007, h 117 × w 61 × dia 58.5 cm
(46 × 24 × 23 in.)
Earthenware paper clay, multi-fired

above, right: **SUSAN COLLETT**
Sway, 2007, h 58 cm (22¾ in.)
Earthenware paperclay, multi-fired

left: **ANGELA MELLOR**
Cretaceous Bowl, 2003, dia 14.5 cm (5½ in.)
Slip-cast bone china with paper-slip inlay

above, left: **KATE MALONE**
Tutti Frutti Flaming Clover, 2007, h 24 cm (9½ in.)
Pebble-glazed earthenware

above, right: **KATE MALONE**
A Big Boy Gourd, 2007,
h 42 × dia 26 cm (17 × 10¼ in.)
Crystalline-glazed stoneware

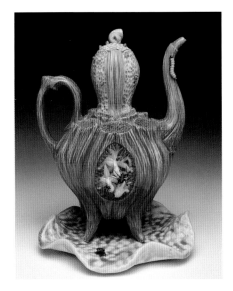

top: **BONNIE SEEMAN**
Untitled Teapot and Tray, 2008,
16.5 × 14 × 23 cm (6½ × 5½ × 9 in.)
Porcelain and glass

above: **BONNIE SEEMAN**
Pitcher and Tray, 2005, h 37 cm (14½ in.)
Porcelain and glass

above: **YING-YUEH CHUANG**
Plant-Creature, 2003, 11.5 × 30 × 30 cm
(4½ × 12 × 12 in.)
Ceramic, multi-fired, 2 stacked elements

GUNHILD RUDJORD
Untitled, Dish, 2007, dia 45 cm (17¾ in.)
Earthenware with oxides and glazes

RALPH BACERRA
Untitled, Platter, 2005, dia 58 cm (22¾ in.)
Ceramic

left: **ZAHARA HAREL**
Fragment of Interior Images, detail, 2006,
h 36 × w 67 × dia 25 cm (14 × 26¼ × 10 in.)
Ceramic

above: **ZAHARA HAREL**
Valentine's Mood, detail, 2006
Ceramic

left: **MATTHIAS OSTERMANN**
Balancing, 2004, h 23 cm (9 in.)
Earthenware, thrown and altered, clay sgraffito
through vitreous engobe, with interventions
of copper, coloured stains and saturated colour
engobes multi-fired in oxidation to 1040°C

above: **KAREN ATHERLEY**
Dish, 2006, dia 35 cm (13¾ in.)
Earthenware, slip, pigment

above: **STEPHEN BOWERS**
Icarus in the Antipodes, Platter, 2007,
h 5 × dia 60 cm (2 × 23½ in.)
Earthenware, wheel-thrown, underglaze colours
and cobalt blue, 1170°C with on-glaze gold lustré

right: **STEPHEN BOWERS**
*Links of Charmshire (an Antipodean Homage to
Grayson Perry),* 2007, d 7 × 65 cm (2¾ × 25½ in.)
Earthenware, wheel-thrown, underglaze
decorated, 1170°C, some with on-glaze gold lustre

above: **LIDIA BOSEVSKI**
Lace, Bowl, 2007
Terracotta, constructed from handmade spirals,
wooden mould, made on CNC based on 3-D model,
980°C

right: **LIDIA BOSEVSKI**
Nest, Bowl, 2007
Brown clay, constructed from handmade clay
'spaghetti' on wooden calote mould, 1000°C

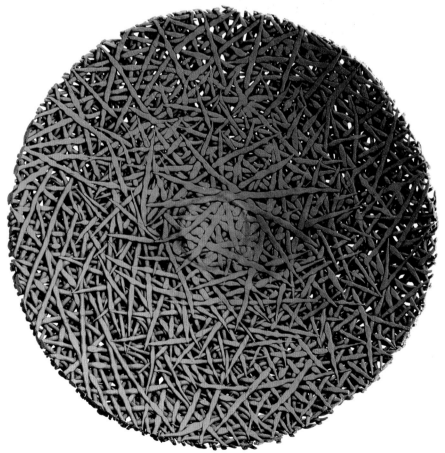

top: **TOR ALEX ERICHSEN**
The King and I, 2007, h 27 cm (10½ in.)
Earthenware, slip and glaze

above, left: **JANICE TCHALENKO**
Yellow Leaf Bowl, 2007, h 13 × d 25.8 cm (5 × 10 in.)
Earthenware, thrown, yellow glaze

above, right: **ASHLEY HOWARD**
Tea Bowl, 2007, 10 × 10 cm (4 × 4 in.)
Porcelain, thrown and altered, enamel collage and gold lustre

top: **ROBIN BEST**
Best Baker, Settlement, 2007,
tallest approx. 33 cm (13 in.)
Porcelain, printed/painted decoration

above, left: **ROBIN BEST**
Coral Vase and Hydra Vase, 2007,
tallest approx. 32 cm (12½ in.)
Porcelain, printed/painted decoration

above, right: **ROBIN BEST**
Oriental Kangaroo, 2007,
h approx. 40 cm (15¾ in.)
Porcelain, printed decoration

opposite, left: **SIN-YING HO**
Bella, 2005, 47 × 30.5 cm (18.5 × 12 in.)
Porcelain, wheel-thrown, hand-painted cobalt blue, enamel,
lustre, computer decal transfer, high-fire reduction

opposite, top right: **SIN-YING HO**
Gibberish III, 2005, 39 × 25.5 cm (15½ × 10 in.)
Porcelain, wheel-thrown, hand-painted cobalt blue,
computer decal transfer, high-fire reduction

opposite, bottom right: **SIN-YING HO**
Binary Code – the Link, 2004, 2 × 8 × 1.5 cm (5 × 21 × 4 in.)
Porcelain, wheel-thrown and slip-cast, hand-painted cobalt blue,
computer decal transfer, terra sigillata high-fire reduction

above: **ALICE MARA**
Dog Track, 2007, 18 × 36 cm (7 × 14 in.)
Rectangular porcelain plate (Maxwell and Williams) digital print

right: **ALICE MARA**
Sink Plate, 2007, 26 × 26 cm (10¼ × 10¼ in.)
Bone china plate (Wedgwood), digital print

top: **SASHA WARDELL**
Sand Coral Bowls, 2007–2008,
h 20 × 9 cm (7¾ × 3½ in.)
Slip-cast bone china, water erosion technique

above: **TAKESHI YASUDA**
Pale Blue Bowl, 2007, h 8 × dia 29 cm (3 × 11¼ in.)
Porcelain, thrown, ying ching glaze, reduction-fired, cone 11

left: **SASHA WARDELL**
Space Bowl, 2007–2008, dia 40 cm (15¾ in.)
Slip-cast bone china with layering and slicing technique

above: **DAVID POTTINGER**
Neriage Tea Bowls, 2007, 80 × 110 × 75 cm
(31½ × 43 × 29½ in.)
Porcelain, coloured lamination, high-fired

right: **DOROTHY FEIBLEMAN**
Sake Cups, 2007, h 5 cm (2 in.) max.
Porcelain, laminated

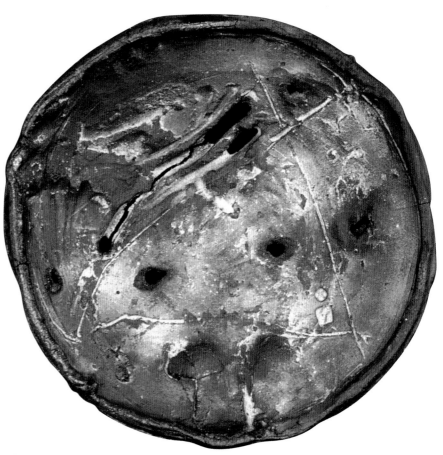

top: **GARETH MASON**
Jar, 2005, h 61 cm (24 in.)
Stoneware and porcelain, thrown, altered, crackle
celadon and copper red glaze with underglaze
vitreous slips, reduction-fired

above: **GARETH MASON**
Jar, Appended Iron Stone Series, 2007,
h 66 cm (26 in.)
Stoneware and porcelain, thrown, altered,
vitreous slips, glaze, mineral, oxide, iron stone,
reduction-fired

above: **CHARLES BOUND**
Plate, 2004, dia 55 cm (21½ in.)
Stoneware, thrown, reduction-fired

left: **MORTEN LØBNER ESPERSEN**
Installation View at Galleri Nørby, 2006
Stoneware and earthenware

below: **TOSHIKO TAKAEZU**
Five Pots, 2007, h approx. 13 cm (5 in.)
Porcelain and stoneware

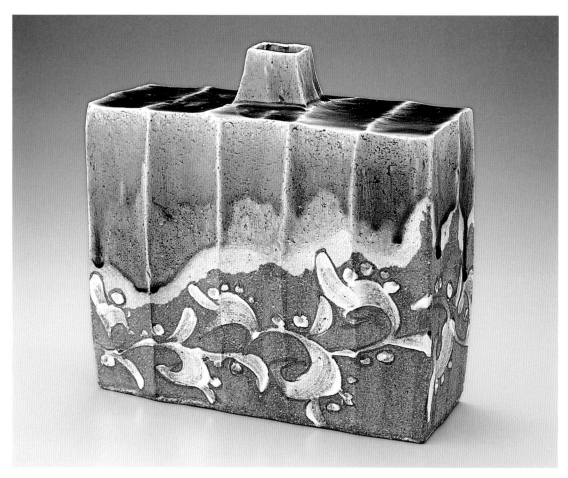

above: **KEN MATSUZAKI**
Narumi Oribe, Rectangular Vase, 2007,
h 28 cm (11 in.)
Stoneware, reduction-fired

right: **KEN MATSUZAKI**
Yohen Shino, Rectangular Vases, 2007,
h 28 cm (10 in.)
Stoneware with natural ash glaze

above, left: **NIC COLLINS**
Three Bottles, 2007, h 20 cm (8 in.)
Stoneware, thrown, wood-fired

above, right: **PHIL ROGERS**
Faceted Bottle, 2008, h 23 cm (9 in.)
Stoneware, thrown and carved, wood-fired,
made from a clay body constructed from
the chemical analysis of Shigaraki clay

right: **JANET MANSFIELD**
Lidded Jar, 2007, h 28 cm (11 in.)
Stoneware, thrown, wood-fired in
anagama kiln, natural ash glaze

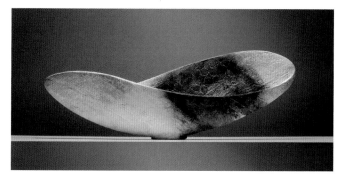

top: **MARTIN MCWILLIAM**
In Out Blue, 2007, h 30 cm (11¾ in.)
Stoneware, reduction-fired

above: **MARTIN MCWILLIAM**
Sway, 2007
Stoneware, reduction-fired

above, left: **SIMCHA EVEN-CHEN**
Square Enigma, 2007, h 24–33 × w 28 × dia 19 cm
(9½–13 × 11 × 7½ in.)
Stoneware and porcelain mix, hand-built from
slabs, burnished, terra sigillata 'Naked Raku'

above, right: **SIMCHA EVEN-CHEN**
Double Sequence, 2008, h 13.5 × w 60 × dia 40 cm
(5¼ × 23½ × 15¾ in.)
Stoneware and porcelain mix, hand-built from
slabs, burnished, terra sigillata 'Naked Raku'

above: **ASHRAF HANNA**
Angular Bowl, 2007, dia 40 cm (15¾ in.)
Earthenware, hand-built, raku

right: **ASHRAF HANNA**
Carved Vessel Form, 2007, h 55 cm (21½ in.)
Earthenware, hand-built, raku

opposite, left: **MAGDALENE ODUNDO**
Vessel Series III, no. 3, 2007,
51.2 × 24 cm (20 × 9½ in.)
Red clay, carbonized and multi-fired

opposite, top right: **MAGDALENE ODUNDO**
Freund, Vessel Series III, no. 4, 2005–2006,
55.3 × 26.5 cm (21¾ × 10½ in.)
Red clay, carbonized and multi-fired

opposite, bottom right: **MAGDALENE ODUNDO**
Vessel Series II, Assymetrical no.1, 2005–2006,
56.4 × 29.7 cm (22 × 11½ in.)
Red clay, carbonized and multi-fired

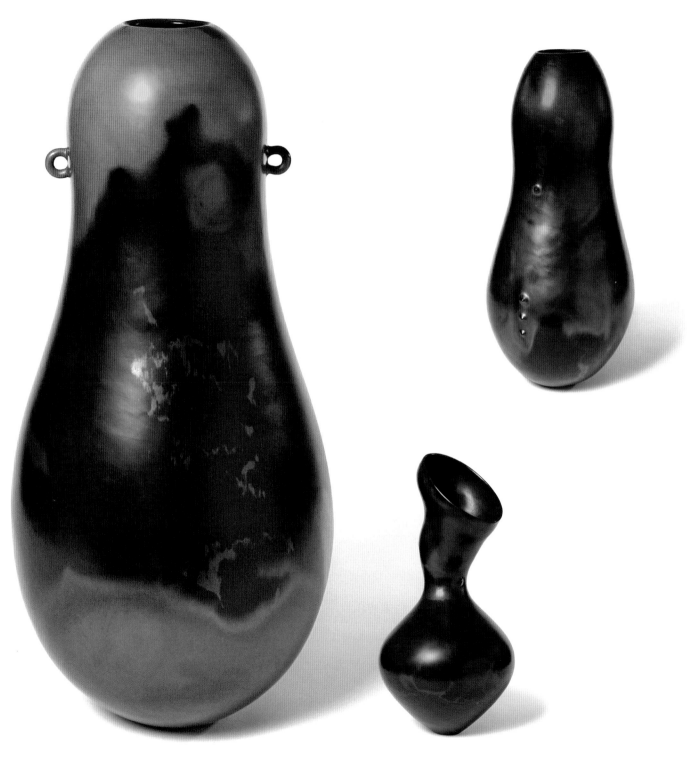

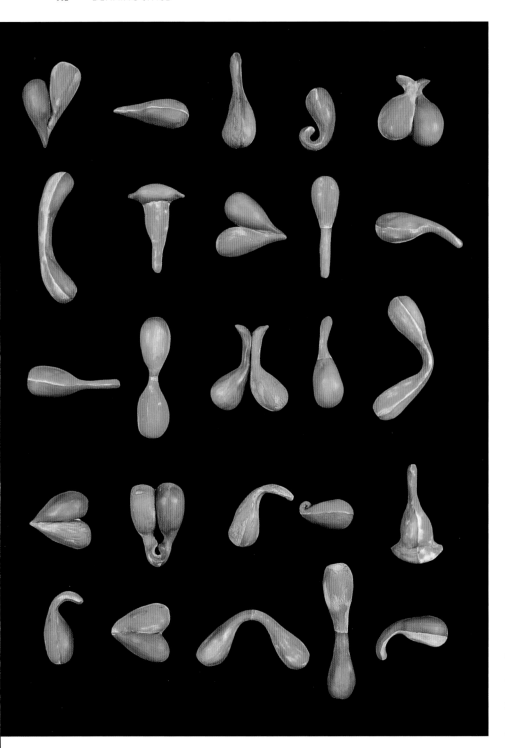

above: JOHN NUTTGENS
Leaf, 2004, h 25 cm (10 in.)
Smoke-fired terra sigillata

left: MADHVI SUBRAHMANIAN
Hieroglyphs, 2007, w 10 × l 134.5 cm (4 × 53 in.)
Earthenware

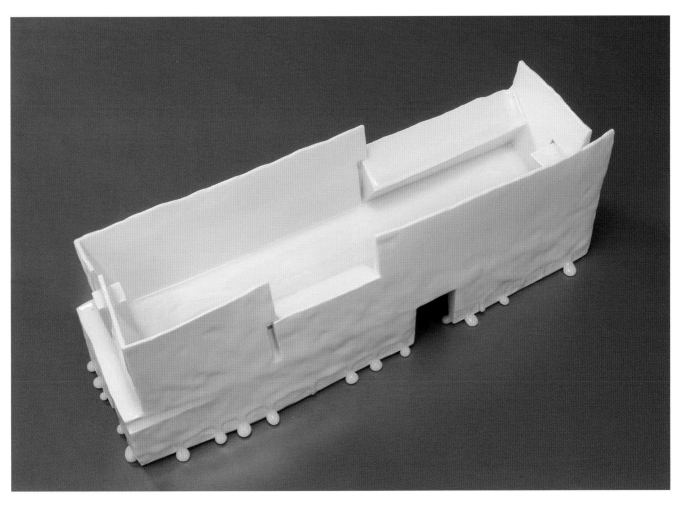

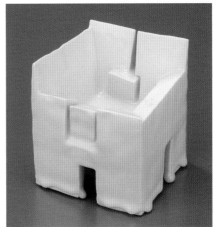

above: **MASAMICHI YOSHIKAWA**
Vessel, 2007, 161 cm (24 in.)
Porcelain, blue celadon glaze, reduction-fired

right: **MASAMICHI YOSHIKAWA**
Kayho, 2007, h 16 × w 14 × l 14 cm
(6¼ × 5½ × 5½ in.)
Porcelain, blue celadon glaze, reduction-fired

above: **BODIL MANZ**
Six Cylinders, 2005,
each 8 × 9 cm (3 × 3½ in.)
Slip-cast porcelain, decals

right: **BODIL MANZ**
The Architectual Volume, 2007,
each dia approx. 7 cm (2¾ in.)
Slip-cast porcelain, decals

above, left: **KRISTINA RISKA**
Bath, 2007
Ceramic

above, right: **KARIN BABLOK**
Vessel, 2007,
h approx. 10 cm (4 in.)
Porcelain, thrown, manipulated, cobalt

left: **KARIN BABLOK**
Two Vessels, 2007,
h approx. 10 cm (4 in.)
Porcelain, thrown, manipulated,
black pigment

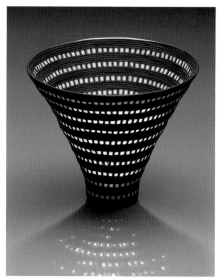

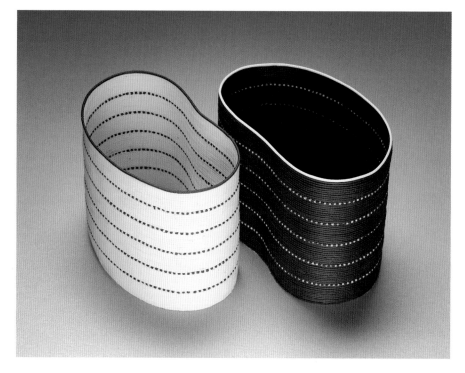

above, left: **KRISTINA RISKA**
Basket, 2007
Ceramic

above, right: **LUT LALEMAN**
Vessel, 2006, h 13.5 cm (5¼ in.)
Ceramic

right: **LUT LALEMAN**
Vessel, 2007, h 14 cm (5½ in.)
Ceramic

top: **HENK WOLVERS**
Vessel, 2007, 30 × 24 cm
(11¾ × 9½ in.)
Porcelain, pigment

above: **HENK WOLVERS**
Vessel, 2006, 17 × 12 cm
(6¾ × 4¾ in.)
Porcelain, pigment

right: **GUSTAVO PEREZ**
Vase, Untitled, 1995, 31 × 21.5 cm
(12 × 8½ in.)
Stoneware

far right: **GUSTAVO PEREZ**
Vase, Untitled, 2000, 36.8 × 26.6 ×
26.6 cm (14½ × 10½ × 10½ in.)
Stoneware

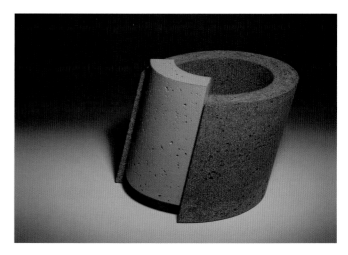

above, left: **SARAH-JANE SELWOOD**
Eye of the Storm – Horizontal Inset Inversion, 2007,
h 18 × dia 30 cm (7 × 11¾ in.)
Porcelain, thrown and assembled

above, right: **RON NAGLE**
Tea and Krumpin, 2005, 8 × 11 × 7.5 cm
(3¼ × 4¼ × 3 in.)
Ceramic, glazed

right: **WIM BORST**
Cone Series, 2007, 24.5 × 8 cm (9½ × 3 in.)
Porcelain

above, left: **KEN EASTMAN**
Slowburner, 2006, 47 × 41 × 33 cm
(18½ × 16 × 13 in.)
Ceramic, hand-built

top right: **CHRISTINE FABRE**
Retour de Chine, Terre Textile, 2006,
30 × 21 cm (11¾ × 8¼ in.)
Ceramic

above, right: **JOHN HIGGINS**
Vessel, 2007, h 30 × w 25 cm (11¾ × 10 in.)
Grogged clay, slab-formed, oxides, slips,
underglaze colours, 1120°C

above, left: **SIMON CARROLL**
Vessel, 2007, h 84 cm (33 in.)
Earthenware, thrown and assembled

above, right: **SIMON CARROLL**
Vessel, 2007, h 70 cm (27½ in.)
Earthenware, thrown and assembled

above, left: **DYLAN BOWEN**
Platter, 2006, 54 × 10 cm (21 × 4 in.)
Red earthenware, thrown, slip decoration, clear glaze

right: **JIM MALONE**
Globular Jar with Three Lugs and Two Ridges, 2008,
h 30 cm (11¾ in.)
Stoneware, thrown, engraved, ash and iron glaze

ARDMORE CERAMICS
Vessel, 2007, h approx. 25 cm (10 in.)
Earthenware, thrown, modelled, painted

above: **ARDMORE CERAMICS**
Teapot with Leopard, 2005,
h approx. 20 cm (7¾ in.)
Earthenware, thrown, modelled, painted

left: **ARDMORE CERAMICS**
Plate, 2007, dia approx. 25 cm (10 in.)
Earthenware, painted by Wonderboy Nxumalo

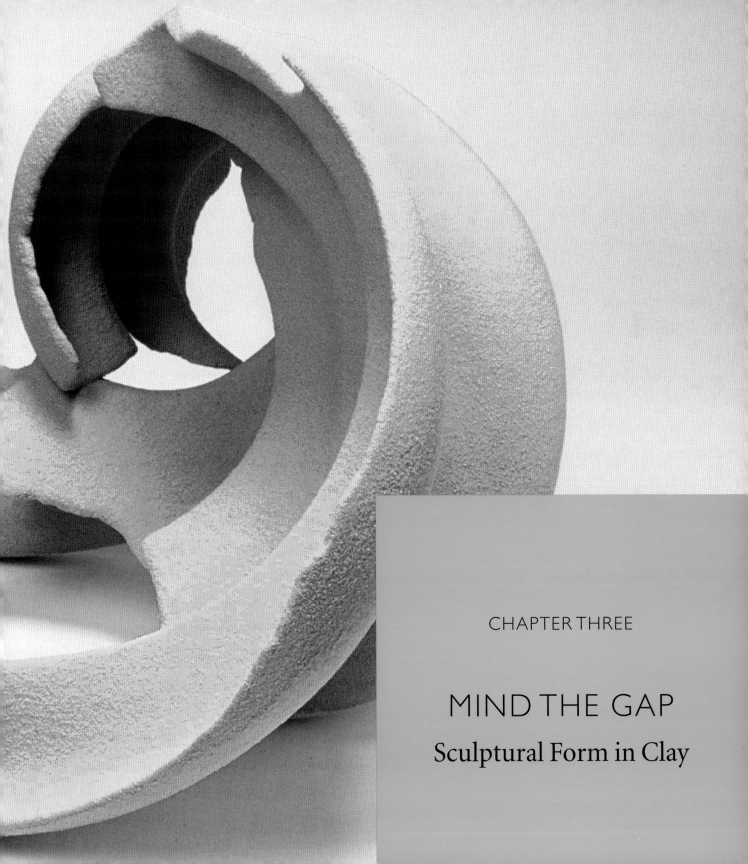

MIND THE GAP

Sculptural Form in Clay

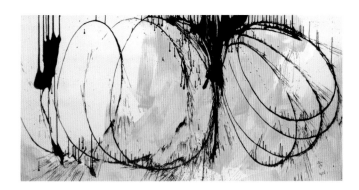

Traditionally sculptors have rarely used clay as a material in its own right, generally preferring to work in bronze, precious metal, marble and wood, although clay has often been used as a staging post for work that has been subsequently cast in metal. Today, one of the basic claims by artists is the freedom to employ any material that seems most appropriate. This has led to an upsurge in interest in clay as a material with qualities of its own, provoking a rethink of its status within the visual arts.

Such issues give rise to the question of what to call such work? It would be rash to claim that just because an object is non function-al it is sculpture. The borderline between painting and ceramics is particularly blurred in two-dimensional work. Ole Lislerud's panels, with their dramatic, expressionistic use of colour and multi-layering create powerful narratives, with titles such as *Another Ugly Day on Wall Street* (2007) and *Growth Prospects* (2007) suggesting the here and now. In a different mood, the splash of colour and light across Sun Chao's panels could be seen as cellular, snow or some heavenly vision that is at once mysterious and elusive.

Much of the work illustrated is so profoundly involved in the techniques, materials and forms of conventional functional crafts that these remain a powerful frame of reference. In addition, some work makes use of the concepts of craft to explore a range of mean-ings, often by making use of the binary oppositions 'function present/function absent' or 'function offered/function denied', to employ Howard Risatti's useful phrase, as a conceptual approach.[1] The chair built by Goro Suzuki is a case in point. This pastiche of Oribe ware of Japan is clearly not intended to be utilitarian but is an idea around a chair.

The blurring of the line between sculpture and craft has been one of the concerns of the highly influential European Ceramic Workcentre in 's-Hertogenbosch, the Netherlands, which was set up to encourage experiment within ceramics. Visitors have included leading artists such as Antony Gormley, Anish Kapoor, Richard Deacon, Richard Wentworth and Tony Cragg. Artists at the Centre spend time pursuing projects that make use of the sophisticated equipment available to explore a diverse range of ideas. In addition to providing first-class facilities, the Centre carries out and publishes research into various technical aspects of ceramics.[2]

STILL LIFE

Representations of inanimate objects, for example fruit, flowers, domestic utensils or food, have long engaged artists, a way of reflecting and commenting on the familiar world of the every day. Adopting the credo of modernism, sculptors in clay produce still life, not primarily as a visual anecdote or the reproduction of something in nature outside itself, but as the creation of new dispositions of shape and appearance.

Today artists such as Richard Shaw, Sylvia Hyman and Bertozzi & Casoni have further perfected this form, Hyman working with themes that arose in the Netherlands in the seventeenth and eighteenth centuries. For Shaw, the selection of the objects he portrays is just as significant as the way they are produced, part of a bringing up to date of a borrowing from history. Working on a larger scale, Bertozzi & Casoni create complex bricolage that may include Brillo boxes, parrots, dogs and life-sized oil barrels to comment on issues around the crisis of the environment, the history of art or the hopelessness of life.

left: **MAREK CECULA**
Air, Mutant, Set 3, 2000,
28 × 28 × 4 cm (11 × 11 × 1½ in.)
Industrial porcelain, alternated

below: **TONY MARSH**
*Untitled (Radiance and Abundance
Series)*, 2007, h 23 cm (9 in.)
Ceramic

Not all artists seek such verisimilitude. In the work of David Regan familiar objects, such as hands and teapots, take on surreal life, their highly detailed decorated surface adding to the overall effect. Tony Marsh assembles finely made objects or containers that may relate to fruit placed in bowls, or may be merely a way of keeping things tidy. The wall pieces created by Isobel Egan recall the shelves of a domestic setting but here are honed and simplified, shelves as starting points for an idea or thought.

The still-life groups assembled by Marek Cecula, using pots produced from redundant factory moulds, are a mediation that touches on industrial production, on consumerism and the studio pottery tradition of wood-firing, among other issues. These ostensibly conventional forms are subtly transformed into a wayward and disturbing version of normality. Some are assembled into piles, others fired in an *anagama* firing, turning the forms into brown and golden burnt offerings, adding further distortion to these still-life assemblies. In bringing a new awareness of the manufacturing process and the market it serves, Cecula questions consumerism and what it represents.

The groups that Annette Corcoran put together are exotic in both their choice of contents and in the use of colour and finish. These larger-than-life close-ups of such things as flowers, birds and plants are both eerily engaging and unsettling. Equally unnerving are the groups assembled by Wendy Walgate. These near life-sized assemblies may involve everyday objects, whether children's toys such as wheelbarrows, toy boxes and chairs piled high with colourful toy animals in nightmarish confusion, which are anything but reassuring or playful.

A major influence on the work of several artists are the paintings of Giorgio Morandi. In seeking to avoid literary or symbolic content, he concentrated on a form of plastic expression that has been read by many as poetic, subtle, restrained and intimate. Such qualities certainly imbue the groups of thrown bottles, beakers, bowls and jugs by Gwyn Hanssen Pigott. Precisely thrown in porcelain, Pigott's carefully arranged vessels conjure up their own quiet worlds, describing a narrative around collectivity that we must decode for ourselves. The precise placing of containers to be more than the sum of their parts is also evident in work by Chun Liao and Pippin Drysdale.

Taking as her starting point everyday objects and transforming them into art is one of the concerns of Betty Woodman. In recent work she has reduced the forms of such things as vessels and ribbons to flattened, low-relief forms and mounted them on the wall to combine the work of both painter and sculptor. Free-flowing, colourful and exuberant, Woodman takes us on a metaphorical – and joyful – voyage of discovery. Low relief is also the approach used by Sheryl McRoberts, whose modelled bowls and fruits create a clay-like interpretation of a conventional still life, one in which components are happily united. Equally evocative in defining the space they occupy are the arrangement of teacups and teapots on a stand by Julian Stair. These create private, self-contained worlds that quietly allude to ritual and ceremony.

MINIMALIST OPTIONS
One of the basic tenets of the minimalist art movement is the absence of evidence of the human hand. With surface and

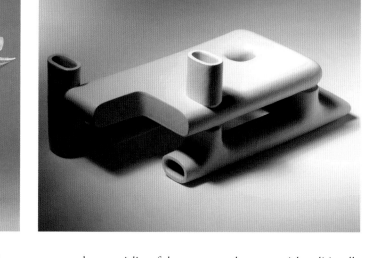

right: ANNETTE
CORCORAN
*Banana Flower, Royal
Flycatcher Teapot,*
2005, h 32 × w 29 ×
dia 20 cm
(12 ½ × 11½ × 8 in.)
Porcelain, hand-built,
underglaze, glaze and
overglaze

shape honed down to essential elements, these often make use of geometrical form as a way of distancing the work from any emotional reference, so permitting a particular involvement with the chosen material as a key signifier of meaning. Within ceramics, this often involves the use of polished rather than glazed surfaces such as in David Binns's geometrical forms, where the stone-like surface adds a further dimension to the monumental, soaring works. By contrast, Tyler Lotz creates spring-like forms full of energy and movement, which, despite their acid colours, owe more to industry and the machine than nature. Twisted as if ready for action, these are objects that hold meaning and form as one.

Equally involving are Wouter Dam's circular, flowing forms. Crisply constructed with engineered precision, Dam's work leads the eye inside and out, forever discovering new facets, new surfaces to retain visual interest. Forms morphing and parting are other themes explored, and just some of the ambiguities in the work of Mieke de Groot, Michael Cleff and Barbara Nanning. Part organic and part architectural, Cleff leaves us to make sense of these intriguing forms. Nanning twists and turns the form, often using bold, primary colours to contrast with the suggested sense of growth. There is a similar ambiguity in the work of Philippe Barde and André Hess. Barde's twin form, *Copy,* is part organic, part human and part geological, while Hess builds objects that are also reminiscent of freely interpreted natural form. Osamma Eman creates architectural forms that morph the vessel with the built environment.

The articulation of interlocking forms is confidentially explored by artists Martin Smith and Inger Södergren. Smith often combines both ceramic and glass in architecturally referenced structures that contrast the materiality of the terracotta clay – material traditionally used within the building industry – with the hard, reflective surface of the coloured glass. The application of silver, aluminium or gold leaf on inside surfaces picks up the colour of the glass, creating further reflections on the luscious surfaces. Dealing as much with the formal concerns of sculpture, such as line, form and colour as with feeling or emotion, Smith brings to his work an awareness of the significance of his chosen material as part of its cerebral meaning. In contrast, Södergren's carefully articulated forms combine a suggestion of the natural world with precision engineering. Like certain types of coiled spring, or the back of an armadillo, the parts interconnect to form a convincing whole. Artists, including Karen Bennicke and John Mason share an interest: their carefully crafted shapes are meticulously worked, their sense of monumentality an important part of their quality.

One of the characteristics of minimalist-based work is the primacy it places on opticality – the importance of the look – over substance. This is brought to near perfection in the work of Ken Price and Ron Nagle. Both work on a small scale, offering a particular sort of intimacy with the object. Technique, in controlling and perfecting the forms and the application of either glaze for Nagle or acrylic for Price, is an essential ingredient in the work. Both artists achieve a painterly quality that is given resonance by the three dimensionality of the object. In a different mood, Robert Winokur creates buildings that are simplified and abstracted to the point where illusion and structure are successfully combined.

More relaxed but equally taut in its concept and making is work by Susan Disley, the gentle slopes and details of the forms evoking

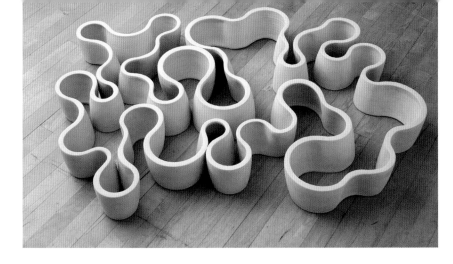

opposite, right: **KAREN BENNICKE**
Construction no. 1, 2004,
h 17.5 × w 30 × l 50 cm (7 × 11¾ × 19½ in.)
Low-fire stoneware with matt glaze

left: **RICHARD DEACON**
Ribbon Bow, 2004, l 118 cm (46 in.)
Unglazed ceramic

a complex narrative of stillness and movement. Architecture and parts of machinery could also be the starting point for these abstracted forms. Maciej Kasperski's tall, totemic-like forms and his curved rocking shapes appear to be built up from multi-layered additions, combining simplicity with an organic sense of growth.

SIZE MATTERS

Scale and the impact it makes are often seen as important defining aspects of sculpture, raising the question of whether small objects, however beautiful, can be deemed sculpture. While this poses questions about the way scale determines the way we can appropriate objects, it is only one factor. Traditionally, clay has been seen as having domestic associations, but artists have discovered its potential for making effective large-scale work that can be sited either indoors or in the landscape. The vast interior works that are created by artists such as Wayne Higby and Ruth Duckworth, whether in porcelain or other ceramic material, attest to the ability of clay to be effective no matter what the scale.

Richard Deacon, a sculptor best known for his work with wood and metal in various forms, also works with clay, attracted by its material qualities and its ability to be modelled and shaped as well as glazed. In some pieces he incorporates abstracted forms placed on solid plinths, which become a crucial part of the piece, or, in other works, stand, more informally, on the ground.

The sense of the organic, of forms appearing to grow and accrete on their own, is a crucial part of the soaring forms of Lawson Oyekan, who builds his pieces by coiling to create a larger-than-life-

sized presence. Some, standing 2.5 m (8 ft) high, are objects to engage with at many levels. In their cultural references, to African and European forms, Oyekan successfully brings together diverse influences to create objects that merge the constructed and the organic. Claudi Casanovas uses the primary, unsophisticated qualities of clay as a major part of his work. He exploits its qualities of roughness, earthiness and rock-like qualities to create seductive, monumental forms that contain a sense of the essence of the material with an eye for shape and volume. He, like Rafa Perézi, evokes the powerful forces of nature to build work that is both spectacular and accessible.

Diverse cultural and material influences also inform the tall vessels by Felicity Aylieff. These were made during a six-month residency in China at the 'porcelain capital' of the country, Jingdezhen. Some vessels have smoothly flowing shapes, others have a more articulated structure. The outcome is a hybrid of Chinese and European sensibility. The forms with cobalt blue painted decoration also recall aspects of traditional work, but are given a modern thrust with broad brushstrokes that move and flitter over the surface to create multi-layered patterning.

The idea of taking familiar forms and enlarging them to monumental proportions is central to the work of artists such as Aylieff, Nicholas Rena and Marit Tingleff. The vastly oversized jugs and bowls constructed by Rena take up iconic forms, which, in their simplicity, reflect on themes such as plenty, abundance and fecundity to transcend any purely domestic associations. Tingleff's huge dishes, measuring some 140 cm (55 in.) in length, take the idea of the serving dish as a starting point but push it to giant proportions. Decorated with abstracted pours and overlaps of slips and glaze, the

FERNANDO CASASEMPERE
Under the Forest, 2007, 5 sections,
each one 3.2 m (10½ ft) high and
approx 1 ton in weight
Ceramic
On show in Ragley Hall, Jerwood
Foundation commission

work could be seen to be allied to the Pattern and Decoration Movement of the 1970s, but the use of the dish form prevents any such easy reading, other than it is a domestic form taken to its outer limits. Pushing ideas to the limits is part of handling large-scale works, with artists taking calculated risks. Fiamma Colonna Montagu has produced forms that convincingly morph trees and clouds into sculptures standing some 2.4 m (8 ft) high, which sit easily within, while also disrupting, their surrounding landscape. Scale is also handled with confidence and assurance by Fernando Casasempere on abstract forms, some of which bear figural references. Both Montagu and Casasempere incorporate an awareness of the organic that is abstracted and distilled.

The relationship between spectacle and scale is imaginatively explored by many artists who push the handling of clay to its limits. Such work may comment on issues such as change in the environment, consumer culture and the abiding power of nature. The broken-down, decrepit automobile that features in Kristen Morgin's work is both spectacular and cautionary and touches on many of these concepts. At one level the sculpture can be seen to be addressing environmental concerns, while also commenting on ageing and decay, particularly of consumer possessions. In contrast, Daphné Corregan's vessel forms and cloud-like wall pieces conjure up a quieter, more serene space, where the objects can be seen as metaphors for the individual either alone or in a group.

Scale plays a significant part in the sculptures of Sandy Brown. The tall, abstracted rounded forms can be seen as making reference to the female figure, an impression enhanced by the bold and fresh use of colour that explores and affirms aspects of the 'feminine'. The

fractured and reassembled large vessels by Claudia Clare also address issues of gender and inequality, their sure graphic sense asserting the relevance of pictorial imagery. The large vessels, painted with naturalistic images of women, broken into fragments and reassembled bear visible evidence of shattered histories.

GROUNDED

Nature and the organic in all its diversity have been one of the enduring touchstones of art. Forms mutating, morphing, growing and changing suggest both growth and expansion as well as danger. Bente Skjøttgaard builds forms that are organic but might have morphed with buildings, but the final impression is one of change and uncertainty, while the organically derived forms by Redo Del Olmo are part plant, part fantasy. Nature is the starting point for the work of Petra Wolf, whose twisting, gyrating forms appear to have mysterious inner life. The vast panels of broken clay, the huge horn suspended in the centre of a gallery and the broken vessel created by Pekka Paikkari touch on the conflicting aspects of nature, something we may or may not be able to control. Aneta Regel Deleu imbues her rock-like forms with rich, saturated pigment, removing any obvious references to the natural world.

A sense of the inner structures of nature inform Natasha Lewer's colourful, cell-like spherical objects. These recall grains of pollen or seeds imbued with heightened technicolour that appear to be tumbling round, their saturated hues redolent with danger and delight. The cellular-like sculptures by Jonathan Keep and Michael Geertsen spread and push in different directions. Both assemble and

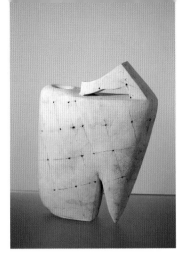
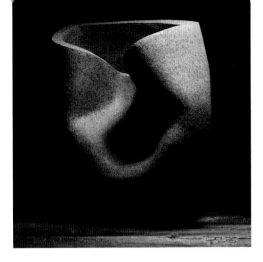

far left: **GORDON BALDWIN**
An Alchemical Vessel V, 2006, approx.
60 × 50 × 15 cm (23½ × 19½ × 6 in.)
Stoneware, hand-built

left: **FERNANDO CASASEMPERE**
The Wall Series, 2007, h 80 × 75 × 49 cm
(31½ × 29½ × 19 in.)
Stoneware clay with industrial waste

morph forms from individual parts, both incorporating thrown components in their work. Geertsen's slightly clown-like patterning on some pieces adds a touch of humour to these mutant beings. Colour, which plays such a significant part in Geertsen's form, is equally important in the tall pieces by Maggi Giles. Like trees exhibiting growth rings, these anthropomorphic shapes, with their bright, unapologetic bands of colour, have all the richness and excitement of lush tropical climes.

The idea of the cell as emblematic of life is also taken up by James Evans and Claire Lindner, both of whom give their own response, some, such as those by Evans, hard-edged and finite. Others are more root-like in their sense of growth. In contrast, the merging of geometrical and expanding form as in the work of Regina Heinz, Tanya Engelstein and John Kørner are explored in forms that appear to have a powerful inner life. All evoke internal tension, space that succeeds in asserting its own presence, as significant in its own way as external appearance.

The notion of the web, the trap, the device for concealment and capture can be architecturally engaging and, at the same time, sinister. Such qualities are evident in the work of artists Annie Turner and Ruth Borgenicht who use the idea of mesh to create some sort of cave, inner spaces that can be seen but cannot be entered. Some forms are more solid, others more open, but all draw us into, while excluding us from, the interior: metaphors, perhaps, for opportunities and pitfalls for the unwary. The pattern-like quality of the form and the use of repeated shapes add to the sense of industry and endeavour.

For Antonia Salmon, the forms are more abstracted than representational, but their starting points are the basic structure of the animal or vegetable world in which anything superfluous has been stripped away. What remains is a sort of skeleton, a memory, a reminder of what lies beneath. These can be more explicit or subliminally expressed, nature, abstracted and simplified as a way of responding to and understanding the world. The work embodies intriguing qualities in which balance and counterbalance keep our eye and mind returning to them time and time again. The sense of the organic that underlies the forms is taken in a different direction by Gordon Baldwin. Working on a much larger scale, his carefully constructed, abstracted forms, with their dry, honed surfaces and occasional marks, have echoes of both the figure and the landscape, evoking a subtle sense of place and time.

DOMESTIC UNCERTAINTIES

The environment, whether centred around the home, the street or its wider concerns, is an issue that has been tellingly explored in clay. For Neil Brownsword it is the demise of the industrial base, in particular the collapse of the once mighty ceramic industry in Stoke-on-Trent that he highlights so poignantly in these evocative fragments. Born in Stoke-on-Trent and trained at the vast Wedgwood Factory, Brownsword has first-hand knowledge of the industry. Over recent years he has been saddened and appalled as shrinking production has resulted in highly talented workers being made redundant, with skills honed over years having been lost as production moves to Asia, a development symptomatic of many Western countries.

The products of the ceramic industry, whether consisting of cheap crockery printed with traditional patterns or small figurines,

LEOPOLD L. FOULEM
Yes, I Do, 2004–2005, h 31.5 ×
w 23 × d 15 cm (12¼ × 9 × 5¾ in.)
Ceramic

have been taken up by artists attracted by their rich social history and also because they are intriguing on their own account. Caroline Slotte uses commercially produced plates printed with the conventional Willow pattern as her starting point. Carefully cutting through areas of the dishes, she creates a multi-layering reminiscent of a stage set, in which one layer is almost indistinguishable from another. Like the Willow pattern, Slotte's layering draws parallels with the mysteries of life. There are no such mysteries in the sand-blasted plates manipulated by Karen Ryan. In a take on the plaques produced in Victorian times bearing uplifting texts, she has emblazoned her plates with emotive words such as fear, guilt and grief, words that are in strong contrast to the cheerful message of the patterning on the plates.

The figurines, produced in quantity by the ceramic industry, are often pastiche renderings of classical figures by such notable companies as Meissen and are redolent with social and historical references. They constitute a kind of sophisticated folk art that is industrially made and predicated on a combination of good taste and sentimentality in which kitsch and camp are essential ingredients. Artists Pauline Wiertz and Barnaby Barford use industrially related objects as their raw material to produce one-off pieces. These are assembled from, for instance, mass-manufactured objects or antique porcelain figurines.

Wiertz brings together beautifully made natural forms to create objects that are both beguilingly attractive yet oddly sinister. Barford makes use of factory-made figurines, an interest he shares with artists such as Konstantin Grcic, Hella Jongerius and Ingo Maurer. Like Barford, they find such trinkets evocative of time and taste, re-assembling them into modern 'kitsch' statements about social class and commercial production. Although charming at first glance, such

pieces often possess a dark side that is anything but humorous. For Barford the titles play an important part in offering an unexpected and often subversive take in presenting a totally unlikely viewpoint, constructing his objects by adapting the found originals, either by painting on to them, adding additional parts or cutting the pieces up before re-assembling, ingeniously enticing people to look again at something they might, as a matter of course, have dismissed.

The low-key sense of anxiety allied with humour that imbues work by Barford is pushed further into the domestic scene by Anders Ruhwald, who makes use of the idea of absence as much as presence. Items of furniture or other everyday objects may be suggested, indicating a sort of functionality, but they have metamorphosed almost beyond recognition. Benches, stools, tables, standard lights may all form part of the world created, but it is one that is indirect and distanced, an uncanny and disturbing angle on the everyday.

While making oblique reference to the domestic environment, artists such as Léopold L. Foulem, Adrian Saxe and Richard Milette create their own commentary on the familiar. In their work everyday objects such as teapots, vases and lidded boxes take on a grand, ritual quality. The uninhibited use of colour and pattern, which owes much to the richly decorated work of factories such as Sèvres, is ornate and ceremonial, a celebration of both process and ordinariness. They create a sense of the absurd with beguiling meticulousness. Lively figurative decoration animates the forms, adding a further layer of meaning. Food and its rituals inform Mervi Kurvinen's work. The decorated chocolate cake that sits tidily in the centre of a plate appears to be both an invitation to eat and a sort of *memento mori*, the portrait, set in an ornate frame, commemorating absence rather than presence.

left: **DAMIAN O'SULLIVAN**
Elderly Lady with Crutch, 2003,
crutch 115 × 15 × 10 cm
(45 × 5¾ × 4 in.)
Slip-cast in porcelain

below: **CHRISTIN JOHANSSON**
Untitled, 2007, 10 × 12 × 30 cm
(4 × 4¾ × 11¾ in.)
Porcelain, metal wire, panties, leatherette

The objects that Jim Thomson produces are also those with which we are familiar – funnels and such like – that are simulacra of the real thing, the colours, textures and surface more emblematic than real. There is also something mysterious but intriguing in the wrapped parcels and sample box by Barbara Hashimoto, the neatly ordered tablets resemble a manual storage system such as might have been found in a library or an archive. The gradations of hue and the texture of the clay may invite inspection but this is a classification about which we can only speculate. A similar sense of mystery imbues the work of Márta Nagy. With titles such as *Melting Snow* (2007) and *Water Filter in the Desert* (2007) we can only begin to guess the narratives they embody, but the complexity of the objects invites curiosity.

The wider concerns of the environment are evident in work such as that by Jenny Beavan, who uses clay to evoke the drama of the natural world. Her emotive wall pieces recall the lapping of water, the swell of tides or the melting of ice caps together with the articulation of the striations which take on geological significance while referring to elemental forces that can be disturbed by the action of humankind. Nina Jun's disintegrating book, its pages eroded and worn as if by age and weather, embodies complex ideas so the piece can be seen as a metaphor for the ending of certainties; belief, family and the basic institutions of civilized life appear to be disintegrating.

The history of ceramics is cleverly employed by artists such as Paul Scott to comment on contemporary issues. In particular Scott takes as his starting point the two-hundred-year tradition of blue and white designs that were produced on tableware in great quantity in Stoke-on-Trent. Designs, such the Willow pattern, originally derived from Chinese originals, are adapted by Scott to comment on modern social, political or environmental issues. These may include the destruction of landscape by capitalist exploitation, the insensitivity of consumerism, the arms market and the omnipotence of international business.

Although the ornaments and knick-knackery produced in quantity by the ceramics industry often serve as amusing if telling starting points for social comment for Richard Slee as well as other artists, he is also fascinated by commonplace, everyday objects such as brooms, radio sets, Easter eggs and suitcases that stir his imagination. The resulting sculptures are a wry, satirical commentary on the domestic, the familiar and the ordinary as a way of both exposing and celebrating issues such as national identity and fairy stories in an often surreal juxtaposition of different elements. With great economy, his finely wrought hand-built forms give the impression that they have been mould-made, appearing so smooth and accomplished. This impression is enhanced by the carefully sprayed glaze that avoids runs or overlays to create blemish-free surfaces. Ambiguous, engaging and witty, Slee's seemingly innocent images, with their use of quotation marks and parentheses, emerge from deep felt emotions.

While Slee's wry look at life is both witty and engaging, Shannon Goff and Christin Johansson offer a more unorthodox view of the familiar. Goff's squashed and distorted telephone

right: **STEPHEN DIXON**
Chimera, Teapot, 2003, h 24 cm (9½ in.)
Ceramic, earthenware

far right: **AKIO TAKAMORI**
Empress and Queen, 2003, Empress:
135 × 59 × 43 cm (53 × 23 × 16¾ in.);
Queen: 107 × 82 × 43 cm
(42 × 32 × 17 in.)
Stoneware with underglaze

and her softly built car dashboard seem to have morphed into eerie, uncanny and unsettling nightmarish objects. The uncertainties to which Goff refers are given a crisper, more clinical finish in the lavatory basins and urinals by Johansson. Bodily functions take on new meanings in these pieces, their meticulous construction aping the precision of these everyday objects. Medical concerns are also the theme of Damian O'Sullivan's work. Aware of the way things such as plaster casts or crutches associated with accidents, particularly for older people, are crude and lacking in a sense of pride, he has created objects that are smart and stylish. There is also a vague medical/laboratory feel in the work of Cindy Kolodziejski, her precisely made, flask-like forms, one of which is supported by a scientific clamp, are sinisterly engaging.

The forms that are made by artists such as Conor Wilson relate to, among other issues, desire and perception, the witty, cartoon-like objects gently satirizing male and female alike. A lemon squeezer, for example, in the form of a set of male genitalia, with a bright yellow glaze and a gold interior, is amusing while also evocative of some sort of painful experience, an ingenious spoof of macho power. The ceramic jock strap by Kati Nulpponen is also an ironic take on one of the most intimate items of male attire. De-sexed by the addition of decorative roses, the item is a gentle satire on masculinity and gender.

REPRESENTATION/ABSTRACTION

The approach adopted by Rodin in his preference for modelling and expression of character finds many followers, artists interested in clay for its own sake and the freedom it offers. Michael Flynn brings life to his grappling couples caught up in their own world, successfully achieving a sense of movement and tension that recalls Rodin's dance figures. There is a similar sense of movement and tension in the figurative and animal studies of Naomi Mathews, seemingly trapped in odd, psychologically fraught, unexpected situations. By contrast Anna Noel's carefully observed figures and creatures capture inner as well as outer strengths, seemingly untroubled by the world around them. Stephen Dixon combines figures and familiar vessel forms to look at social conventions around a variety of political issues. Kathy Venter's floating or suspended figures in her series *Immersion* (2006) are in the act of either moving in or out, the pose of the figure remaining ambiguous. Movement is subtly suggested by Claire Curneen in her quasi-religious figures such as *St Sebastian* (2001). Standing like a Renaissance saint with weight on one leg, the devotional qualities of these studies of this enigmatic figure are both real and emblematic. In her single and group figures Patricia Rieger evokes both ambiguity and reality, figures caught in movement but seeming to be self involved and distant.

There is a greater sense of formality in Ruth Duckworth's maquette for two standing figures and in the single figures by Vladimir Tsivin. Like the stylization of Egyptian shabti, Duckworth's heterosexual couple are both human and god-like, their simplified, regal stance arresting in their simplicity. Alessandro Gallo's anthropomorphized besuited figure also brings together the real and the mythologized worlds. Others artists such as Mo Jupp adapt a strong sense of ritual that borrows from stylization of Ancient Egyptian forms to address both the past and present. Jupp's use of clay is a significant aspect of his figures.

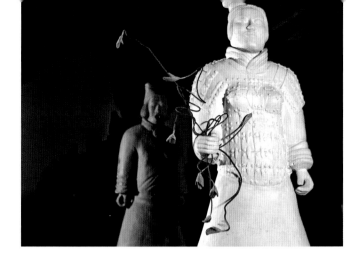

left: **MARIAN HEYERDAHL**
The Terracotta Woman, Tree of Life,
2007, h 1.85 m (6 ft)
Clay, iron, plaster

below: **CINDY KOLODZIEJSKI**
Floral Fountain, 2006, 18 × 13 × 46 cm
(7 × 5 × 18 in.)
Glazed earthenware

Narrative plays a significant part for some artists, especially when they involve groups of figures caught up in complex relationships. The magnificent tableaux created by Akio Takamori make ingenious references that touch on Eastern and Western culture as well as social relations. Simplified and with minimal use of colour and line, Takamori creates complex screnarios. The near-life-sized figures assembled by Christie Brown appear to be caught up in some formal, ritualistic relationship that may be part religious and part secular, the rawness of the terracotta clay giving them an earthy, primitive-like quality. Different dramas are the subject of Carole Windham's work. Based on nineteenth-century flat back figures produced in quantity in Stoke-on-Trent and other places, she pokes gentle fun at contemporary personalities.

Gender issues are raised in a different way in the work of Marian Heyerdahl. While impressed by the strength and power of the terracotta army of the tomb dedicated to the Emperor Qin Shihuangdi, she noted the absence of women. Taking the historical figures as her model, she has created a female equivalent in almost every detail. By changing the sex of her figures, Heyerdahl's stately army enacts a different drama and tells a different – more modern – story.

There are other narratives played out in the work of Louise Hindsgavl and Chris Antemann. Although they adopt different approaches, both artists consciously set out to confront expectations with figures behaving badly, questioning any notion of 'good taste', their preference is for creating battle grounds of excess and indulgence. The irony of the scenes depicted is heightened by being modelled in dazzlingly white porcelain, a material usually associated with ideas around purity. The issue of taste touched on by Hindsgavl

and Antemann is raised in different ways by Justin Novak and Vipoo Srivilasa, both of whom play with elements of kitsch. Novak combines aspects of the sentimental with an ironic twist on the normal. One conventionally glamorous-looking female nude is seen to be sewing up her wrist. Novak's two cartoon-like rabbits, one sporting machine guns, appear to be parodying nationalism with unthinking bravado. Equally bizarre are the toy-like androids, fantasy vases and hands by Srivilasa, which parody both ritual and convention.

The ability of the figure to confront and question is employed by several artists. In Nick Renshaw's *Terrestrial Being* (2006) the figure in question is standing firmly seeming to defy our gaze, despite its blue head. The life-size figures are part alien, part human. The enigmatic is a powerful aspect of much work, whether in Patricia Rieger's saluting or waving figure, in Tony Moore's *In the Age of Innocents* (2007), of two heads with death-like faces confronting each other, or in the doll-like heads by Mariana Monteagudo.

Mythology is the theme of Pamela Leung's near life-sized anthropomorphized creatures. Calling on her extensive knowledge of Chinese mythology, which involves figures that may be part human, part animal, Leung builds armies of exotic figures that may protect us from evil, their presence a reassurance in a strange, alien world. Leung carefully applies colour and glaze to highlight the sense of reality she wishes to evoke. Other artists make use of poured glaze and strong colour to suggest

right: JAMES COQUIA
Regarding the Vessel (detail), 2001,
24 × 19 × 21.5 cm (9½ × 7½ × 8½ in.)
Earthenware, copper oxide, terra sigillata

below: PATRICIA VOLK
Lineage, 2007, h 36 × w 60 × d 230 cm
(14 × 23½ × 90½ in.)
Ceramic

both destruction and creation. This quality is used inventively by Xavier Toubes on a series of monumental heads that are covered with multiple layers of poured coloured glaze, which both define and obscure the form.

Intricacies of Dreaming (2007), Tanya Batura's disturbing open-mouthed head, lolling to one side as if asleep, is given a deep red blush, an indication of danger as much as love. Equally unnerving are the 'comic' figures by Patti Warashina. Their jokey, clown-like appearance appear to offer amusement while evoking a more sinister edge. The four heads by Gert Germeraad, *The Four Temperaments: Choleric, Phlegmatic, Sanguine and Melancholic* (2007), while touching on the way the ancient world attempted to make sense of the body, reflect the way individuals continue to respond to mood and emotion. In Ivan Albreht's work the heads are like memories, skins that have been collected and squashed, heads seemingly without content, merely piled up. Anonymous, white and bland, they have a trophy-like quality that is the stuff of nightmares. A similar sense of alarm imbues the stylized heads of Tony Bennett, an artist who plays with form and surface as social commentary.

The heads created by Paul Mathieu are turned upside down, literally empty headed, but their surfaces are covered with photographic imagery or areas of strong pattern. Pattern and surface quality are also significant aspects of the heads fashioned by Patricia Volk. The use of strong colour and pattern transforms the anonymous, elongated faces, with their closed eyes, into mysterious creatures that suggest ritual and ceremony. By contrast, the figures created by Michael Kalmbach explore the notion of hyper-realism, the detailed modelling and convincing colouring have the outward appearance of 'the real', the figures seeming to represent familiar 'types' without being anyone in particular.

The influence of Surrealist thought in seeking to explore the frontiers of experience and to broaden the logical and common sense view of reality by combining it with instinctual, subconscious and dream experience in order to achieve a 'super-reality' is used by artists, especially those working with portrait heads. The work of Hans Bellmer in creating provocative work around dolls, sexualizing and sometimes mutilating them, exerts a powerful influence. Bretton Sage Binford's dream-like figures touch on desire and taboo, a combination of the real and the fantastic, creating powerful creatures that are part human, part mythical and part animal, the doll/baby forms adding further unsettling dimensions. The disturbing figures created by Kim Simonsson are also a combination of human, animal and myth, one recalling the sort of figure used as half-sized replicas, part of appeals to collect money, their presence both discomforting and oddly reassuring.

Artists Margaret Keelan and Shirley Leslyn Sheppard make effective use of doll-like imagery to comment on perceptions of gender, sexuality and desire. The doll-like figures created by

far left: **SUSAN HALLS**
Shirley, 2006, h 50 × w 24 × d 28 cm
(19½ × 9½ × 11 in.)
Paper clay

left: **MARGARET KEELAN**
Blue Boat, 2007, 25 × 18 × 30.5 cm
(10 × 7 × 12 in.)
Clay, stains, glaze

Cynthia Consentino are anything but benign, but their touting of guns, donning of animal heads or sprouting flowers are at odds with their innocent appearance. Composite assemblies, with figures part of complex if often colourful worlds such as in the work of Stephen Bird, evoke their own involved, multi-layered existences in which the construction of individual identities must strive to assert itself. The animals and figures in the work of Carolein Smit seem to emerge from or covered by some sort of coating.

Continuing the Surrealist theme, artists morph components to create otherworldly objects. Artists such as Sergei Isupov, László Fekete and James Coquia bring together disparate forms to highlight desire, fear and confusion. The couple kissing in Isupov's *To Kiss* (2007) appear to be exchanging more than bodily fluids as figures appear to flow literally from one to the other. The double heads that make up Coquia's *Dicephalopod* (2001) look both perplexed and surprised to discover they are part of the same whole. With its suggestion of the alter ego, *Dicephalopod* is both amusing and slightly alarming. In works such as *The Thief of Baghdad* (2002–2003) Fekete makes a pun on the traditional story and the weight of tradition. The single figures by Debra Fritts lend themselves to many psycho-dynamic readings, touching as they do on issues such as the notion of self, feelings of loss and cultural and personal identity, memory, dream and fantasy. Her figures seem almost to float and drift, combining illusion with a sense of the real.

Just as various traditions have developed around Surrealism, many artists have responded to the way figures can be both humorous and profound. Susan Halls's anthropomorphized dog, *Shirley* (2006), literally takes on a dog's life, the ears looking crestfallen. While we can feel sympathy for, or even empathize with, the chimera, it is still a humorous look at the human condition. Gitte Jungersen's found figures and animals that people her red and pink clouds set up unlikely juxtapositions. In *The Longings of Spiderman* (2006) the figure is so ludicrously small and so precariously perched on the edge of the cloud that we feel for his safety. Few ambiguous feelings are conjured up by Peter Rasmussen, in pieces such as *Hansenstein* (2007), a delightful narrative in which the rabbit takes on the role of potter and decorator possibly to portray the actual artist. Craig Mitchell brings a similar sense of the joyful cartoon to his stick-like figures, detailed portraits of carefully observed characters rendered with verve and unapologetic charm.

1 For a wider discussion of such issues see Howard Risatti, *A Theory of Craft: Function and Aesthetic Expression*, The University of North Carolina Press, Chapel Hill, 2007.
2 For a full account see Anton Reijnders, *The Ceramic Process: A Manual and Source of Inspiration for Ceramic Art and Design*, European Ceramic Workcentre, A & C Black, London and University of Pennsylvania Press, Philadelphia, 2005, which illustrates the range of work produced.

above: **MAREK CECULA**
Fire, In Dust Real (Burn Again),
Set 7, 2005, 28 × 28 × 4 cm
(11 × 11 × 1½ in.)
Industrial porcelain, wood-fired

left: **FERNANDO CASASEMPERE**
The Wall Series, 2007, h 80 × 75 × 49 cm
(31½ × 29½ × 19¼ in.)
Stoneware clay with industrial waste

right: **PIPPIN DRYSDALE**
Kimberley Series, Lines of Site, 2007
Porcelain, thrown, size variable

below, left: **GORDON BALDWIN**
Strange Vessel, 2006, 43 × 56 × 26 cm
(16¾ × 22 × 10¼ in.)
Stoneware, hand-built

below, right: **PIPPIN DRYSDALE**
*Kimberley Series, Tablescape –
After the Rain*, 2007, h 14–55 cm
(5½–21½ in.)
Porcelain, thrown

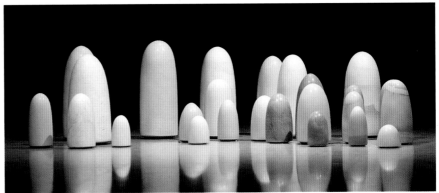

right: **JENNY BEAVAN**
Energised Water 2, 2007,
w 35 cm (13¼ in.)
Porcelain, glazes

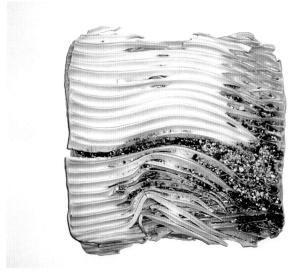

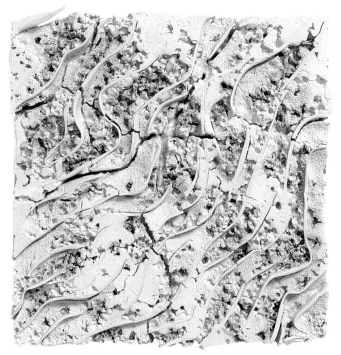

above, left: **JENNY BEAVAN**
Water in Action, 2001–2002,
56 × 56 cm (22 × 22 in.)
China clay with porcelain and molochite, incorporating marsh grass,
gorse and other vegetation from the Fal Valley Clay Pits, Melbur,
Virginia and Wheal Remfry; glaze and glass

above, right: **DAVID BINNS**
Cast Standing Form, 2006,
48 × 32 × 6 cm (19 × 12½ × 2¼ in.)
Kiln-cast mixed ceramic aggregates, glass-forming oxides, 1170°C,
ground and polished after firing

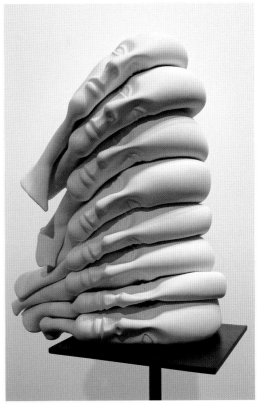

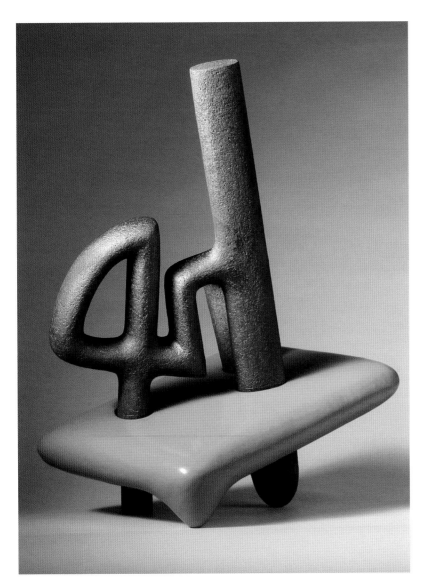

above: **IVAN ALBREHT**
Stack, 2007, h 158 × w 25 × d 25 cm
(62 × 10 × 10 in.)
Porcelain, steel, found object, slip-cast and
hand-built porcelain fired in high-range
oxidation, welded steel

left: **KAREN BENNICKE**
A Sign from Le Corbusier, 2004,
h 42 × w 23.5 × l 30 cm (16½ × 9¼ × 11¾ in.)
Low-fired stoneware with matt glaze and stains

above, left: **BARNABY BARFORD**
Salads?! I'll Give them Fucking Salads!, 2007,
h 30 × dia 29 cm (12 × 11 in.)
Bone china, porcelain, enamel paint, other media

above, right: **BARNABY BARFORD**
Come on you Lightweight – Down It!, 2007,
h 29 × w 38 × l 28 cm (11¼ × 15 × 11 in.)
Bone china, porcelain, other media

opposite, left: **BRETTON SAGE BINFORD**
Flowerchild, 2005, 41 × 20 cm (16 × 8 in.)
Slip-cast, altered, assembled, white stoneware,
overglaze decals

opposite, top right: **BRETTON SAGE BINFORD**
Aspirations, 2006, h 51 cm (20 in.)
Slip-cast, cut and altered porcelain body

opposite, bottom right: **TANYA BATURA**
Intricacies of Dreaming 1, 2007, h 23 cm (9 in.)
Clay, acrylic paint

above, left: **STEPHEN BIRD**
Raining Magic Flowers, 2008,
65 × 41 × 25 cm (25½ × 16 × 10 in.)
Earthenware, slips, glaze, decals

above, right: **STEPHEN BIRD**
Monkey Boy, 2005, h 35 cm (13¼ in.)
Earthenware

opposite, left: **CHRISTIE BROWN**
Small Cat Woman, Cat Woman 2, Cat Woman I,
2007, 64 × 15 × 11 cm (25 × 6 × 4 in.), 93 × 26 ×
23 cm (36½ × 10 × 9 in.), 88 × 24 × 21 cm
(34½ × 9½ × 8¼ in.)
Ceramic

opposite, top right: **TONY BENNETT**
England 1 (Greenhalf), *Engerland!*, 2006,
h 54 × w 45 × d 45 cm (21 × 17¾ × 17¾ in.)
Press-moulded red earthenware and T material

opposite, bottom right: **TONY BENNETT**
Hairy Beast Teapot, 2006, h 61 × w 40 × d 11 cm
(24 × 15¾ × 4¼ in.)
Extruded red earthenware

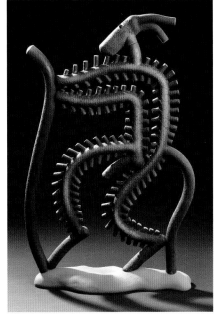

above: **NEIL BROWNSWORD**
Buller, 2007, 25 × 30 × 62 cm (10 × 12 × 24 in.)
Ceramic and salvaged factory detritus

right: **NEIL BROWNSWORD**
Crank, 2007, 25 × 80 × 64 cm (10 × 31½ × 25 in.)
Ceramic, industrial archaeology

top left: **CLAUDI CASANOVAS**
Ermitò de Sant Sebastià, 2003–2004,
h 77 × w 50 × d 30 cm (30¼ × 19½ × 11¾ in.)
Porcelain

above, left: **CLAUDI CASANOVAS**
Castellar, 2003, 45 × 64 × 45 cm (17¾ × 25 × 17¾ in.)
Porcelain, mixed media

above, right: **PHILIPPE BARDE**
Barde 3, 2000, 60 × 60 cm (23½ × 23½ in.)
Porcelain, 1280°C

above, left: **CLAUDIA CLARE**
Dancing, from Shattered, 2007, h 190 cm (75 in.)
Earthenware, slip, lustre, enamels

above, right: **FELICITY AYLIEFF**
Chasing Black, 2006, h 193 × 67 × 67 cm (76 × 26¼ × 26¼ in.)
Porcelain, thrown in sections and joined, glazed, cobalt
and iron oxide, black on-glaze enamel, reduction-fired

left: **SANDY BROWN**
Goddess, 1990, h 1.7 m (5½ ft)
Grogged stoneware clay, coiled, white slip, cobalt oxide lines

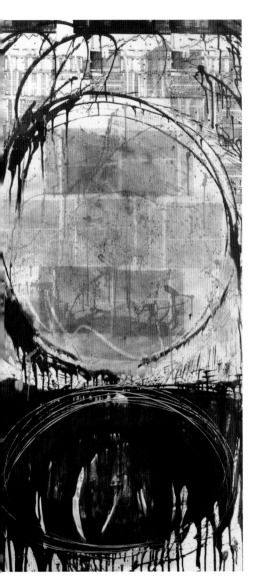

left: **OLE LISLERUD**
Growth Prospects, 2007, h 2 m × w 1 m × d 1 cm
(78½ × 39¼ × ½ in.)
Porcelain, silkscreen and brushwork

below: **SUN CHAO**
Snow in Early Spring, 2006, w 71 cm (28 in.)
Ceramic slab

above: **CYNTHIA CONSENTINO**
Self Portrait with Gun, 2005,
56 × 18 × 39 cm (22 × 7 × 15½ in.)
Clay, slip, oils, wax, epoxy

right: **CYNTHIA CONSENTINO**
Flower Girl VI, 2007, 102 × 38 × 51 cm
(40 × 15 × 20 in.)
Stoneware, glaze, oil, cold wax

CYNTHIA CONSENTINO
Rabbit Girl IV, 2005,
104 × 47 × 34 cm
(41 × 18½ × 13½ in.)
Clay, glaze, oils, cold wax

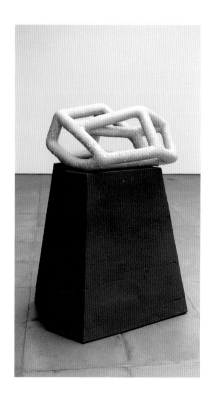

above: **RICHARD DEACON**
Range E, 2005, h 104 cm (41 in.)
Glazed ceramic on unglazed plinth

right: **DAPHNE CORREGAN**
*Dress, with Glass Roses, Gush (Two Tubes),
Wall Piece,* 2008, h 150 cm (59 in.) max.
Ceramic

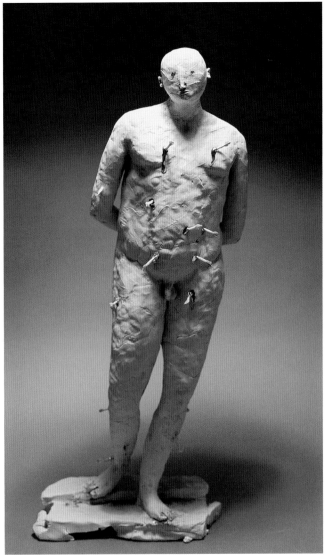

above, left: **CLAIRE CURNEEN**
Daphne, 2006, 55 × 30 × 20 cm
(21½ × 12 × 8 in.)
Porcelain

above, right: **CLAIRE CURNEEN**
St Sebastian, 2001, h 69 cm (27 in.)
Porcelain

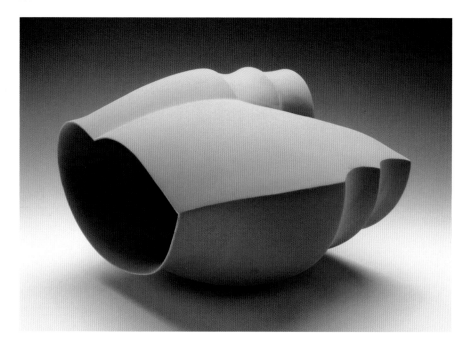

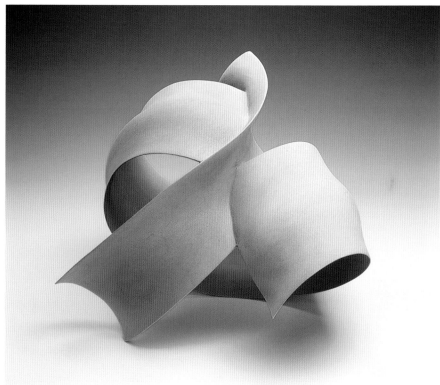

above: **WOUTER DAM**
Light Blue Shape, 2000,
18 × 25 × 25 cm
(7 × 10 × 10 in.)
Ceramic

right: **WOUTER DAM**
Yellow Sculpture, 2005,
24 × 35.5 × 34 in.
(9½ × 14 × 13½ in.)
Ceramic

above: **ANETA REGEL DELEU**
Escape 2, 2008, h 32 cm (12½ in.)
Porcelain

right: **ANETA REGEL DELEU**
Pulsing, 2007, h 40 cm (16 in.)
Stoneware, basalt

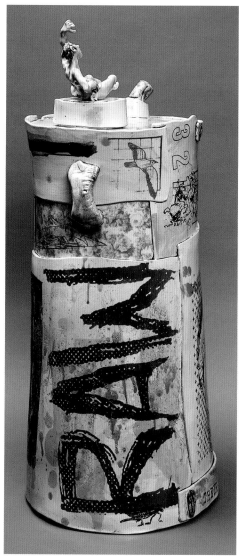

above, left: **ANNETTE CORCORAN**
Chickadee, Mountain Chickadee, Warbler and Titmouse Teapot, 2007, h 31.5 × w 25 × dia 32 cm (12⅜ × 10 × 12½ in.)
Porcelain, hand-built, underglazes, glazes and overglazes

above, right: **STEPHEN DIXON**
Their Finest Hour, 2004, h 73 cm (28¾ in.)
Ceramic, lidded vessel

left: **ANNETTE CORCORAN**
Hummers Teapot, 2007, h 23 × w 34 × d 18 cm (9 × 13½ × 7 in.)
Porcelain, hand-built, underglaze, glaze and overglaze

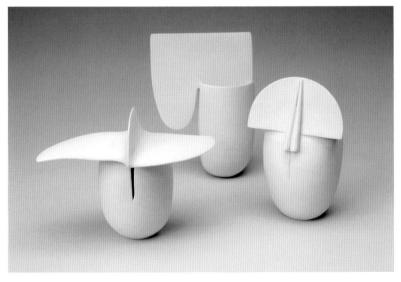

top: **OSAMMA EMAN**
My Wall of Fire, 2004, 250 × 100 cm (98 × 39 in.)
Earthenware white, copper sulfate, iron (ferro) sulfate, iron chloride, pit
firing, different-sized tiles, bisque

above: **RUTH DUCKWORTH**
Three Porcelain Vessels, 2003, h 23 cm (9 in.) max.
Ceramic

right: **RUTH DUCKWORTH**
Maquette for Life-Size Standing Figures, c. 2002, h 42 cm (16½ in.)
Ceramic

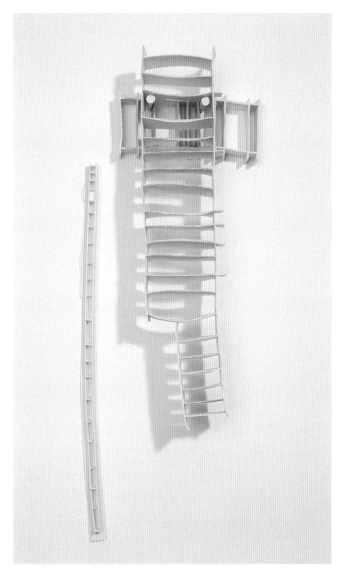

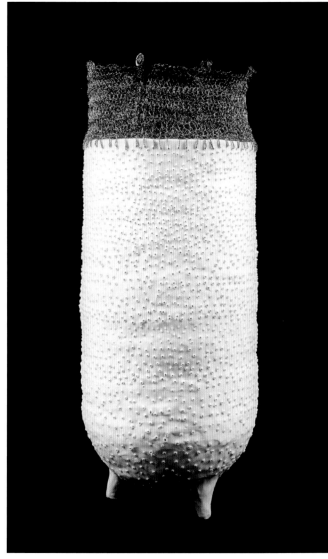

above, left: **ISOBEL EGAN**
Intimate Spaces, 2005, overall size h 50 × w 20 cm
(20 × 8 in.)
Individual hand-built porcelain, ceramic fibres
combined with porcelain slip, three separate
slab-built pieces, 1260°C

above, right: **TANYA ENGELSTEIN**
Veils, 2007, h 45 cm (17¾ in.)
Porcelain hand-built, knitted copper wire

opposite, top left: **JAMES EVANS**
Auberge, 2007, 30 × 36 × 36 cm (12 × 14 × 14 in.)
Ceramic

opposite, bottom left: **JAMES EVANS**
Plaisantin, 2007, 64 × 27 × 35 cm
(25 × 10½ × 14 in.) Ceramic

opposite, top right: **MICHAEL CLEFF**
From the Series 'On Addition', 2005,
h 28 × 31 × 25 cm (11 × 12 × 10 in.)
Stoneware, hand-built

opposite, bottom right: **SUSAN DISLEY**
Open Cellular Form, 2007, d 17 cm (6½ in.)
Stoneware, hand-built, pinched and coiled, white
engobe painted in layers on surface, edges
enhanced with copper carbonate, 1260°C

above, left: **LASZLO FEKETE**
Wildlife Memorial Soup Tureen, 2001, h 60 cm (23½ in.)
Glazed porcelain

top right: **LASZLO FEKETE**
The Thief of Baghdad, 2002–2003, h 36 cm (14 in.)
Slip-cast and assembled porcelain, glazes, lustres, decals

right: **LEOPOLD L. FOULEM**
Vase Image with Floral Motif on Gold Ground, 2005–2006,
h 33.7 × w 20.5 × d 12 cm (13 × 8 × 5 in.)
Ceramic

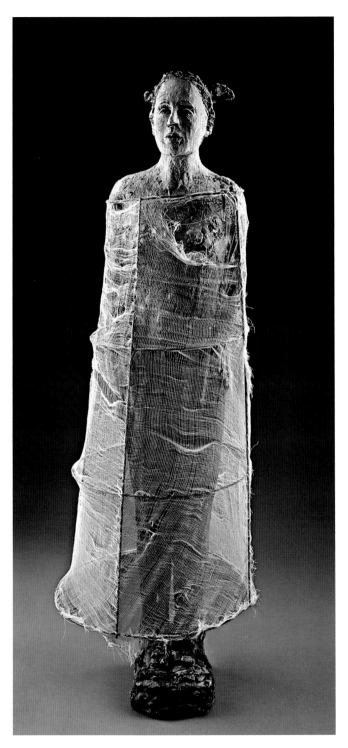

left: **DEBRA FRITTS**
In My Youth, 2007, h 119 × w 40.5 × d 40.5 cm
(47 × 16 × 16 in.)
Terracotta, gauze, metal

top: **MICHAEL FLYNN**
Tickle 2, 2002, h 15 cm (6 in.)
Porcelain

above: **MICHAEL FLYNN**
Black Moth, 2006, h 37 cm (14½ in.)
Porcelain

above:
ALESSANDRO GALLO
The Vain Crow, 2007,
25.5 × 38 × 25.5 cm
(10 × 15 × 10 in.)
Raku

far left:
ALESSANDRO GALLO
Not Again!, 2007,
152.5 × 46 × 51 cm
(60 × 18 × 20 in.)
Ceramic

left: **JAMES COQUIA**
Dicephalopod, 2001,
h 44 cm (17 in.)
Earthenware, copper oxide
and terra sigillata

top: **MICHAEL GEERTSEN**
Dark Blue Wall Object, 2006, h 40 × l 120 × d 30 cm
(15¾ × 47 × 12 in.)
Earthenware, hand-thrown, altered, cobalt blue glaze

above, left: **MICHAEL GEERTSEN**
Corner Object, 2006, h 32 × l 45 × d 35 cm
(12½ × 17¾ × 13¾ in.)
Earthenware, hand-thrown and altered,
white glaze, decals, platinum

right: **MICHAEL GEERTSEN**
Standing Object, 2007, h 31 × l 32 × d 32 cm
(12 × 12½ × 12½ in.)
Earthenware, thrown and altered, white glaze,
decals, platinum

below: **GERT GERMERAAD**
Portrait of Oane T. Postma, 2004,
57 × 32 × 36 cm (22½ × 12½ × 14 in.)
Ceramic

right: **SUSAN HALLS**
Muscleman Rider, 2007, h 30 × l 28 × w 15 cm
(12 × 11 × 6 in.)
Paper clay

bottom right: **GERT GERMERAAD**
*The Four Temperaments: Choleric, Phlegmatic,
Sanguine and Melancholic*, 2007,
h approx. 75 cm (29½ in.)
Earthenware, painted after firing

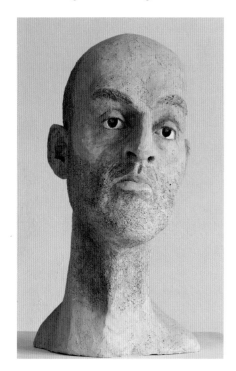

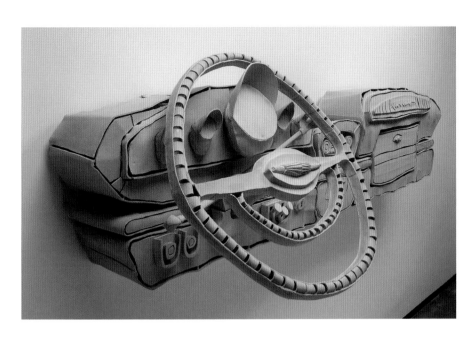

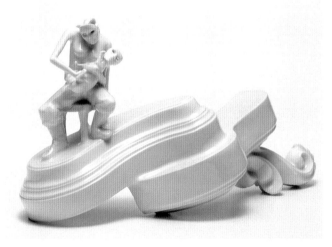

top: **SHANNON GOFF**
Dashboard, 2003, 56 × 224 × 72 cm (22 × 88 × 28 in.)
Ceramic

above: **LOUISE HINDSGAVL**
Who Loves Who, 2007, 22 × 15 × 30 cm (8½ × 6 × 11¾ in.)
Porcelain

left: **LOUISE HINDSGAVL**
Who Believes in Miracles, 2007, 31 × 15 × 31 cm
(12 × 6 × 12 in.)
Porcelain

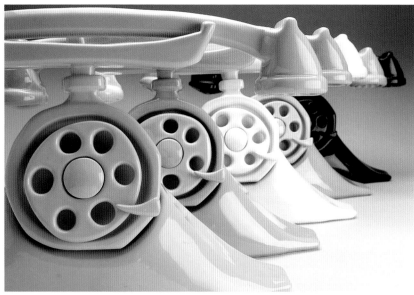

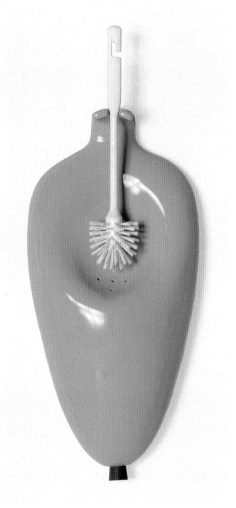

top: **MAGGI GILES**
Dog, Chair, 2007
Ceramic, slip, pigment

above, left: **SHANNON GOFF**
Telephone (Black Telephone, Pink Telephone, etc.),
2005, 76 × 28 × 46 cm (30 × 11 × 18 in.)
Vitreous china

above, right: **CHRISTIN JOHANSSON**
Untitled, 2007, 30 × 13 × 50 cm (12 × 5 × 20 in.)
Earthenware, car paint, rubber plug, toilet brush

WAYNE HIGBY
EarthCloud, 2002–2006, h 11 × w 17 m (36 × 56 ft)
Porcelain, 5,955 hand-cut elements
EarthCloud is a permanent porcelain,
architectural installation, made over four years
specifically for the entrance to the C. D. Smith
Theater, Miller Performing Arts Center, Alfred
University, Alfred, New York (Kallman, McKinnell
and Wood architects)

above: **NINA JUN**
The Perishable, 2004, h 213 cm (84 in.)
Ceramic, projected image

below: **BARBARA HASHIMOTO**
110 Pages, 2007, l 89 cm (35 in.)
Ceramic, book, encaustic, maple box

right: **MIEKE DE GROOT**
Untitled, 2007, 38 × 27 × 30 cm
(15 × 10½ × 12 in.)
Stoneware, gas kiln

below: **MIEKE DE GROOT**
Untitled, 2004, 53 × 30 × 27 cm
(21 × 12 × 10½ in.)
Stoneware, gas kiln

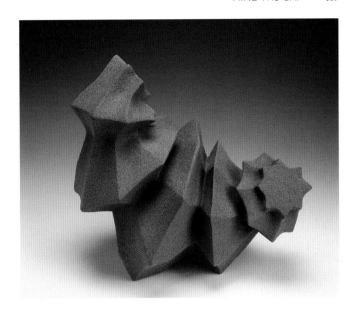

left: **REGINA HEINZ**
Space Map, 2002, h 10 × w 32 × d 28 cm
(4 × 12½ × 11 in.)
Ceramic

below, left: **REGINA HEINZ**
With a Twist, 2005, h 63 × w 55 × d 30 cm
(24¾ × 21½ × 11¾ in.)
Ceramic

below, right: **RUTH BORGENICHT**
Watery Landscape, 2005, h 30 cm (12 in.)
Stoneware

above: **GITTE JUNGERSEN**
*The Longings of Spiderman
(Red with Spiderman)*, 2006,
h 18 × w 42 × d 18 cm (7 × 16½ × 7 in.)
Ceramic

left: **GITTE JUNGERSEN**
Place to be Proud (Green with Stag), 2006,
h 54 × w 32 × d 20 cm (21 × 12½ × 8 in.)
Ceramic

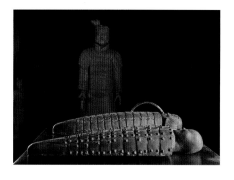

above: **MARGARET KEELAN**
Goose, 2007, 56 × 15 × 18 cm (22 × 6 × 7 in.)
Clay, stains, glaze

above, right: **MARIAN HEYERDAHL**
From *The Terracotta Women Project*,
h 1.85 m (6 ft)

right: **MARIAN HEYERDAHL**
The Terracotta Woman, Head Hunter, 2007,
h 1.85 m (6 ft)
Clay, iron, plaster

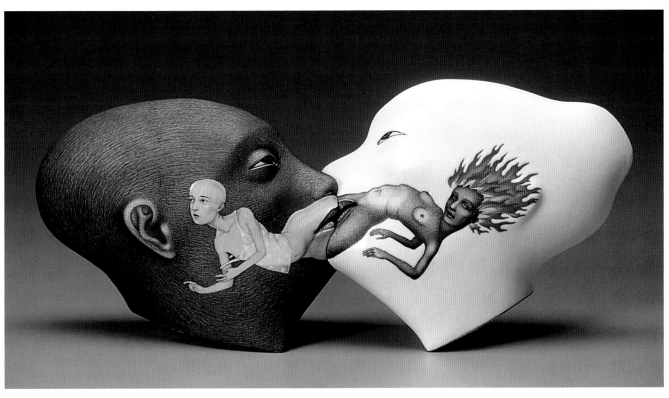

above: **SERGEI ISUPOV**
To Kiss, 2007, h 17 cm (6½ in.)
Porcelain

right: **MICHAEL KALMBACH**
Liebscher, 2007, approx. 27 cm (10½ in.)
Ceramic, glaze

far right: **MO JUPP**
Seated Figure, 2005, h 36 cm (14 in.)
Stoneware

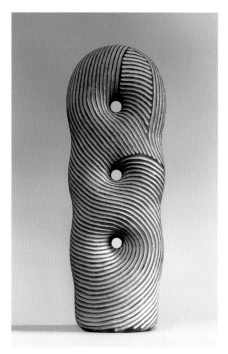

above: **MACIEJ KASPERSKI**
Triplex System, Ninja Cuts 2, 2007,
101 × 36 × 20 cm (40 × 14 × 8 in.)
Ceramic, chamotte, electric kiln, 1200°C

top: **JONATHAN KEEP**
Earth Cloud (Foreground), 2008,
100 × 68 × 49 cm (39 × 27 × 19 in.)
High-fired terracotta

above: **MACIEJ KASPERSKI**
SHC, Simplex Horizonatal Coil 04, 2005,
19 × 60 × 22 cm (7½ × 23½ × 8½ in.)
Ceramic, chamotte, electric kiln, 1200°C

left: **TONY MOORE**
Who Knows Why? 150 Body-cast Human Heads
(detail), 2006, 2.3 × 8.5 sq m
(84 × 300 sq ft), size variable
Steel, architectural stoneware, barium glaze,
wood-fired 5 days to cone 12

below: **KRISTEN MORGIN**
Hearse, 2004, h 165 cm (65 in.)
Unfired clay, wood, wire, cement, glue, salt

top: **PAMELA LEUNG**
Three Tiger Heads, 2003, h 30 cm (12 in.)
Stoneware

above: **FIAMMA COLONNA MONTAGU**
Cloud Trees, 2006, h 320 cm (126 in.)
Ceramic

above, right: **PAMELA LEUNG**
Girl on Donkey, 2006
Stoneware, glaze

above: **CLAIRE LINDNER**
Mandragotte, 2008, 29 × 9 ×11 cm
(11 × 3½ × 4 in.)
Porcelain

right: **CLAIRE LINDNER**
Leviathan 2, 2007, 124 × 30 × 12 cm
(49 × 12 × 5 in.)
Porcelain

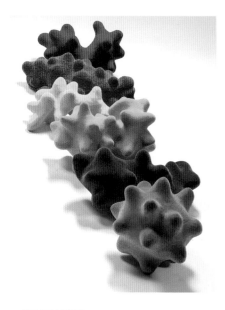

top: **TYLER LOTZ**
Tendril Series 1, 2004, h 38 cm (15 in.)
Clay, acrylic

above: **NATASHA LEWER**
Mutations, 2006, l 140 cm (55 in.)
Flocked ceramic

above: **TYLER LOTZ**
Filament, 2007, 17 × 18 × 19 cm (6½ × 7 × 7½ in.)
Ceramic, slip-cast, assembled, fired around cone 1,
acrylic, applied by pouring many layers

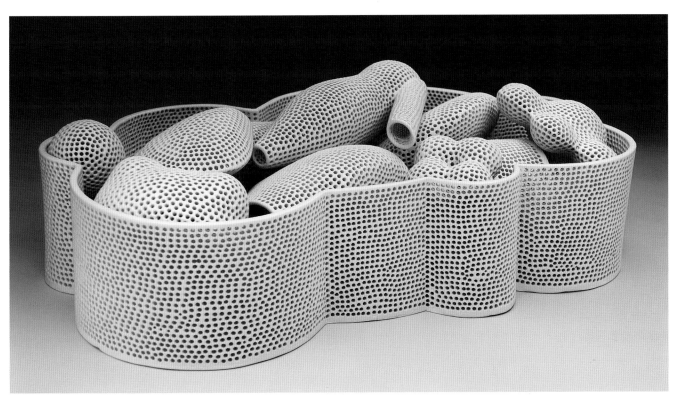

above: **TONY MARSH**
Floating and Dreaming Series, 2004,
l 76 cm (30 in.)
Earthenware

right: **JOHN MASON**
Figure Blue, 2002,
150 × 60 × 60 cm (59 × 23¾ × 23¾ in.)
Ceramic

NAOMI MATHEWS
Dog and Chimp, 2003,
h 120 cm (47 in.)
Earthstone clay, hand-built,
coiled with coloured clay
and slip

below: **CRAIG MITCHELL**
Bird Vendor, 2007,
h 83 × l 22 × w 22 cm (32½ × 8½ × 8½ in.)
Hand-built earthenware, wood, galvanized wire

right: **CRAIG MITCHELL**
Shoemaker, 2007,
h 65 × d 20 cm (25½ × 8 in.)
Hand-built, earthenware, wood, thread

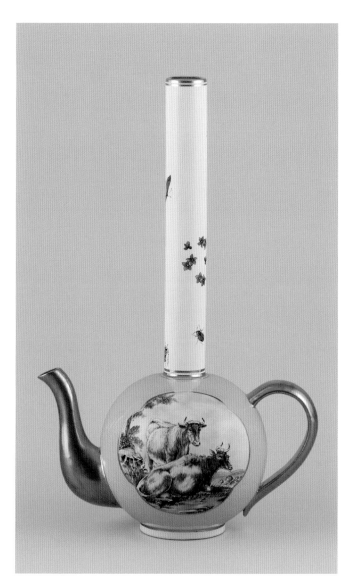

top: **PAUL MATHIEU**
Flower Vase with Matisse, 2005, h 40 cm (15¾ in.)
Porcelain

above: **RICHARD MILETTE**
Skyphos with Blue and White Lid in Mounts, 1996,
h 29.5 × w 32.5 × d 22.5 cm (11½ × 13 × 9 in.)
Ceramic

above: **RICHARD MILETTE**
Meissen Bottle Teapot, 2003,
h 36.9 × w 23.4 × d 13.8 cm (14½ × 9 × 5½ in.)
Ceramic

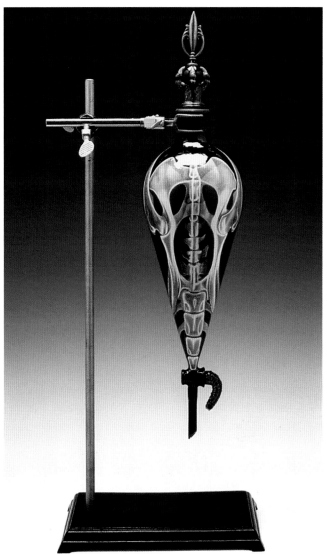

top left: **MERVI KURVINEN**
The Grandmother, 2006, 16 × 8 cm (6 × 3 in.)
Hand-painted miniatures, ceramic, silver, pearls

above, left: **CINDY KOLODZIEJSKI**
Pearl Necklace, 1999, 43 × 15 × 13 cm (17 × 6 × 5 in.)
Earthenware

above, right: **CINDY KOLODZIEJSKI**
Untitled, 2001, 72 × 28 × 16.5 cm (28½ × 11 × 6½ in.)
Earthenware, mixed media

top: **KAREN RYAN**
Guilt and Grief, Pair of Plates, 2007, h 26 × w 52 cm (10 × 20½ in.)
Ceramic, second-hand

above, left: **BARBARA NANNING**
Transmutations, 1999, h 46 cm (18 in.)
Earthenware, lacquer, stoneware, pigment, sand coating

above, right: **REDO DEL OLMO**
Santibanco, VI, 1999
Sculpture clay, coil and slab construction, sprayed application of
engobe, smoke, cone 01

above: **MARTA NAGY**
Melting Snow, 2007,
8.5 × 30.5 × 26 cm
(3¼ × 12 × 10 in.)
Stoneware, porcelain

right: **MARTA NAGY**
Water Filter in the Desert, 2007,
10 × 47.5 × 16 cm (4 × 18½ × 6 in.)
Stoneware, porcelain, silver leaf

above: **ANNA NOEL**
The Young Lady of Bute, 2007,
approx. h 36 × w 39 × d 14 cm (14 × 15 × 5½ in.)
Hand-built, sculpted high-fired earthenware

right: **ANNA NOEL**
Horse and Rider, 2003, h 40 cm (15¼ in.)
Ceramic

opposite, top left: **KATI NULPPONEN**
Fragile, 2004, 30 × 12 cm (12 × 4¼ in.)
Hand-painted porcelain, textile

opposite, top right: **JUSTIN NOVAK**
21st Century Bunny (Diptych), 2007, 20 × 13 ×
13 cm (8 × 5 × 5 in.)
Slip-cast porcelain objects with china paint
and decals

opposite, bottom: **JUSTIN NOVAK**
Disfigurine #46, 2006,
28 × 2.5 × 20 cm (11 × 1 × 8 in.)
Raku-fired ceramic piece with metal attachments

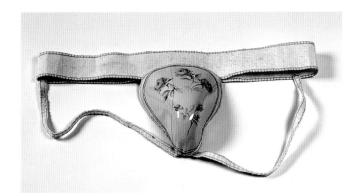

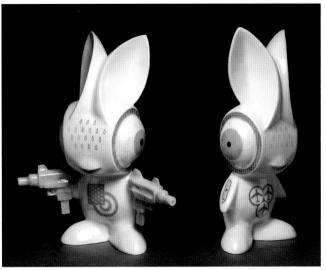

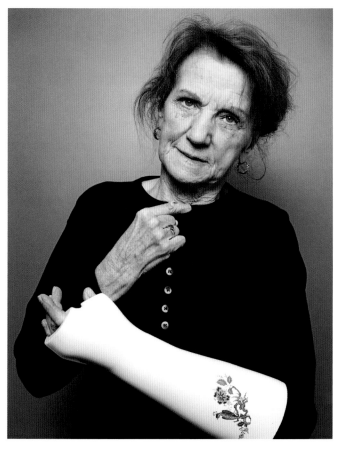

above, left: **DAMIAN O'SULLIVAN**
Elderly Lady with Eyepatch, 2003,
33 × 11 cm (13 × 4¼ in.)
Slip-cast in porcelain

above, right: **DAMIAN O'SULLIVAN**
Elderly Lady with Arm in Cast, 2003,
7 × 4 cm (2¾ × 1.5 in.)
Slip-cast in porcelain

above, left: **LAWSON OYEKAN**
Pictured with Coming Up for Air Series,
2000–2001, h 200 cm (79 in.)
Red German clay, unfired

above, right: **LAWSON OYEKAN**
Autonomous Resonator Series, 2004,
h approx. 45 cm (18 in.)
Baltimore clay, unfired

top: **PEKKA PAIKKARI**
Breaking Up of Ice, 1992, 50 × 150 × 150 cm (20 × 59 × 59 in.)
Ceramic

above: **PEKKA PAIKKARI**
Scream, 2006, h 4 m (13 ft)
Ceramic

right: **PEKKA PAIKKARI**
Fractured Sheet, 2007, 93 × 93 × 2 cm (36½ × 36½ × ¾ in.)
Fired clay

RAFA PEREZI
Untitled, 2006, h 40 × 28 cm (15¾ × 11 in.)
Ceramic, fired above 1150°C

above, left: **PEDER RASMUSSEN**
Hansenstein, 2007, 22 cm (8½ in.)
Ceramic

above, right: **SHIRLEY LESLYN SHEPPARD**
Three Men and their Boot Fetish Dance, 2006,
h 42 cm (16½ in.)
Earthenware, slip-castings re-assembled, glaze with decals

above: **DAVID REGAN**
The Tooth Teapot: Cyanide Leach Goldmine, 2004,
h 14 × w 28 cm (5½ × 11 in.)
Porcelain

right: **DAVID REGAN**
Sink Full of Dishes: Housewife Daydreams, 2007,
h 35.6 × w 58.4 cm (14 × 23 in.)
Porcelain

above: **GWYN HANSSEN PIGOTT**
Float, 2007, h 17.6 × w 156 × d 19 cm
(7 × 61 × 7½ in.)
Translucent porcelain, thrown

right: **GWYN HANSSEN PIGOTT**
Still Life with Two Cups, 2005,
h 29.6 × w 34.3 × d 29.2 cm
(11½ × 13½ × 11½ in.)
Translucent porcelain, thrown

above: **NICHOLAS RENA**
Habits of the Saints 5, 2007,
29 × dia 40 cm (11 × 16 in.)
Ceramic

left: **NICHOLAS RENA**
Habits of the Saints 2, 2007,
65 × 49 × dia 19 cm (25½ × 19 × 7½ in.)
Ceramic

left: **PATRICIA RIEGER**
Soliloquy, He 1. The Expulsion Series, 2007,
h 59 × 25 × 53 cm (22 × 10 × 21 in.)
Fired clay, metal

below: **NICK RENSHAW**
Terrestrial Being, 2006, h 130 cm (51 in.)
Stoneware, multi-fired

opposite, top: **ANDERS RUHWALD**
Between Thought and Expression, 2006,
58 × 41 × 74 cm (23 × 16 × 29 in.), 58 × 43 × 85 cm (22¾ × 17 × 33½ in.)
Glazed earthenware

opposite, bottom left: **ANDERS RUHWALD**
Shelf/Lamp, 2006, 7 × 35 × 34 cm (2¾ × 13¾ × 13¼ in.)
Glazed earthenware, cord, bulb, plug

opposite, bottom right: **ANDERS RUHWALD**
Social Piece of Furniture #5, 2006,
99 × 29 × 24 cm (39 × 11½ × 9½ in.)
Glazed earthenware

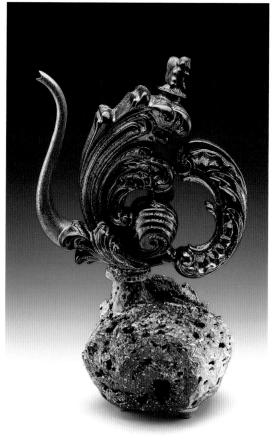

above, left: **ADRIAN SAXE**
1-900 Zeitgeist, 2000, each 88 × 140 × 68.5 cm
(34¾ × 55 × 27 in.)
Porcelain, stoneware, mixed media, six centerpiece
vessels, installation in *Departures: 11 Artists at the Getty*,
J. Paul Getty Museum, Los Angeles

above, right: **ADRIAN SAXE**
Untitled Ewer (BSD), 2004, 33 × 21 × 14 cm
(13 × 8¼ × 5⅝ in.)
Porcelain, stoneware, mixed media

above: **SHERYL MCROBERTS**
Ode to Janet Fish, 2005, 56 × 76 cm (22 × 30 in.)
Low-fire red earthenware (terracotta), modelled, cone 1

left: **JIM THOMSON**
Familiar 37, 2007, 22 × 52 × 54 cm (8½ × 20½ × 21 in.)
Stoneware, cone 6 oxidation

above: **CAROLINE SLOTTE**
Rose Border Multiple, Double Blue II, 2007,
dia 28 cm (11 in.)
Re-worked ceramic, second-hand material

left: **CAROLINE SLOTTE**
Pink Skies (detail), 2007, dia 22 cm (8½ in.)
Re-worked ceramic, second-hand material

right: **PAUL SCOTT**
Three Gorges, After the Dam, 2004, l 52 cm (20½ in.)
T material, slip and glaze with in-glaze screenprint,
decal college

below: **PAUL SCOTT**
Tea Cup and Saucer from Cockle Pickers Tea Service,
2006, dia 13 cm (5 in.)
Ceramic

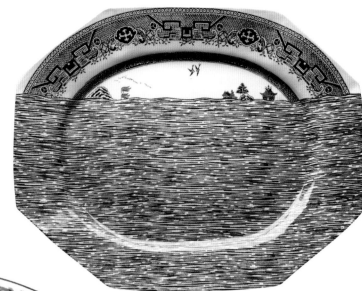

above: **KIM SIMONSSON**
Steel Rabbit, 2007, 110 × 100 × 145 cm
(43 × 39 × 57 in.)
Ceramic, glass, platinum, bondo

right: **KIM SIMONSSON**
Girl Baptized in Gold, 2007, 110 × 50 cm
(43 × 19½ in.)
Ceramic, glass, platinum, bondo

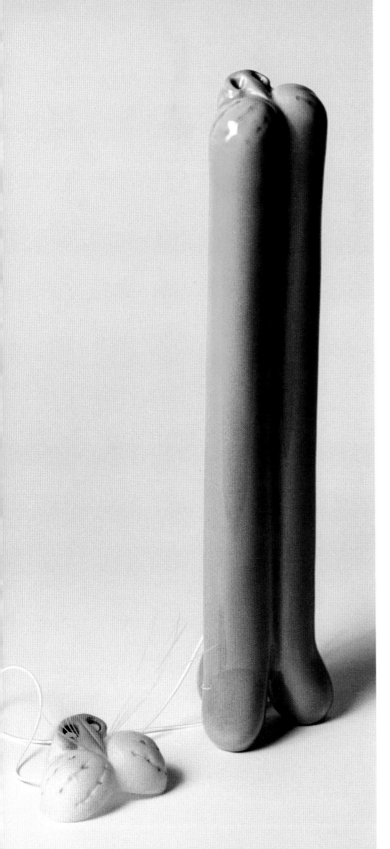

above: **RICHARD SLEE**
Bean, 2006, l 33 cm (13 in.)
Ceramic, found mask

left: **RICHARD SLEE**
Dog/Naked, 2005, h 29 cm (11½ in.)
Ceramic, found mask

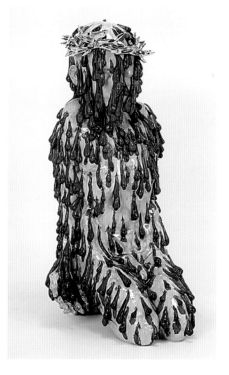

above: **CAROLEIN SMIT**
Man of Sorrow, 2008, h 59 cm (23 in.)
Earthenware, red glaze, gold lustre, hand-built

left: **BENTE SKJØTTGAARD**
White Rocks no. 0803, 2006, 67.5 × 41.5 × 36.5 cm
(26½ × 16 × 14 in.)
Stoneware

above, right: **VIPOO SRIVILASA**
For the Future, Natural Therapeutic, 2008,
h 60 × l 33 × d 16 cm (23½ × 13 × 6 in.)
White earthenware, hand-built, glaze
on glaze, 1160°C

right: **VIPOO SRIVILASA**
Fortune Teller, 2007, various sizes
h 10–15 cm (4–6 in.)
Cool Ice Porcelain, hand-built, cobalt
and ceramic pigment, 1200°C

left: **RICHARD SHAW**
Upside Down, 2003,
38 × 23 × 19 cm (15 × 9 × 7½ in.)
Porcelain

below, left: **RICHARD SHAW**
C.P.'s Paint Box, 2001,
11 × 33 × 29 cm (4¼ × 13 × 11½ in.)
Porcelain

below: **SYLVIA HYMAN**
Narragansett Bay, 2005,
h 47 cm (18½ in.)
Stoneware and porcelain

above: **INGER SÖDERGREN**
The Miser, 2007, h 58 × w 63 × d 36 cm
(22¾ × 24¾ × 14 in.)
Smoke-fired T material

right: **CHUN LIAO**
Installation, 2008, h 10 × dia 28 cm
(4 × 11 in.)
Porcelain, thrown

above: **MARTIN SMITH**
Sound and Silence 5/2, 2005, dia 66 cm (26 in.)
Ceramic, glass

right: **MARTIN SMITH**
Triptych in Four Parts, 2007,
157 × 37.7 × 8.5 cm (62 × 15 × 3¼ in.)
Ceramic and aluminium leaf

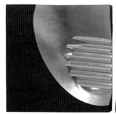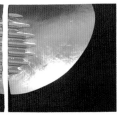

AKIO TAKAMORI
Boat, Installation View of 15 Figures, 2001,
h from 84–103 cm (33–40½ in.)
Stoneware with underglaze

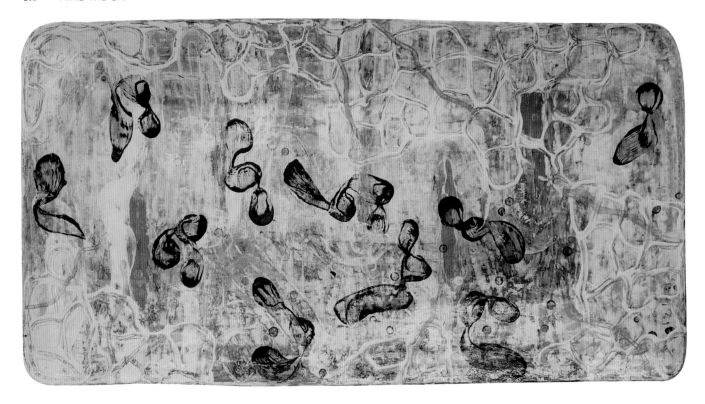

left: **GORO SUZUKI**
Oribe Chair, 2001,
46 × 23 × 22 cm (18 × 9 × 8½ in.)
Ceramic

below: **GORO SUZUKI**
Oribe Stacked Boxes, 1999,
37 × 22 × 20 cm (14½ × 8½ × 8 in.)
Ceramic

opposite, top: **MARIT TINGLEFF**
Dish, 2006, l approx. 150 cm (59 in.)
Ceramic, slip, glaze

opposite, bottom: **MARIT TINGLEFF**
Dish, 2006, l approx. 140 cm (55 in.)
Ceramic, slip, glaze

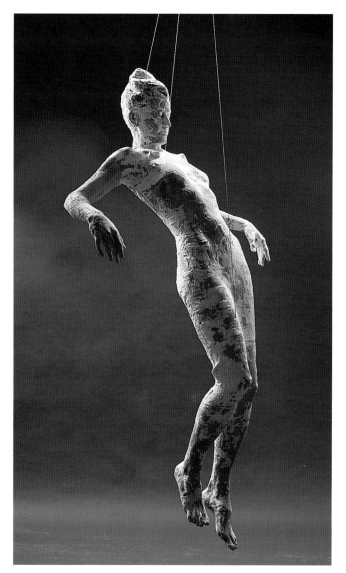

above, left: **KATHY VENTER**
Immersion 17, 2006, 183 × 109 × 137 cm (72 × 43 × 54 in.)
Terracotta, wood (chair), gypsum cement

above, right: **KATHY VENTER**
Immersion 16, 2006, h 84 cm (33 in.)
Terracotta and polychrome

right: **KATHY VENTER**
Immersion 11, 2006, 162 × 68.5 × 73.5 cm (64 × 27 × 29 in.)
Terracotta, gypsum cement

ANNIE TURNER
Martello Towers, 2007, h 18 × w 18 cm (7 × 7 in.)
Red grogged clay, lithium carbonate stoneware
glaze, 1230°C

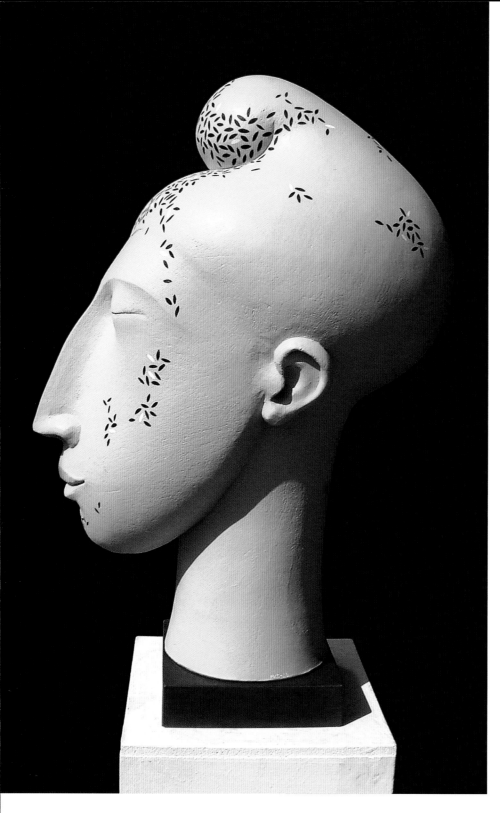

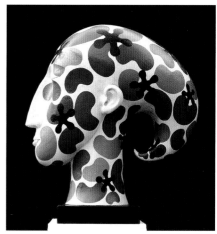

above: **PATRICIA VOLK**
Trickster, 2007, h 60 × w 26 × d 53 cm
(8 × 10¼ × 21 in.)
Ceramic

left: **PATRICIA VOLK**
Sentinel, 2006, h 71 × w 26 × d 46 cm
(28 × 10 × 18 in.)
Ceramic

above: **WENDY WALGATE**
Pax Express, Robin Redbreast Wagon, 2006,
h 43 × w 43 × d 23 cm (17 × 17 × 9 in.)
White earthenware, slip-cast, glazed,
vintage metal toy wagon

right: **WENDY WALGATE**
Envoy Chair, 2006, child's chair,
h 71 × w 35.5 × d 30.5 cm (28 × 14 × 12 in.)
White earthenware, slip-cast, glazed,
vintage wooden and metal

above, left: **PAULINE WIERTZ**
Zoutslak, 2006
Glazed porcelain with transfers

above, right: **PAULINE WIERTZ**
Chicken, Crab and Lobster-legged Cups, 2003,
h 13 cm (5 in.)
Glazed porcelain with transfers

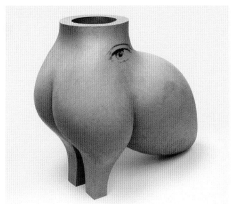

above: **CONOR WILSON**
Lemon Squeezer, Edition of 9 Yellow/9 Pink,
1998–2001, 37 × 36 × 23 cm (14½ × 14 × 9 in.)
White clay, yellow glaze, gold lustre

right: **CONOR WILSON**
Shubutt (prototype), 2002, h 28 cm (11 in.)
Ceramic

above: **BETTY WOODMAN**
Balustrade Relief Vase, 2005–2006,
h 145 cm (57 in.)
Glazed earthenware

right: **BETTY WOODMAN**
Gaugin's Nude, 'His/Her' Vase (detail), 2005,
h 74 cm (29 in.) max.
Glazed earthenware, epoxy resin, lacquer, paint

CAROLE WINDHAM
Roy, Vicky and Benday Dots, 2006,
h 21 cm (8¼ in.)
Ceramic, slip-cast

above: **PETRA WOLF**
Stretching, 2008, d 35 cm (13¼ in.)
Clay body, hand-built, 1180°C, electric kiln

right: **ROBERT WINOKUR**
Two Barns on the Wall: White Washed, 2006,
h 40 × 73 × 10 cm (16 × 28¾ × 4 in.)
Ceramic, slab constructed, engobe

above, left: **KEN PRICE**
Thirteen Balls, 2006,
22.2 × 15.2 × 12.7 cm (8¾ × 6 × 5 in.)
Acrylic on fired ceramic

above, right: **KEN PRICE**
Bloato, 2004,
h 61 × 61 × 55.9 cm (24 × 24 × 22 in.), base size,
h 111.8 × 86.4 × 76.2/81.3 cm (44 × 34 × 30/32 in.)
Acrylic on fired ceramic

CHAPTER FOUR

A SENSE OF SPACE

Installation, Site Specific,
Environmental

preceding pages: **THOMAS WEBER**
Koerbe (Baskets), 2007,
h 65 cm (25½ in.) max.
Coiled-built white clay with glazes,
1060°C

below: **LEE RENNINGER**
Lace1, 2005, 122 × 76 × 1 cm
(48 × 30 × 0.4 in.)
Porcelain; fibre, unglazed, hand-

wrought porcelain units, fired at
cone 10 reduction, tied together
with cotton crochet

right: **RICHARD LONG**
*Wall Installation 7, Firth of Forth
Mud Arc*, 2007

When the UK artist Richard Long covers a wall in an art gallery with hand prints using river mud, the resulting art work can take on any one of several identities – be they installation, site-specific, site-aware, site-sensitive, environmental and performance art – or all of them. So widely applied is the term installation that almost any arrangement of objects can be described as such. All embracing, it directs as much attention to the staging as to the objects it includes. As a result, attempting to devise a useful or workable definition presents various challenges.

Any dscussion of installation art that focuses on work in clay poses a number of problems because, of all the forms used by ceramists, it moves furthest from 'craft production', which is often seen as being defined as much by its material qualities as its expressive content. Yet, despite this, many artists working primarily with installation and ceramics define themselves as ceramists, upholding and maintaining the powerful links to their chosen material and the craft tradition.

Installation, site-specific, site-sensitive, site-aware, environmental and performance have become something of a mantra denoting various ways of presenting ideas, concepts and objects with subtle but

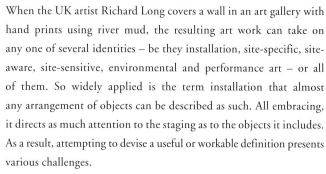

significant differences, though there are often important overlaps. In its broadest meaning, installation is generally taken to signify a group – or even a single object – placed within a defined space. In general the installation is temporary and, most significantly, related to the space occupied.

As such, the relationship between the space and the object(s) evokes complex and multiple associations, tempting a variety of thoughts and associations and even moods. The work of Lee Renninger, for example, combines a sense of the organic with a theatrical quality to create drape-like fabrics in the form of dresses and garment.

Significantly, one of the overall unifying characteristics is a profound commitment to, and understanding of, their chosen material – to an awareness of clay-ness, surface treatment and to social and domestic references in evolving ideas. In one of the few exhibitions to look seriously at, among other work, installation art and its role within contemporary ceramic practice, *A Secret History of Clay: From Gauguin to Gormley* (Tate Gallery, Liverpool, 2004) included the work of several installation artists. Amongst other issues, they addressed questions around fragility, the positioning of the vessel, cultural borrowings, performance and the inherent qualities of unfired clay. Nobuo Sekine, one of the exhibitors, showed a vast mound of oiled clay, some 2 m (6½ ft) high, the surface of which visitors were invited to model.[1]

One of the works on show was *Porcelain Wall* (2004) by Edmund de Waal, which consisted of rows of similar-looking porcelain cylindrical forms, some 10 cm (4 in.) high, with a pale blue celadon glaze; it raised issues concerned with repetition as a comment on the craft of ceramics, its role in providing useful objects and its cultural heritage in form, material and firing. In 'borrowing' some of the formal language of ceramics from the Far East, de Waal was echoing the long history of exchange of goods, ideas and cultures that have been, and continue to be, a part of Western culture. De Waal's work is discussed in more detail later in this chapter.

far left: **CLARE TWOMEY**
Consciousness/Conscience,
Collaboration with Royal Crown Derby, 2003
Bone china

left: **JENNY STOLZENBERG**
Strong at the Broken Places (detail), 2005
Ceramic and wood

below: **PIET STOCKMANS**
Cape, 2007, 200 × 200 cm (78½ × 78½ in.)
Porcelain, slip-casting

TREAD SOFTLY

When the ceramic artist Clare Twomey walked across the floor in her installation *Consciousness/Conscience* (2003), which was also on show in *A Secret History of Clay*, she could, to all intents and purposes, have been smashing 10,000 years of ceramic history. Part of the installation consisted of a carpet of tiles and to enter the space the viewer had to walk over them and by so doing crushed and destroyed them. With its pun on the notion of bone – the floor tiles were made of a low-fired bone china body, a product that is made up of fifty per cent calcined animal bone – at one level *Consciousness/Conscience* addressed profound issues such as life and death, as well as construction/destruction.

The fragility of ceramic is one of its major characteristics, but, apart from its ability to be relatively easily broken or, in this case, trampled under foot, fired clay will remain largely unaffected for thousands of years. Even when buried in the ground, objects will decay or change little, with many ancient treasured forms retaining a freshness that belie their long history. Twomey, working in the early years of the twenty-first century, exploits both the ability of clay to be formed into a seemingly enduring, hard material and also its vulnerability, turning it from a permanent to a transient material of little value save as sophisticated archaeological remains, evidence of some exotic but long-gone construction.

Twomey's installation can be seen as indicative of the way many ceramists approach the material in bringing to the work a deep understanding of its intrinsic qualities. While well aware of the long and complex history of clay, artists see it as offering opportunities for the exploration of ideas, whether about vulnerability, fragility or the desire to 'make a mark' even if this involves destroying the object

itself. To see only Twomey's installation rather than to walk across it is to limit experience of the work, yet the very act of engaging physically with it ruins it, literally for ever.

Not all artists working with clay offer such a dramatic or creative/destructive experience, but explore similar aspects of the material. Most artists, however, are deeply, if obliquely, concerned with its history, whether social, economic, technical or aesthetic and the idea of real or emblematic function. Just as Twomey set up a paradox between use and destruction, in her piece, *Between* (2005), Phoebe Cummings creates a similar conflict between use and impossibility. In the piece *Between* Cummings has created what looks like a lush stair carpet running down the centre of a staircase, a sort of arrested escalator that seems as if it might burst into life at any moment. Made up of hundreds of fat coils of unfired clay placed close together resembling exaggeratedly large tufts of wool, it runs almost like a river down the stairs. The velvet-like surface, while inviting the viewer to ascend the stairs, also denies them that possibility because to walk on the 'carpet' would be to destroy it. Cummings's use of clay is intrinsic to the work, its fragility an important part of the effect.

A similar sort of paradox informs the objects placed on the shelves in Belinda Berger's *Country Life* (2006). They are almost deliberately out of reach, tempting us to touch

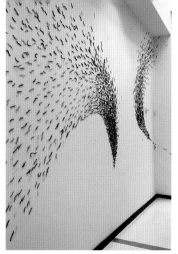

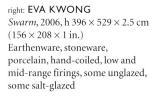

right: EVA KWONG
Swarm, 2006, h 396 × 529 × 2.5 cm
(156 × 208 × 1 in.)
Earthenware, stoneware,
porcelain, hand-coiled, low and
mid-range firings, some unglazed,
some salt-glazed

far right: JEFF SCHMUKI
Scatter, 2004–2008
Earthenware, glaze, size variable

while at the same time making this virtually impossible. The installations of shoes and dresses created by Jenny Stolzenberg explore both absence and presence, work that touches powerfully on individual and collective tragedy.

Formal concerns that are central to the practice of some artists are handled with great conviction by Xavier Toubes, Piet Stockmans and Marek Cecula. Toubes's installation of 200 or so dishes placed on the wall in ordered array creates a monumental effect by its sheer scale, converting the modest individual components into something spectacular. Stockmans also makes use of the repetition of shapes, for instance, in *The Belgian Shore* (2007). It is made up of swaying rows of blue jug forms weaving their way across the floor in an elegant movement reminiscent of the sea. With a characteristic minimalist use of colour and form, Stockmans creates an air of mystery and magic. His trademark combination of blue and white is continued in *Wall Installation, Stockholm* (2007), which uses components of square white boxes each with a 'lid' in blue. Placed on the wall, these change according to the position from which they are seen and the shadows they cast. The arrangement may appear simple but is visually and conceptually effective: Stockmans sets up reverberations with modernist ideas along with traditional associations with blue and white, whether with Ming Dynasty China or eighteenth-century Wedgwood.

Marek Cecula offers a different take on internationalism, the domestic and consumerism. In his magnificent 'Persian Carpet' series he plays on the use of the fragility of the medium, the technical ability of ceramic transfers, or decals, to reproduce almost exactly the appearance of a Persian carpet and the ability of the eye to make

sense of what it can see. Like the magic Persian carpets that feature in Middle Eastern myth, Cecula's carpet is one we can see but, like Cummings's stair carpet, it cannot be walked on. Through the use of printed decals or transfers fired onto mass-produced china plates, the visually striking sculptures touch on aspects of cultural exchange and the illusionistic qualities that ceramics can so effectively create.

Mapping the world, literally and metaphorically, is a theme found in much installation work and is used to great effect by Jeanne Quinn. Working with both wall-based pieces and suspended forms, Quinn creates work that offers her own response to the world. In installations such as *Lacemap* (2008), Quinn pins shapes onto a background, vaguely recalling conventional geographical mapping, and creates another map – one of her own making. Quinn's abstracted, elusive territory is multi-layered and complex. The mapping that takes place in the work of Maria Nuutinen is more personal and autobiographical. Photographic imagery, fragments of half-seen, half-remembered faces create a kaleidoscope of impressions with which most of us can begin to identify. Other works also incorporate old photographs, effective triggers of memory, associations and family that are powerfully evocative and redolent with emotion. The wall installations devised by Eva Kwong and Jeff Schmuki are, by comparison, distant and controlled. While using the flatness of the surface as a ground, their appearance is changed by building up patterns of form. In pieces such as *Swarm* (2006), Kwong literally creates a crowd that appears to mill and move over the surface, the small, curved components wriggling and weaving their own way. Kwong's work is, paradoxically, minimal but also suffused with information, a curious hybrid of the organic and the constructed. Honed and

far left: **ANGEL GARRAZA**
Things from Memory, 2004
Ceramic

left: **FIRTH MACMILLAN**
Pink Grow Green, 2006, 109 ×
30.5 × 2.5 cm (43 × 12 × 1 in.)
Ceramic, hand-built, slip-cast
whiteware, cone 04 oxidation

simplified, her work has a sense of inner life and energy. In the large-scale, sculptural installations of Firth MacMillan clay is handled with a directness and a physicality that demonstrates a sense of both authority and discovery. The work offers a physical experience that makes use of colour and scale to touch on deeply buried emotions. Placed on the wall much like paintings or photographs, these works exceed the illusion of the two dimensional to face the viewer with their unambiguous presence.

PLACE/POSITION

Just as installation has become a recognized form in art, a way of presenting ideas/objects within anonymous gallery or museum contexts, so ceramics have long had a place in the home, which for many involves careful display. Pots sitting on a dresser, arranged inside a china cabinet or hanging on hooks in the kitchen can often seem to take on aspects of installation. One of minor pleasures of owning pots is to arrange them to heighten their qualities, for some an act done without a huge amount of thought, while for others it is an important part of enjoying the full qualities of pots, with much satisfaction in getting such a display right. The work of Anne Helen Mydland touches on the domestic aspects of display within the domestic setting and the personal context it evokes. She places selected objects in cabinets and room settings, the self-conscious assemblies evoking a sense of unease as well as pleasure.

In addition to arranging ceramics within the home, a further characteristic of making pots for the potter is the performative aspect. One of the fundamental features of working on the wheel is the ability to produce pots rapidly using the technique of throwing, which to the casual observer might almost appear to be installation/performance in its own right. The skilled potter can fascinate onlookers with the seeming ease and speed of production, and the resultant rows of identical pots. These rapidly fill up shelves with forms that in their similarity and slight differences seem to embody narrative. Even a skilled hand-builder can fashion coils or slabs of clay with remarkable speed.

In contrast, industrial techniques such as slip-casting offer no such variations because the nature of the process means it can only replicate identical objects in any desired quantity. It is also a process that allows casts to be made of almost any object, be they ornaments, guns, flowers, animals, fruit or figures and repeat them ad nauseum, such as in the work of Charles Krafft. Sentiment and danger are brought together in his deceptively attractive slip-cast machine guns. Despite the brightly coloured and cheerful floral decoration and classic blue and white patterning, it is a reference to a weapon of destruction and aggression, although here transformed into a sophisticated 'ornament'. The use of the same, or similar, objects is often a significant aspect of ceramic installation.

Repeating forms and the sense of repetition, together with the rhythms they set up, are significant aspects of installations by artists such as Angel Garraza. Garraza's strange pairings and couplings of oddly shaped, ambiguous objects occupying the floor in his installation *Mentiras* (2002) appear like mechanical tops, caught up in their individual dramas, wending their own way within the confines of the gallery, occupying their own space, alien beings in their private worlds. Using titles such as *Synthetic Reality* (2008), Susan Beiner

right: **THOMAS WEBER**
Rollen, Rolls, 1992–95,
dia 52 cm (20½ in.) max.
Coiled, different clay with
different glazes, 1060°C

below: **ANDREW BURTON**
Resurrection, 2006,
7 × 5 m (23 × 16½ ft) max.
Ceramic, mortar

suggests the interface between constructed or made objects and nature. She takes us to a world where little is as it seems. The lavish-looking flowers and crowded wall pieces appear to echo nature but a closer look quickly reveals their manufactured origin.

Ready-made ceramic objects are used by Kerry Harker to great effect; she decorates them as a 'ceramic canvas' for her 'paintings', such as in *Bud* (2004–2008), where she adds her own 'voice' to the pieces. The use of similar as opposed to identical pieces can be highly effective in suggesting both the delights of intimacy and the fear of loss of 'personal space'. The sense of anxiety that pervades the work of Alexander Brodsky is partly because familiar objects are seen in unfamiliar ways. The 'archaeology' of his installation reveals a diverse range of objects that might include toys, bones and footwear, all finished without glaze, the raw, white surfaces adding a further bleached quality to these finds.

A powerful sense of environmental concerns informs the work of artists Satoru Hoshino and Sofia Beça. Hoshino creates a convincing sense of growth in installations that seem to invade and take over gallery space to evoke a sense of the organic without replicating any particular aspect. Beça's work makes allusions to such things as standing stones, objects that may be the result of natural activity or carefully created and placed by human endeavour. The use of earth colours, such as terracotta and burnt brown, are the colours of earth, the reassuring, quiet tones of land. The forms put together by Makoto Hatori combine an awareness of organic form with a constructed and considered

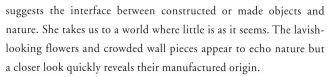

structure. Like forms that mutate and grow out of control, Hatori's work touches on the real and the imagined. Inspired by time spent in India, Andrew Burton has built large structures incorporating hand-made bricks that are part container, part architecture and part vessel.

The ambiguities evident in Burton's work are taken in different directions by Eva Mileusnic. The tall, figure-like forms that make up the group in *A Working Cast* (2007) are wrapped around with wool or cloth saturated in slip. The result is a hybrid, a blending of materials that relates to both the body and to industrial manufacture. The tall forms recall the sort of skeins used when weaving, but are here rendered obsolete, out of action, out of time. Like Mileusnic, Thomas Weber puts together groups of objects that, collectively, tell a different story than each of the individual objects. Some, such as *Koerbe* (2007), feature full, fat rounded vessels with pointed tops, their upper part brightly coloured. Others, like *Das Dorf* (2006), make use of the natural colour of the clay in an installation that stretches the full length of the gallery. The group *Rollen* (1992–95) uses simple coiled, rounded, brightly coloured clay forms. Like children's toys they call out to be played with, rearranged and sorted.

The sense of inhabiting an area and making it your own, evident in the work of Mileusnic and Weber, is also a fundamental part of installations by Lubna Chowdry and Anne Tophøj. Chowdry's carefully placed assemblies of toy-sized buildings evoke urban sprawl, towns or cities, spread out to offer a bird's-eye view of where we live and who we are. The dishes and containers put together by Tophøj stretch out, tempting us to make our own selection. The vessels snuggling together on a single plinth in work by Dorothee Schellhorn crowd up, almost jostling for position. The use of stereotypical vase

far left: **EDMUND DE WAAL**
Permanent installation at
Chatsworth House, Derbyshire,
2007, tallest approx. 76 cm (30 in.)
Porcelain, reduction-fired

left: **SATORU HOSHINO**
*Beginning Form – Met Spiral
05I–1*, 2005, h 290 × w 280 ×
d 150 cm (114 × 110 × 59 in.)
Mixed black clay, 1210°C,
reduction-fired

forms in bright, rich colour add to the cartoon-like quality of the assembly, though each vessel retains its individuality.

The complex structures based round the vessels that Nicole Cherubini assembles combine fired ceramic with wood, metal and other materials. Aware of the conventions of presentation through the use of plinths and pedestals, Cherubini exaggerates and expands to create larger-than-life pieces. Colourful and with a welcome sense of the uninhibited, the objects are exotic confections, flights of fancy that gently satirize the convention of both craft and high art. As such they can be enjoyed as a rococo extravagance and as a celebration of the plastic qualities of clay and glaze.

SITE/SIGHT

Site-specific installations – or interventions – that relate to identified locations not only open up new opportunities for introducing new audiences to ceramics, but also offer alternative ways of encountering them. Part of Liu Jianhua's site-specific project at Oxburgh Hall, Norfolk, UK involved the complex installation *Regular/Fragile* (2005–2006). Shown in the Venice Biennale, it was re-created in a new form and included the placing of hundreds of pieces of broken porcelain, modelled figures around the hall. The top of a table, standing in the centre of one of the grand rooms, was filled with pale blue porcelain forms. The chairs placed round the table suggest that this might be in preparation for a meal, but the quantity of crockery on the table, which amounts to a positive cornucopia, indicates that the actual serving of food may be a problem. In other assemblies Jianhua incorporates found and made objects to look at the concepts of waste, collecting and desire. The large-

scale works by Zhu Legeng use the colour and textures of clay to animate the impersonal walls of auditoria to create a powerful visual effect.

The placing of pots in unexpected places has been one of the thoughtful themes explored by Edmund de Waal. He has refined the concept of the temporary intervention within established spaces, be they houses, museums or galleries, to what he identifies as 'site-sensitive' work. For this he carefully places pots in and around particular institutions such as museums and historical houses which quietly disrupt the status quo. At Blackwell, the Arts and Crafts house, in England's Lake District, de Waal's cylindrical porcelain forms were carefully arranged on shelves, in window bottoms and shelves with seemingly no obvious display intended, an understated but abiding presence.

In contrast, a commission for an installation in the magnificent interior of Chatsworth House in Derbyshire involved placing vessels inside and in front of the grate and on the mantelshelf of a grand eighteenth-century fireplace. The fireplace became home to tall, slender, lidded porcelain jars nearly a metre in height with a soft, pale blue glaze. The tall, slim containers seem to lean and sway appearing to grow and take root in their new surroundings, all perfectly settled and at home, quietly but firmly asserting their presence.

An installation at Kettle's Yard, Cambridge was equally ambitious. Within the gallery special installations were devised, some self-contained, some making use of the gallery architecture that touched on themes such as the seasons or on the domestic context for pots. Within the house – once the home of collector and curator Jim Ede – de Waal placed objects around the interior, some replacing pots on shelves, others standing on tables, all, to some extent, disrupting the space with their retiring but assured presence.

right: VICTORIA EDEN
February 5 2004, 2007
Ceramic, hand-built, moulded.
Screenprint of image taken from
press cutting

far right: KEITH HARRISON
Last Supper, 2006, 8 × 1.2 × 1 m
(26 × 4 × 3 ft)
Egyptian paste, brick clay, heating
elements, electric cabling,
insulation blocks, timer switches

The significance/relevance of place inevitably has a profound effect on the work produced. Artists often spend much time in a particular location, absorbing the ambience, noting the detail and identifying any useful space. This was particularly the case with Clare Twomey's installations at the Victoria and Albert Museum, London, the Great Ormond Street Hospital for Children, London, and at the Eden Project in Cornwall. For her installation *Trophy* (2006) set in the prestigious and stately space of the Victoria and Albert's Cast Court Twomey produced hundreds of tiny blue birds, barely 4 or 5 cm (1½–2 in.) in diameter, fashioned from Wedgwood's famous blue jasper clay. These were placed on shelves, around sculptures, nestling on the floor and in corners, converting the gallery into an exotic aviary of life, providing the ideal opportunities for direct audience participation. Members of the public were invited to admire and also to take individual pieces of work away with them. In so doing, the blue birds, emblematic of happiness, took flight, moving to different spaces, taking on new lives. Participants were asked to send photographs of the birds in their new habitat resulting in Twomey being inundated with images that affirmed the continuing life of the project.

For an installation concerned with environmental issues at the Eden Project in Cornwall – a highly popular project set in the vast space of a redundant clay pit – Twomey devised the idea of making hundreds of roses in white bone china. Traditionally these were made by hand, petal by petal, in Stoke-on-Trent and applied to a variety of ware, whether on the side of vessels, used as knobs or as decorative elements generally. Skilled workers produced them in quantity. Although speedily made, they have a convincing, realistic quality.

At the Eden Project Twomey 'planted' the roses she made, which were not fired, in the garden to create a field of unlikely but intriguing blooms. Over time the unfired roses disintegrated and were washed back into the earth from where the material had come.

The 'issue-based' concerns, a characteristic of installations such as Twomey's Eden Project, were taken up by Victoria Eden who was greatly moved by the tragic death of 18 Chinese cockle pickers in Morecambe Bay in 2004. Caught by the rapidly rising tide and unable to reach land, the cockle pickers were swept out to sea and drowned. The tragedy was the starting point for Eden's installation which involved making casts of the ripples left on the sand by the sea which were used as the basis for a series of 18 flattened shapes that bore the incised names and images of the cockle pickers. These fired forms were subsequently placed in the bay and allowed to be washed by the sea, a memorial and tribute to a devastating event that was often overshadowed by questions around illegal immigration and exploitation by unscrupulous 'gang masters'.

STAGE/STAGED

Not all site-sensitive installations are as controlled as those discussed above, but they can involve an element of drama and performance. The two installations at the Victoria and Albert Museum by Keith Harrison made inventive use of the space and location which, for their full effect, required the presence of an audience to realize his idea fully. For his installation *M25 London Orbital* (2006) Harrison constructed a scale model of the M25, the ring road that runs around the city some twenty-five miles from the centre. Harrison's model, which weaved its

far left: **GREG PAYCE**
Albedo, 2006, each
vase, h 35.5 cm (14 in.)
Porcelain

left: **NICOLE
CHERUBINI**
Alabastron, 2007,
91 × 76 × 114 cm
(36 × 30 × 45 in.)
Ceramic, terracotta,
porcelain, wood,
enamel, lustre,
crystal ice

way through the sculpture court and the garden, was filled with a cargo of Egyptian paste in which electrical elements were buried. When charged with electricity it was intended to fire slowly and change colour over several hours, the slow combustion witnessed by an attentive audience. Although, on this occasion, an electrical failure prevented the firing from taking place, the tension and suspense, together with the fascination of the 'road', created an effective site-specific piece. It was later reconfigured and successfully fired.

On the same occasion, and taking his cue again from the museum setting, Harrison devised *Last Supper* (2006), which was set up in the grand Raphael Gallery. It took on quasi-religious aspects in addition to looking at issues concerning waste and consumerism. Thirteen blocks of different-coloured Egyptian paste, their shapes cast from the inside of discarded electrical cookers, were fitted with electrical elements that were also recovered from redundant cookers. As in Leonardo da Vinci's depiction of the Last Supper, these were placed in a row on a long table creating a sort of family. As they were fired, much to the amusement of the on-lookers, steam and vapour was slowly given off causing the Egyptian paste to change colour with the heat. The magnificence of the setting and the dramatic if slow firing all added to a spectacular event.

Audience participation is a key element for some artists. In Andrew Livingstone's installation *Tacit* (2006), which involved CCTV, a monitor, plastic clay and a sheet of instructions, participants were asked to construct a basic clay pot following a set of instructions while being monitored by CCTV. Making the pot was more difficult

than it might first appear, often causing participants to struggle, so re-calling an episode of the popular television programme the *Generation Game* in which guests were invited to throw a pot on a potter's wheel much to the amusement of the audience. *Tacit* also alerted visitors to the fact that in any public space we are subject to constant monitoring by the ubiquitous CCTV. For Bonnie Kemske, her rounded, abstract sculptures are only brought to life when they are handled, caressed and nursed, an intimate form of audience participation. In contrast, the performative element of Nina Hole's work is strictly for observation only. Hole builds vast structures that are part house and part kiln. These are then fired, engulfed by spectacular flames which then convert them into permanent/temporary structures.

Hole's spectacular structures – a meditation on the destructive/creative force of fire – are hard to match, but other artists explore other ways of animating form. One of Greg Payce's installations con-sists of a circle of vessels that stood on the top of a circular wall, which was enlivened by the use of projected images. In some images a naked woman appears, on others the pots are covered in a richly coloured tree-like image. The impressive installation, with its formal arrangement of components, is partially disrupted by projections that open up a variety of interpretations, a metaphor for the way we 'read' and see.

1 *A Secret History of Clay: From Gauguin to Gormley* was one of the first international exhibitions to pres-ent the work of artists who have worked with clay from the beginning of the twentieth century to the present day. It followed on from the equally pioneering exhibition *The Raw and the Cooked: New Work in Clay in Britain*, 1993, which was curated by Alison Britton and Martina Margetts and shown in London, Oxford, Wales, Japan, Taiwan and France.

above: **LEE RENNINGER**
Wrap1 Porcelain, 2007, 86 × 244 × 5 cm
(34 × 96 × 2 in.)
Fibre unglazed hand-wrought porcelain units,
fired cone 10 reduction, sewn with fibre

right: **LEE RENNINGER**
Boho1, 2007, 152 × 152 × 152 cm
(60 × 60 × 60 in.)
Porcelain, hemp, unglazed, hand-wrought
porcelain units, fired at cone 10 reduction, tied
together with hemp

above: **PHOEBE CUMMINGS**
Between, 2005, 40 × 240 cm (15¾ × 94 in.)
Stoneware sprayed with porcelain

above right: **BELINDA BERGER**
Country Life, 2006, dia 22 cm (8½ in.) max.
Porcelain

right: **EDMUND DE WAAL**
A Change in the Weather, 2007, h 159 cm (62½ in.)
Porcelain, wood

above: **LIE FUNG**
Wandering Souls 2, 2003–2005,
160 × 45 × 11 cm (63 × 17½ × 4 in.)
Partially glazed porcelain and stoneware, wire,
painted plywood box, electric lights

right: **LIE FUNG**
Soaring V.2, an 8-piece constellation, 2003–2005,
each approx. 16–30 × 23–42 × 16–23 cm (6–12
× 9–16½ × 6–7 in.), except for 'ball' piece, approx.
30 × 30 × 30 cm (12 × 12 × 12 in.)
Partially glazed porcelain, various wire, chain

above: **CLARE TWOMEY**
Blossom, 10,000 Hand Made Unfired China
Flowers, Eden Project/Cape Farewell, 2007
Bone china

left: **CLARE TWOMEY**
Trophy 4000, Wedgwood Blue Jasper Birds, 2006
blue jasper clay, modelled, installation at the
Victoria and Albert Museum, London

top left: **XAVIER TOUBES**
Melodien, 240 plates, 2004–2007, h 195 cm (77 in.)
Glazed ceramic with lustre

Piachea, h 152 cm (60 in.)
Enamel with lustre

bottom left: **MARIA NUUTINEN**
First Aid Kit, 2005
Mixed material, installation

above: **JENNY STOLZENBERG**
Forgive and Do Not Forget, 2002,
457 × 91 cm (180 × 36 in.) max.
Mixed clays, each shoe individually hand sculpted,
some shoes fired to point of almost collapse

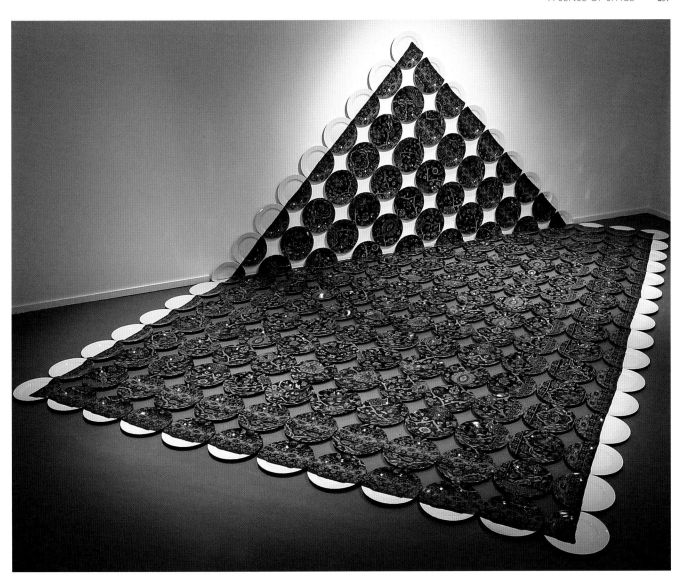

MAREK CECULA
The Porcelain Carpet, 2002,
4 × 5.50 m (12 × 18 ft)
Ceramic, decals

above: **EVA KWONG**
Lament, 2005–2007, h 305 × 1524 × 8 cm
(120 × 600 × 3 in.), can be variable in size
and arrangement
Porcelain clay, press-moulded, celadon glazed

right: **PIET STOCKMANS**
The Belgian Shore, 2007, 200 × 600 cm
(79 × 236 in.)
Porcelain, slip-casting

above: **FIRTH MACMILLAN**
Big Grass, Little Grass, Quince, 2005,
$61 \times 61 \times 5$ cm ($24 \times 24 \times 2$ in.)
Ceramic, hand-built, whiteware,
cone 04 oxidation

right: **FIRTH MACMILLAN**
Big Grass, Little Grass, Quince
(detail), 2005, $13 \times 7.5 \times 5$ cm
($5 \times 3 \times 2$ in.)
Ceramic, hand-built, whiteware,
cone 04 oxidation

above: **JEFF SCHMUKI**
Mirage, 2008, size variable
Earthenware, lustre

right: **JEFF SCHMUKI**
Scatter, 2004–2008, size variable
Earthenware, glaze

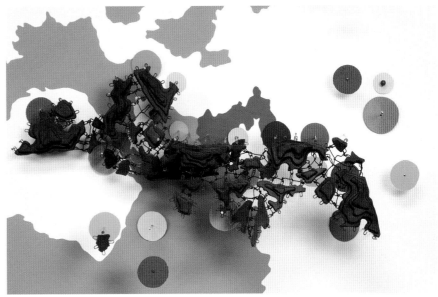

above: **JEANNE QUINN**
Where I Live, This is What the Sky Looks Like,
2003, h 3.6 m × w 3.6 × 5 (12 × 12 × 16 ft)
Porcelain, nylon cord, plywood, paint

right: **JEANNE QUINN**
The Perfect World, 2007, h 3.3 × w 8.5 × d 1.3 m
(11 × 28 × 4½ ft)
Porcelain, wire, paint, plywood

above: **ALEXANDER BRODSKY**
Grey Matter (Table), 1999, 155 × 91 × 1267 cm
(61 × 36 × 498¾ in.) overall
Unfired clay

right: **ALEXANDER BRODSKY**
Grey Matter (Table) detail, 1999,
155 × 91 × 1267 cm (61 × 36 × 498¾ in.) overall
Unfired clay

above, left: **ANNE HELEN MYDLAND**
Stigmata (detail), 2007, h 30 cm (12 in.)
Stoneware, children's trinket, furniture, lights

above: **ANNE HELEN MYDLAND**
Relicshrine, 2007, h 17 cm (7 in.)
Stoneware, lights, furniture, plaster

left: **CHARLES KRAFFT**
Never Look a Gift Shoppe in the Mouth, 2006,
l approx. 25 cm (10 in.)
Hand-painted porcelain

SUSAN BEINER
Synthetic Reality, 2008,
various sizes,
highest 152 × 41 × 41 cm
(60 × 16 × 16 in.)
Installation, porcelain, foam,
polyfil, plexiglass, floor stems

above: **MAKOTO HATORI**
5-7-5, 1998, h 172 × w 200 × d 15 cm
(68 × 79 × 6 in.)
Ceramic, wood and wire additions; a number of
vessels are thrown in stoneware on the wheel. The
vessels are put in frames, made flat. The pieces are
painted with slip and salted water, fired in a gas
kiln, 1380°C, oxidized atmosphere, two-day firing

right: **MAKOTO HATORI**
Spread, 2005, h 51.5 × w 79 × d 19.5 cm
(20 × 31 × 7½ in.)
Ceramic, wood and metal stand additions;
fired in traditional Japanese bank kiln, 1250°C,
reduction-fired, eight-day firing

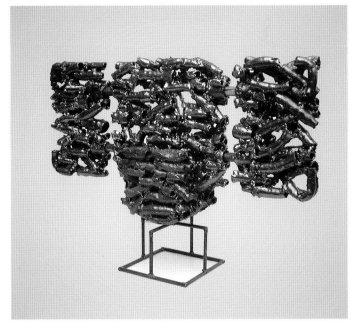

NICOLE CHERUBINI
Installation view, 2007, at the Institute
of Contemporary Art, University
of Pennsylvania, Philadelphia

ANGEL GARRAZA
Mentiras, 2002, h 50 cm
(19½ in.)
Ceramic

top left: **KERRY HARKER**
Bud, 2004–2008
Bone china, on-glaze transfers

top right: **ANNE TOPHØJ**
Dinner – Set Vision II

above: **DOROTHEE SCHELLHORN**
Still Life VII, 1998, h 30 cm (12 in.)
Earthenware

opposite: **THOMAS WEBER**
*The Village, Installation with More
than 1000 Pieces, Work in Progress*, 1992
until today, average size of pieces approx.
20 × 20 × 20 cm (8 × 8 × 8 in.)
Terracotta, 1160°C

above: **SOFIA BEÇA**
Assembleia, 2006, h 34 cm (13¼ in.) max.
Sandstone, engobes, gas-fired, 1150°C
and electric-fired to 1100°C

right: **SATORU HOSHINO**
Beginning Form – Met Spiral 06, 2005,
h 300 × w 600 × d 400 cm (118 × 236 × 157 in.)
Mixed black clay, 1210°C, reduction-fired

top: **ANDREW BURTON**
Stell, 2006
Ceramic, mortar

above: **ANDREW BURTON**
Harkers Wall, 2007

right: **ANDREW BURTON**
Skyqutb, 2005, h 3 m (10 ft)
Brick, mortar

top: **EVA MILEUSNIC**
A Working Cast, 2007, various heights from 50–70 cm (20–27½ in.)
Slip-cast stoneware, stoneware glaze, wool fibres and fabrics
impregnated with stoneware slip

above: **LUBNA CHOWDHARY**
Acknowledged Sources, 2001
Second-hand ceramic over-printed crockery

above, right: **LUBNA CHOWDHARY**
Metropolis, 2000 onwards
Ceramic, multi-object work of over 1,000 pieces

above, left: **ZHU LEGENG**
Rhapsody of Time and Space (detail), 2003,
171 × 70 m (561 × 230 ft)
Stoneware, reduction-fired, 1330°C

above, right: **ZHU LEGENG**
Rhapsody of Time and Space, 2003

above: **LIU JIANHUA**
Regular/Fragile, 2002–2007
Installation view at Oxburgh Hall, Norfolk
Porcelain

right: **LIU JIANHUA**
Dream, 2005–2006, 1200 × 900 × 80 cm
(472 × 354 × 31½ in.)
White porcelain, DVD projection

above: **KEITH HARRISON**
M25 London Orbital, 2006,
1000 × 1100 × 5 cm (393 × 432 × 2 in.)
Promasil and Duratec technical ceramics, cobalt
oxide, glaze, frit, electric cabling. The track is
a 1:5000 scaled version of the M25 motorway
and negotiates the inside and outside of the Victoria
and Albert Museum, London, Sculpture Court

left: **KEITH HARRISON**
Grand (Final 3), 2008, 214 × 160 × 56 cm
(84 × 63 × 22 in.)
Egyptian paste, brick clay, heating elements, electric
cabling, fireproof board, steel bench, steel tray

above: **ANDREW LIVINGSTONE**
The English Scene, 2008, approx.
h 24 × w 20 × l 200 cm (9½ × 8 × 79 in.)
Slip-cast figures, fired and unfired,
glass, castors, ready-made plate

right: **ANDREW LIVINGSTONE**
Tacit, still shot of live relayed CCTV image
to monitor, 2006, variable size
CCTV, monitor, clay

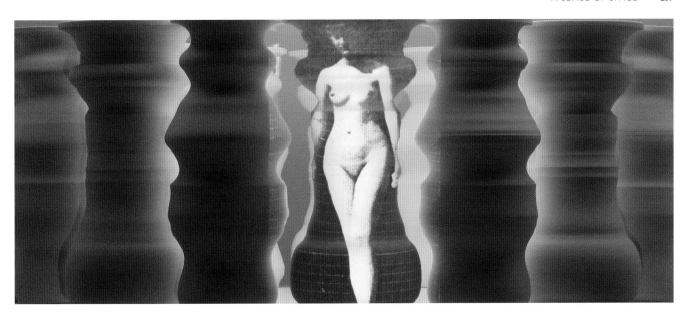

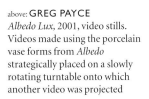

above: **GREG PAYCE**
Albedo Lux, 2001, video stills.
Videos made using the porcelain
vase forms from *Albedo*
strategically placed on a slowly
rotating turntable onto which
another video was projected

right: **GREG PAYCE**
Al Barelli, 2001, h 213 cm (84 in.)
Earthenware, terra sigillata

above, left: **BONNIE KEMSKE**
Cast Hug, 2008, l 56 cm (22 in.)
Ceramic, press-moulded

above, right: **VICTORIA EDEN**
February 5th 2004, 2007
Ceramic, screenprint;
photographed on Morecambe Bay

above: **NINA HOLE**
Two Towers, Two Taarns, 2006, 350 × 165 × 165 cm
(138 × 65 × 65 in.)
Ceramic, terra sigillata, mixed media, wood-fired,
Appalachian State University, North Carolina

right: **NINA HOLE**
Two Towers, Two Taarns, 2006, at night

CHAPTER FIVE

THE LINE OF BEAUTY

Studio, Design, Industry

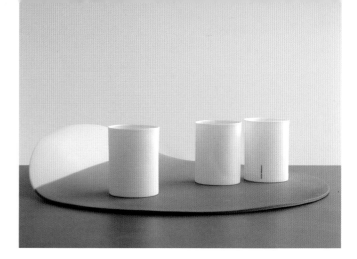

preceding pages: **YONG PHILL LEE**
Tableware, 2007
Porcelain

right: **PIET STOCKMANS**
Veni, Tableware, Royal Boch, 1998
Ceramic, pigment, blue spot design

below: **HELLA JONGERIUS**
Bowl with Bird, Animal Bowls, 2004, dia 21 cm (8¼ in.)
Porcelain, hand crafted, hand-painted

Twenty or even ten years ago significant creative partnerships between the ceramic industry and individual makers were very few. Ceramists – those who actually work with clay as opposed to designers working for ceramic manufacturers – and industry have tended to view each other with suspicion. This has been altered by two major factors – changes within the market and the advent of new technologies, particularly with regard to design. The development of highly sophisticated computer design programs has enabled shapes to be constructed in virtual reality on screen to give a clear indication of the three-dimensional form while rapid prototyping systems allow these forms to be turned into models. Such processes enable techniques such as piercing as well as fine detail to be incorporated into the form.[1]

Such far-reaching change has prompted major manufacturers such as Wedgwood, Royal Copenhagen, Delft, Lenox Porcelain, Royal Boch, Nymphenburg, Royal Tichelaar Makkum and Thomas Porcelain to look at different kinds of production, for example, more innovative design, with shorter runs aimed at a more specialist market. In comparison with traditional production cycles, manufacturers no longer commit to maintaining patterns in stock indefinitely, but want new ranges, sometimes annually, to stimulate the market continually. Part of this opening up has involved looking for different kinds of designers with manufacturers approaching individual makers for design concepts. This has resulted in the creation of shapes and decoration that have a lively modern feel, an imaginative hybrid of shape, colour and decoration.

For Carol McNicholl using an industrial technique such as slip-casting was a way of reproducing modelled or found objects and re-assembling them into bizarre, even surreal compositions. Slip-casting offers a useful means of playing about with familiar objects whether pistols, children's toys or popular ornaments in the form of animals such as dogs, horses or cats and reassembling them in different ways.

Collaborations with industry can broadly be categorized as follows: conceptual – in which ceramists respond to, make use of, or adapt the products of industry – and design, where potters design wares for industrial production. One of the joys for artist/makers designing for industry is that the production details of setting up, casting, jiggering or pressing, decoration and firing are resolved by workers in the factory who have the knowledge and expertise to do this. The downside of the arrangement is that the demands of production often involve compromises, which means the finished work may not fully match the original idea. In some factories the need for speedy introduction of new styles is so pressing that the move from design to manufacture precludes making ceramic prototypes.

RETHINKING DESIGN

One of the most revolutionary approaches to everyday ceramics that evolved in the 1990s is that of Droog Design, a company based in the Netherlands. Initially led by Gijs Bakker and Renny Ramakers, the group of radical designers, while distancing themselves from the

YONG PHILL LEE
Parting Vases, 2007, h 15 cm (6 in.)
Porcelain

conventional craft identity, were inspired by newly available materials as well as by found objects. Experiments were made with industrial manufacturing techniques that could be manipulated to recall those made by hand without attempting to create a handmade look. Hella Jongerius, for instance, designed a set of porcelain bowls that were fired differentially to obtain unique asymmetrical shapes while Dick van Hoff designed plates extruded from a randomly blended two-tone porcelain. Bakker also devised designs for the high-profile Duch firm Cor Unum in 's-Hertogenbosch. To be economically viable, both Bakker and Ramakers had to face the difficulty of setting up wider distribution and a cheaper range without becoming over populist and loosing their radical edge.[2]

While Droog Design succeeded by acting as its own independent company, many ceramic factories saw the potential for incorporating such work within their own production. One of the leading designers within this field is Hella Jongerius. Bringing together the handmade and the industrial, Jongerius has designed individual pieces that might, for example, incorporate wool or thread as well as ranges of work for large-scale production. In so doing she has looked carefully at various aspects of the attractions of traditional work, seeing this as a major selling point, but bringing it up to date. For the Delft factory in the Netherlands, Jongerius has drawn on conventional forms to revitalize a range that places elements of tradition within a modern framework.

The factory has long been respected for its traditional wares with blue and white decoration, but they now appear staid and of little interest to a younger generation. Jongerius took the strongest shapes – rimmed plates and full rounded jugs and vases – and decorated them by leaving part of the red earthenware body bare to contrast with the pure white glaze and leafy decoration in Prussian blue. The range proved a popular success. Jongerius has produced designs for factories that include Royal Tichelaar Makkum and Nymphenburg. Other artists designing for factory production include Piet Stockmans and Olav Slingerland.

One enterprising initiative by the Royal Tichelaar Makkum factory was to commission four artists to respond to the classic traditional pyramid vase used to display tulips. Known for its great attention to detail and its ability to reproduce classic forms with expert skill, the Makkum factory also produced a pyramid with blue and white decoration, but the invited artists responded very differently, uncowed by the tradition they were invited to contemplate. Jurgen Bey, known for designing furniture as well as ceramics, combined both concerns by placing ceramics in a cabinet for one piece. Jongerius transposed the pyramid into a giant jug, while others used the principle of stacking objects on top of each other to create unlikely but fascinating juxtapositions.[3]

The opportunity to create minimalist forms that rely on the simplicity of material and a sense of sculptural form are evident in the work of Lola Dimova, Kenji Uranishi and Yong Phill Lee. Although all produce highly distinctive, individual pieces, they share a concern with function and ergonomic design while allowing the method of manufacture and the material to have a part in the final product.

Given the traditionally uneasy relationship between the maker – who is primarily concerned with both artistic expression and financial viability – and industry, which must be economically profitable, the initiative for a more imaginative approach has come primarily from industry as it looks for different ideas to nourish a market or

right: **PEKKA PAIKKARI**
Tea Set, 2000
Stoneware

below: **BRIAN ADAMS**
Oak and Ceramic Vase, 2007,
h 30 × w 9.6 × d 5.6 cm
(12 × 3¾ × 2¼ in.)
Slip-cast earthenware and
CNC routed European Oak

even identify new ones, commissioning a maker/designer to produce a range. Sue Pryke designed pots for IKEA, one of the largest and most prestigious companies in terms of supplying modern design for the home. Brightly coloured and neatly designed, the pots are sold at modest prices in stores around the world.

At Royal Copenhagen Ole Jensen helped reinvent the traditional quasi Delftware image with a more streamlined Scandinavian approach. One of his pieces includes a bowl that has been intercut with a strainer, so embracing both the ability to prepare and serve food. For the Finnish manufacturer Arabia, Pekka Paikkari has designed a variety of imaginative wares, from highly decorated teasets, colour-

ful salt and pepper pots, to minimalist fruit bowls, flower containers and cake plates that take on sculptural qualities.

The flourishing economy of China, a country with a low-cost labour force, an enormous reservoir of skilled workers and an expanding middle class, has stimulated several factories to seek new ranges to identify niche markets. Plain white porcelain wares, popular in the West for their minimalist, clean lines, are generally regarded by the Chinese as too ordinary – too much like conventional hotel ware in China – and hence a new interest has developed in the fragility and milky whiteness of bone china, a material little used hitherto in the country.

The Australian studio potter Janet deBoos was invited to design a teaset for industrial production, but she did not use the convention-al method of planning it on a drawing board, but by throwing the forms in her usual way. These were then reproduced in the factory in almost exactly the same style in a strange if unnerving similitude. The first of these was with a Milan-based company, Paola C Ceramics. The second was at the invitation of Huaguang Company's Bone China division in China. Here she worked closely with both the mould makers and the factory workers as the pieces were produced, fascinated by the changes as the original forms were made in porce-lain. The results are eerie, uncanny products, but ones that merge studio and industry in a novel way, though the work can be seen to raise thorny ethical issues concerning the relationship between designing, making and reproduction.

Similar projects in the UK have involved studio potters Chris Keenan and Carina Ciscato, two highly regarded potters well known for their precisely made and poised tablewares. In comparison to the low cost of industrially produced wares, studio pottery is relatively expensive in terms of purchase price, and may seem to be beyond the pocket of many. To bridge this gap and to produce a studio range at modest prices, the UK-based retailer Habitat commissioned Keenan to make a range of tableware – bowls, cups and saucers, mugs and plates – that would be faithfully reproduced in a factory. Again, rather than designing on the drawing board, they wanted Keenan to make the finished prototypes from which Habitat would produce virtually identical lookalikes in Japan. The shape and glaze of the resulting ware almost matched Keenan's originals exactly. The range, marketed under the name *Sora*, was sold in Habitat stores at

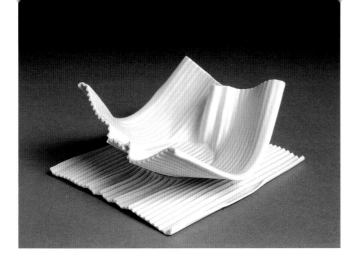

left: **NICOLE LISTER**
A Little Wrap, 2003, 9 × 17 × 19 cm (3½ × 6½ × 7½ in.)
Limoges porcelain, cast using corrugated cardboard
moulds; a small percentage of paper pulp was added
to Limoges porcelain casting slip that was painted
into the constructed mould and slowly built up to
the required thickness, the cardboard mould burnt
out in the bisque firing, cone 8 oxidation

below: **BODO SPERLEIN**
Arcadia Collection, 2007, dia 28 cm (11 in.), small,
dia 22 cm (8½ in.), X-small, dia 15 cm (6 in.)
Fine bone china plates, décor inspired by the
delicate dew on spiders' webs

a fraction of the cost of his handmade wares. Any slight irregularities that are an attractive and desired feature of handmade ware were evened out, the pots, though looking almost identical in style to his standard wares, have an eerie relationship to the handmade originals.

An imaginative commission by the recently opened MIMA (Middlesbrough Institute of Modern Art) in the UK has explored the possibilities of a different kind of collaboration between maker and industry. MIMA commissioned Takeshi Yasuda, a potter well known for his handmade tablewares, to design and produce a range of pots that could be used in the café and sold in their gallery shop.[4] Yasuda, who spends much of the year directing the Pottery Workshop Experimental Factory in Jingdezhen – the 'porcelain capital' of China – realized that to achieve the quantities he was looking for hand-throwing was unworkable and so learnt the techniques of mould making as a way of producing the ware. For the range Yasuda has made inventive use of the classic combination of the white porcelain body and pale blue celadon glaze to produce a handsome range of functional ware that brings together the sensibilities of the potter with industrial production techniques. These are now produced industrially in China partly by hand, partly with the use of the machine.

The studio potter Janice Tchalenko has regularly worked with industry, attracted by the challenge of designing work from the studio potter's perspective that can be faithfully adapted by others, whether in a workshop or factory for quantity production. She has designed for, among others, Dartington Pottery and with the small but enterprising Poole Pottery. Potters turned designers can often bring to the product a sensibility that has some of the qualities of the handmade object. The bone china tableware designed and produced by Bodo

Sperlein is factory-made, but the clean, sensual forms and white glaze give them a crisp modern feel that retains some handmade qualities. Eduard Hermans also looks to small-scale or batch production, which he carries out himself, often making use of industrial methods like jigger and jolly, extrusion or slip-casting as a means of producing sculptural tableware that has social and political references. To a series of pure white plates, Hermans adds a bright red sickle form that signifies both harvest and the idealism of collectivity.

Tavs Jørgensen, who studied and works as a studio potter, designs ranges for, among others, the prestigious firm of Lenox Porcelain. Jørgensen is also at the forefront of exploring the possibilities of new technology, designing forms on computer using CAD (computer-aided design) and producing the model through the use of rapid prototyping to make shapes that would be difficult to create by other means. Brian Adams produces small runs of functional ware also using CAD and rapid prototyping. His ripple plate is an ingenious example of what can be achieved, while Justin Marshall and Nicole Lister make ingenious use of the possibilities of new technologies. Morgen Hall also employs industrial processes and techniques of laser cutting to produce tableware.

The advent of new technologies not only question the gestation of shape and decoration, but also the definition of ceramic itself. A newly invented alumino-silicate material, almost identical in composition to clay, but

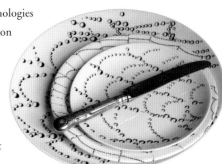

right: **PETER TING**
Vases, 2007
Ceramic

below: **ROBERT DAWSON**
Willow Pattern with Uncertainty, 2003,
dia 27 cm (10½ in.)
Print on bone china; limited edition of 100

which does not need to be fired in order to form a hard body is, to all intents and purposes, ceramic. The body has been used by Michael Eden to produce a range of decorative pieces. Working with a sophisticated computer design program he has designed forms based on a classical Wedgwood urn in black jasper. Once the design has been agreed, the model was made by rapid prototyping, a process that allows for piercing and fine detailing, and subsequently made in the new ceramic material. The result opens up new possibilities for ceramics that look to the future as well as to the past.

Working on a small scale using semi-industrial processes offers new opportunities in the interface between making and design. Using a knowledge of ceramic materials and processes, maker/designer/ producers such as Satyendra Pakhalé and Katy West have evolved a range of odd and unusual but intriguing objects that are part decorative, part functional and part a wry take on the objects of everyday. West's ceramic shelves, although functional, take on a life of their own, as do mugs in what she calls her 'Souvenir Range'. These include a plain white china cup, functional and modern in appearance, which is discreetly engraved with an ornamental Georgian handle, quite different in its references to the actual handle. Producing individual pieces rather than sets, maker/designers such as West evolve proto-types that lend themselves to small-scale production in a small factory.

Like artists working on other areas, ceramists are concerned with environmental issues and explore ways of using ceramics for their low-tech possibilities. The range of objects designed by Martín Azúa make use of aspects of low-fired ceramic, using the fact that they are slightly absorbent to cool liquid, whether on drinking vessels or when potting plants. He is also aware of the muti-functional aspects of shapes that can double up as bowls and pourers. For one range, he buried the forms on river beds which, over a short time, picked up colouring from the water, resulting in individual – and free – surface treatments on decorative rather than useful forms.

Collaboration between factories and studio potters takes a variety of forms, some involving the potter in a more hands on way, while others are more distant. For Prue Venables, the commission to design a teaset for a factory in Japan not only involved creating the shapes, but also meant seeing its resolution through the early stages of production. In tune with concerns about the mountains of ceramic waste being produced, the factory devised a porcelain body that incorporated a sizable proportion of recycled fired porcelain that had been ground and added to the plastic body. The successful collaboration between potter/designer and factory has been put into practice at Royal Crown Derby in the UK. Royal Crown Derby is well known for its fine bone china wares and the use of ornate patterns produced in dark, rich colours often enhanced by gold lustre. Calling on this traditional ware, Peter Ting has designed a range of wares that make use of the decorative style but he has simplified it to give it a modern feel.

For some potters, the fascination with factory production extends not only to the output of identical wares, but also to the idea of mass production in general. The American-based ceramist Marek Cecula

right: **MAREK CECULA**
Liquid Forms, Tall and Long, 2003,
10 × 13 × 5 cm (4 × 5 × 2 in.),
6.4 × 20 × 5 cm (2½ × 8 × 2 in.)
Porcelain

below: **ANGELA VERDON**
Untitled, 2006, h 25 × 135 cm
(10 × 13¾ in.)
Burnished bone china

became involved with a ceramics factory in his native Poland, both as a source of producing a range of smooth, streamlined bowls and jugs that are in keeping with modern life and as a site of industrial production. The factory-produced wares make sensitive use of the fine white body and the shapes are attractive and appealingly functional in feel. Attracted by the idea of quantity production, but well aware of the social and economic structures this represents, working with redundant tableware moulds, Cecula cast up the traditional shapes and then distorted them in alarming ways. He shows this work in a series under the name of *Mutants*.

The almost brutalist 'component' forms designed by Ineke Hans that make use of an over-arching mechanical, machine-like quality are perfectly if quirkily functional. The effect of the metal-like appearance of her coffee set, with its flat plates and cup handles that resemble pipes, is enhanced by the dark, silky matt surface. The theme is also extended to a tulip vase and a five-branched candle holder. Although a similar style is used in other forms cast in porcelain, the effect is softer and more seductive. A cake stand constructed in the form of a mountain has a monumentality that makes the confections even more special.

VERNACULAR VOCABULARIES

For artist/makers curious about the resonance of the ceramic tradition itself, the challenge is to engage with industrial production as an integral part of the concept of the work – with what Justin Novak[5] calls the vernacular visual vocabulary, be it social, cultural or poetic. As part of her installation work, Clare Twomey has successfully collaborated

with both Wedgwood and Royal Crown Derby (discussed in Chapter 4). Wedgwood supplied quantities of their iconic blue jasper clay for *Trophy* (2006). The Wedgwood body, devised by Josiah Wedgwood over 225 years go, is instantly associated with status and quality. For Twomey's installation *Consciousness/Conscience* (2003), the Royal Crown Derby factory, which, as discussed earlier, specializes in bone china wares, produced hundreds of low-fired tiled pieces that were literally crushed underfoot by visitors, a disturbingly satisfying experience in which destruction and enjoyment are uneasy bedfellows.

Although a relatively small factory by international standards, Royal Crown Derby has established a reputation for collaborating effectively with artists. Angela Verdon was commissioned to produce a special window in bone china and has subsequently spent time in the factory working with their renowned bone china body. As a result, given the technical problems of working with the body, she produced astonishingly large, abstract sculptural pieces. When fired these are polished to produce a satin-like finish of great delicacy that, pleasingly, gives the pieces a bone-like quality. Ken Eastman, well known for his vessel-based slab-built forms, has also worked productively at Royal Crown Derby. Adapting his tall vessel forms to bone china production, he has created forms that take on a softer, more organic quality, an

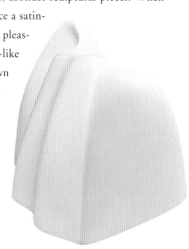

right: **ROB KESSELER**
Bouquet, 2006, 120 × 30 × 100 cm (47 × 11¾ × 39 in.)
Bone china with enamel and gold print, metal
shelving (with support from Royal Crown Derby)

below: **ROB KESSELER**
Blue Willow, 2003, each dia 27 cm (10½ in.)
Bone china with enamel print of microscopic
wood section

impression heightened by the use of carefully chosen floral decoration, a great contrast to Eastman's handbuilt pieces with their toned and textured surfaces.

Residencies at ceramic factories can be productive for both maker and producer. The American maker Justin Novak spent three months at a porcelain tableware factory in Walbrzych, Poland and at the Kohler Company factory in Wisconsin. The Kohler factory is well known as a major producer of commercial bathroom furniture and Novak saw part of this output as a suitable basis for his piece *Confessional Sink* (2004). For this he adorned an existing hand basin and supporting ceramic pedestal with two latticed ceramic panels fitted either side of the basin. These were pierced with the quatrefoil pattern of the confessional screen. The screen is also reminiscent of those used to separate the private quarters reserved for wives and concubines in the harem. The sink was thus transformed into sites of atonement for religious, private and physical cleansing.

Inspired by his time spent in tableware factories and the possibilities it allowed, Novak initiated an experiment in product design and manufacture at the University of Oregon. Taking, as his model, Andy Warhol's engagement with mass-produced imagery in his notorious New York 'Factory' in the 1960s Novak also named his project Factory as it was intended to deal with mass-produced objects. Following Warhol's example, the students became involved in 'commodity production' and were encouraged to appropriate and re-contextualize everyday items and adopt these as the basis for quantity production. One series, the *Sala* collection (2006) by Fern Wiley, was derived from a store display for stockings, an idealized and streamlined leg was dissected to form a series of multi-functional vessels. Another project, *Soup* (2006), was as much about social concerns as aesthetic or economic involvement. For this project 100 bowls, based on the shape of a plastic disposable dish, were reproduced in clay. The finished bowls were filled with soup and sold for a donation, the resulting income was used to help feed the hungry locally.

On a more modest scale, the Berlin Hering factory commissioned UK-based artist Pamela Leung to design a series of mythological figures that were produced in white porcelain. Well known for her fantastic, brightly coloured, near-life-sized figures that combine aspects of Chinese mythical figures, the simpler, smaller, pure white figures, produced in the factory, are quietly effective in evoking the essence of these mysterious creatures.

One of the attractions of working with world-renowned manufacturers such as Wedgwood is their

technical knowledge and expertise. At Wedgwood this has resulted in successful collaborations with artist/designers such as Robert Dawson and Rob Kesseler, both of whom have produced a series of plates with fine decoration. These make use of existing, finely made forms as a basis for applied decoration. For Dawson, who distorts and refocuses surface decoration, it is what he calls the 'gentle violation of expectation' that interests him as he twists and reformulates familiar designs such as the ubiquitous Willow pattern. In another work, a wall of tiles, the patterning gradually moves out of focus, causing the viewer to blink twice, questioning their own sight. By contrast, Kesseler calls on the technical expertise of the factory to produce exquisite reproductions of minute pollen grains enlarged millions of times. Working with scientists at Kew Gardens, Surrey, Kesseler investigated rare and unusual pollens, enlarging them and adding his own, often surreal colouring. Taking the classic Flora Danica dinner service produced by Royal Copenhagen as his model, Kesseler reproduced the fantastic forms, part nature, part invention, on fine bone china plates as a statement about life forces that lie outside our reach.

Thoughtful designs used on wall surfaces can enliven and enrich public spaces. Lubna Chowdhary uses rich, saturated colour printed on standard tiles to evoke a feeling of movement in her tile installations. For Masamichi Yoshikawa the openness of public areas are an opportunity to combine both wall treatments and large rounded vessels that speak to each other without in any sense being obviously related.

At the long-established Spode factory, a company with a reputation for its finely decorated wares, the artist Charlotte Hodes has worked productively, looking at the archive of decoration and patterns to interpret these on existing forms, offering an alternative take on the traditional image of the factory through the use of different kinds of surface decoration. Produced in limited quantities, such objects are marketed through conventional outlets and are intended for the home rather than the museum, as a way of reaching a wider and larger audience.

1 For an intelligent discussion of this subject see Tanya Harrod, 'Otherwise Unobtainable: The Applied Arts and the Politics and Poetics of Digital Technology', in Sandra Alfoldy (ed.), *NeoCraft: Modernity and the Crafts*, The Nova Scotia College of Art and Design Press, Halifax, 2007.
2 For a fuller account see Glenn Adamson, *Thinking Through Craft*, Berg, Oxford and New York, 2007, pp. 33–36.
3 The pieces were exhibited in 2008, the other artists were Alexander van Slobbe and Studio Job.
4 Early prototypes, made at Jing te Chen in China, were on show in the Crafts Council's exhibition *Table Manners: International Contemporary Ceramics*, 2005.
5 Justin Novak, 'Cultural Labor: Notes on the Teaching of Labor and the Labor of Teaching', in *Explorations and Navigations: The Resonance of Place*, NCECA 40th Annual Conference Report, 2006.

above: **HELLA JONGERIUS**
Non-Temporary, 2005, tableware for Makkum, dia 45 cm (17½ in.) max.
Ceramic

above, right: **HELLA JONGERIUS**
Nymphenburg Sketches, Plate with Flower Décor, 2004–2006, dia 30 cm
(11¾ in.)
Porcelain, hand-painted

right: **SUE PRYKE**
Tableware for IKEA, 2000
Earthenware

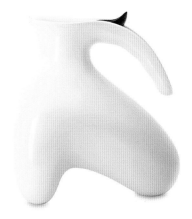

top: JANET DEBOOS
Tea Set, 2004, h 16.5 cm (6½ in.) max.
Bone china, slip-cast; Huaguang Zibo production ware

above: PEKKA PAIKKARI
Salt and Pepper, 2000
Stoneware

right: OLE JENSEN
Teapot, 1998–2008
Porcelain; Royal Copenhagen Factory

above: **CHRIS KEENAN**
Sora Tableware, 2006
Porcelain, sizes variable; Habitat

right: **TAKESHI YASUDA**
Tableware, 2006–2008, dia 29 cm (11 in.)
Porcelain
Collection designed for MIMA
(Middlesbrough Institute of Modern Art)

far right: **BODO SPERLEIN**
Equus, 2008, Bodo Sperlein for Lladró,
pedestal bowl, 10 × 20 cm (4 × 8 in.);
bowl, 6 × 20 cm (2 × 8 in.); coffee cup
with saucer, 18 × 12 cm (7 × 4¾ in.);
teapot, 16 × 21 cm (6 × 8 in.); butter dish,
12 × 20 cm (4¾ × 8 in.)
Handmade porcelain, hand-painted, inspired
by the grace and beauty of the horse

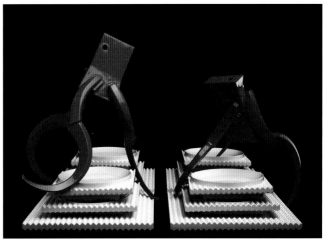

above: **TAVS JØRGENSEN**
Metia™, Stacking Coffeepot, Sugar and Creamer, 2007
Porcelain; Dansk®, Lenox Group Inc.

top right: **EDUARD HERMANS**
Whipped Cream, 2004, h 25 cm (10 in.)
Stoneware

bottom right: **TAVS JØRGENSEN**
U-Cup, 2003, h 11 × dia 19 cm (4¼ × 7½ in.)
Bone china, slip-cast

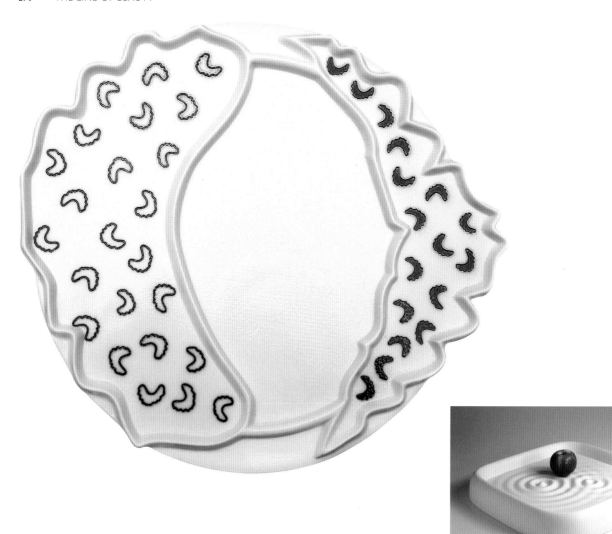

above: **MORGEN HALL**
Celery Plate, 2006, dia 27cm (10½ in.)
Soda-fired porcelain

right, top: **BRIAN ADAMS**
Ripple Dish, 2004, 36 × 36 × 8 cm (14 × 14 × 3 in.)
Slip-cast earthenware

right, bottom: **PRUE VENABLES**
Tea Set, 2006
Porcelain, completed factory production

above, left: **PETER TING**
Table Plates, 2007
Royal Crown Derby bone china plates, transfer design derived
from traditional Imari pattern

above, right: **KATY WEST**
Shelf Bracket Pendant Light, 360, 2006, 34 × 34 × 20 cm
(13¼ × 13¼ × 8 in.)
Hollow-cast vitrified china

Shelf Bracket Shelf, 1000, 2006, 100 × 20 × 17 cm (39 × 8 × 6½ in.)
Hollow-cast vitrified china

opposite, top left:
ANGELA VERDON
Untitled, 2006, h 25 × l 35 cm
(10 × 13¾ in.)
Burnished bone china

opposite, bottom left:
MAREK CECULA
Creamer and Sugar, 2003,
h 15 cm (6 in.) max.
High-fired porcelain

above: **INEKE HANS**
Black Gold Modular Porcelain, 2002,
h 20 × dia 18.5 cm (8 × 7¼ in.),
h 20 × dia 40 cm (8 × 15¾ in.)
Black porcelain; produced by INEKE
HANS/ARNHEM at EKWC (European
Ceramics Workcentre)

right: **INEKE HANS**
*Sugar Candy Mountain, Revolving
Bonbonnière,* 2007
Ceramic, three sizes, S, M, L, colours
black, white glazing; commission,
production, distribution by Cor Unum

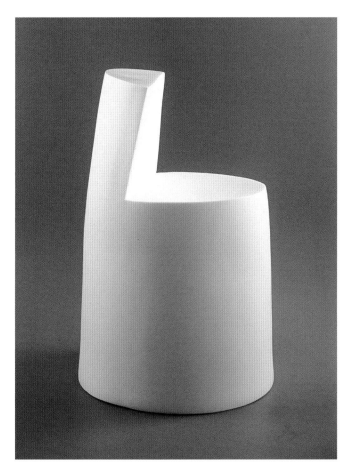

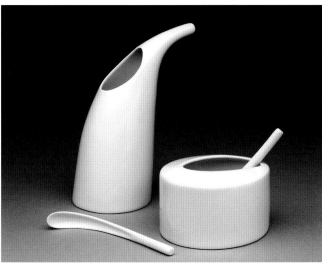

top: **KEN EASTMAN**
Derby Variations, 2007, h 30 × 23 × 23 cm
(11¾ × 9 × 9 in.)
Bone china

above: **KEN EASTMAN**
Derby Variations, 200, h 24 × 23 × 23 cm
(9½ × 9 × 9 in.)
Bone china

above: **PAMELA LEUNG**
Patron, 2005, h 23 cm (9 in.)
Porcelain, cast; limited edition,
Hering, Berlin

right and far right: **JUSTIN NOVAK**
Confessional Sink, 2004
Slip-cast vitreous china; Kohler Factory
through the Arts/Industry Program
at John Michael Kohler Art Center
in Sheboygan, Wisconsin

ROB KESSELER
Harvest (detail), 2001, remade 2007,
plate, dia 27 cm (10½ in.)
Bone china with enamel and gold print,
dried wheat

ROBERT DAWSON
Don't You Know it's Gonna Be All Right, 2004,
1.2 × 4.8 m (4 × 15¾ ft)
Print on ceramic wall tiles; commission for
Voewood, near Holt, Norfolk

ROBERT DAWSON
Roseo, 2003, each, dia 27 cm (10½ in.)
Print on bone china dinner plates;
limited edition of 100

right: **CHARLOTTE HODES**
Fish Dish, 2004, 45 × 24 cm (17½ × 9½ in.)
Bone china, underglaze copper engraved
tissue transfer from the Spode archive on
to Spode bone china

above: **CHARLOTTE HODES**
Left to right, *Green Pools*, 2006,
50 × 25 cm (20 × 10 in.)
Earthenware, coloured slips, digital and hand-
drawn transfers, sprigs

Floating, 2006, 41 × 35 cm (16 × 13¾ in.)
Earthenware, coloured slips, digital and hand-
drawn transfers, sprigs

Vase for Mademoiselle Camargo, 2006,
40 × 28 cm (15¾ × 11 in.)
Earthenware, coloured slips, digital and hand-
drawn transfers, sprigs

above: **CHARLOTTE HODES**
*Coffee Pot, Sugar Bowl and Coffee Cup from Dinner
Set*, 2001, h 23 cm (9 in.) max.
Spode white china, copper engraved tissue transfer
from Spode archive and platinum

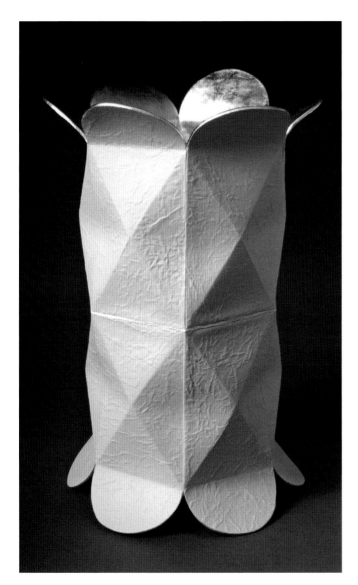

above, left: **NICOLE LISTER**
Mad Queen Monteith, 2007, 45 × 30 cm (17¾ × 11¾ in.)
Porcelain and silver leaf, slip-cast Limoges porcelain,1220˚C, cone 8
oxidation, interiors gilded with imitation silver leaf and painted with
transparent shellac varnish, epoxy adhesive and acrylic paint used for
joining components

above, right: **NICOLE LISTER**
Construct No. 2, 2004, set of 3 containers, 19 × 13.5 cm each (7½ × 5¼ in.)
Limoges porcelain, slip-cast and assembled Limoges porcelain, black
engobe inlay, clear glaze, cone 8 oxidation, yellow on-glaze decals

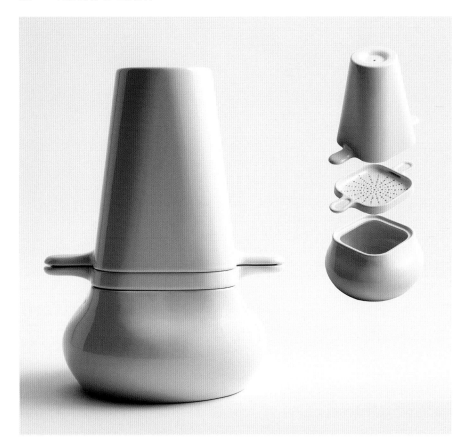

above, left: **SATYENDRA PAKHALE**
Good Food Project, 2006, h 35 × w 27 × d 24 cm
(13¾ × 10½ × 9½ in.)
Ceramic; Bosa Ceramiche, Italy

above, right: **SATYENDRA PAKHALE**
Roll Carbon Ceramic Chair, 2006,
h 79 × w 55 × l 75.5 cm (31 × 21½ × 29¾ in.)
Ceramic; Designer's Gallery, Cologne, Germany

above: **MASAMICHI YOSHIKAWA**
The Water of Life, Nagisa, 2005, 3.1 × 27 m
(10 × 88½ ft)
Porcelain, Cyubu New International Airport

right: **LUBNA CHOWDHARY**
Lantern Tower, 2007
Ceramic; commissioned by Tesco and
Slough Borough Council

far right: **LUBNA CHOWDHARY**
Script, 2006, 100 × 150 cm (39 × 59 in.)
Ceramic; commissioned by Sony for the
Beautiful Script exhibition, the Dray Walk
Gallery, London

above: **KENJI URANISHI**
Tea Set, 2007, h 10 cm (4 in.)
Porcelain, slab-built, inlay fine lines

below: **OLAV SLINGERLAND**
Slow Motion, 2006
Slip-cast

above: **LOLA DIMOVA**
Ki, Sushi, Oriental Food Dinner Set, 2005,
big plate, 35 × 35 × 2.8 cm (13¾ × 13¾ × 1 in.),
plate, 22 × 22 × 2.8 cm (8½ × 8½ × 1 in.),
rectangular plate, 30 × 14 × 2 cm (11¾ × 5½ × ¾ in.),
small plate, 14.5 × 14.5 × 2 cm (5½ × 5½ × ¾ in.),
soy dish, 9 × 9 × 4 cm (3½ × 3½ × 1½ in.),
bowl, 12 × 12 × 7 cm (4¾ × 4¾ × 2¾ in.),
bowl lid, 12 × 12 × 2.5 cm (4¾ × 4¾ × 1 in.),
soy bottle, 6 × 6 × 16.5 cm (2¼ × 2¼ × 6½ in.)
Porcelain

top: **YONG PHILL LEE**
Teapot, Two Mugs, 2006
Porcelain

above, left: **MARTIN AZUA**
Jar, 1999, 1.5 litres, 10 × 15 × 32 cm (4 × 6 × 12½ in.)
Earthenware

above, right: **MARTIN AZUA**
Natural Stain, 2000, 18 × 12 × 30 cm (7 × 4¾ × 11¾ in.),
20 × 8 × 5 cm (8 × 3 × 2 in.)
Ceramic

BIOGRAPHIES

Barbro Åberg, b 1958, Umeå, Sweden; lives in Denmark; Education: Clackamas Community College, Oregon; The School of Arts and Crafts, Kolding, Denmark.
'Most of my pieces are monochrome with a focus on form and surface texture. I experiment with "constructions", and I am fascinated by the contrast that occurs when the weight of the clay meets the lightness of the perforated structures.'

Brian Adams, b 1963, UK; lives in England; Education: Ulster Polytechnic, Northern Ireland; De Montfort University (formerly Leicester Polytechnic), Leicester; Royal College of Art, London.
'I design and produce decorative and functional ceramic objects. Complex yet simple, sculptural yet functional. All objects have their roots in function and have been developed using a combination of the latest computer aided design.'
www.brianadamsceramics.co.uk

Thomas Aitken, b 1967, Prince Edward Island, Canada; lives in Warsaw, Ontario, Canada; Education: Red Deer College, Alberta, Nova Scotia; School of Art and Design, University of Wales Institute, Cardiff.
'My work celebrates the functional object, its history and associations. Each piece of my hand-produced porcelain is intended to delight the eye, to please the touch and to satisfy the owner through time.'

Ivan Albreht, b 1970, Belgrade, former Yugoslavia; lives in Miami, Florida; Education: Academy of Applied Arts in Belgrade, Southern Illinois University, Carbondale.
'In 2000 I moved to the United States of America where I continued to study art. My current work explores issues regarding the human condition by raising questions about individual identity, as well as society at large in a socio-political context.'
www.albreht.com

Tor Alex Erichsen, b 1955, Norway; lives in Norway.

Jennifer Allora and Guillermo Calzadilla, Allora, b 1974, Philadelphia; Calzadilla, b 1971, Havana, Cuba; lives in Puerto Rico; Education: Allora, Massachusetts Institute of Technology, Cambridge, Massachusetts; Whitney Museum Independent Study Program, New York; University of Richmond, Richmond, Virginia; Calzadilla, Escuela de Artes Plásticas, San Juan, Puerto Rico; Bard College, Annandale-on-Hudson, New York.
Collaborating since 1995, Allora and Calzadilla approach visual art as a set of experiments that test whether ideas such as authorship, nationality, borders and democracy adequately describe today's increasingly global and consumerist society.

Chris Antemann, b 1970, USA; lives in the USA; Education: University of Minnesota, Minneapolis; Indiana University of Pennsylvania.
'The designs and images taken from old collectibles, such as porcelain figurines and fine china, evoke palpable shards of memory serving history as humble paradigms. As archetypes, these objects inspire me with their position in the domestic realm.'

Ardmore Ceramics, Founder Fée Halsted-Berning, b 1958, Bulawayo, Zimbabwe; lives in South Africa; Education: Natal University, Pietermaritzburg.
Ardmore Ceramic Art Studios produce unique functional and sculpted ceramics based on a dynamic fusion of African and Western artistic traditions rooted in the identity of the artists and defined by the use of African animal shapes and forms, legends and myths combined with rich colour and exuberant decoration.
www.ardmoreceramics.co.za

Karen Atherley, b 1961, Manchester; lives in Lincolnshire, UK; Education: Rochdale School of Art; Camberwell College of Arts, London (formerly known as Camberwell School of Arts and Crafts).
'My pots are vividly coloured and decorated with flowing, mainly female, figurative nudes and faces wrapped around a diverse range of vases, bowls, cups/saucers and plates, influenced by Greek antiquity and the colours of the Impressionists.'
www.karenatherleyceramics.com

Felicity Aylieff, b 1954, UK; lives in London and Bath; Education: Bath Academy of Art; Goldsmiths, University of London; Royal College of Art, London.
Aylieff's work crosses the boundaries of ceramics and sculpture. The large clay pieces do not aim to be anything other that what they are: the result of a continuing personal enquiry into material and form that she has pursued since her vessel-making beginnings.

Duncan Ayscough, b 1968, Stockport, UK; lives in Wales; Education: Filton Technical College, Bristol; Manchester Metropolitan University (formerly Manchester Polytechnic); School of Art and Design, University of Wales Institute, Cardiff.
'It is the intrigue of opposites that continually informs my practice, especially those of control and chaos, pushing the material to its physical limits – frequently over them – in order to produce structures that reflect both fragility and strength of form.'
www.ayscoughceramics.co.uk

Martín Azúa, b 1965, Basque Country, Spain; lives in Barcelona, Spain; Education: University of Barcelona.
Questions: A question can be a project and achievement in itself.
Utopias: Thinking in the future overcoming problems that today seem irresolvable.
Emergencies: Those things that matter to which we dedicate our attention, time and effort.
www.martinazua.com

Karin Bablok, b 1964, Donauwörth, Germany; lives in Germany.
'The first attempt to throw a form hardly ever fulfils my aim in respect to smooth curves and settled proportions. The pure whiteness as well as the asymmetry tempts me to balance the form by painting onto the surface.'

Ralph Bacerra, 1938–2008, California; Education: Chouinard Art Institute, Los Angeles.
'My pieces are based on traditional ideas and engage in certain cultural appropriations – in form, in design, in glaze choices. However, my work is not postmodern in the sense that I am not making any statements – there is no meaning or metaphor.'
www.frankllloyd.com

Gordon Baldwin, b 1932, Lincoln, UK; lives in the UK; Education: Lincoln College of Art; Central Saint Martins College of Art and Design, London.
'The role I take is Artist as Explorer with the vessel as my basic structure (like the structure of a Haiku). I suppose the compulsion comes from things heard, things seen, things read, things done by drawing and previous work.'
www.bmgallery.co.uk

Philippe Barde, b 1955; lives in Geneva, Switzerland; Education: Art School, Macon, France, Applied Art School, Geneva, Switzerland.
'Feeling is creation. Feeling is creating without ideas. That is why feeling is understanding, as the universe has no ideas. (Fernando Pessoa) I think that to learn the craft of ceramic is to forget it.'

Barnaby Barford, b 1977, UK; lives in England; Education: University of Plymouth; ISIA Art and Design School, Faenza; Royal College of Art, London.
Barford creates unique narrative pieces working primarily with found objects, which he chops and changes to create sinister and deeply sardonic sculptures.
www.barnabybarford.co.uk

Tanya Batura, b 1974, Hartford, Connecticut; lives in Los Angeles, California; Education: University of California, Los Angeles; University of Washington, Seattle; Manchester Community Technical College, Manchester, Connecticut.
'I use clay to create psychological and dark figures. These figures are derived from abstracted close-ups and headshots of plastic surgery, pornography, burn trauma, facial prosthesis, and dental procedures.'

Svend Bayer, b 1946, Uganda to Danish parents; lives in the UK; Education: Exeter University; apprenticeship with Michael Cardew.
'I invest my soul in making tableware. It is like obsessive behaviour, I'm addicted to it. I'd like to make pots that are so tactile that people would want to take a bite.'

Jenny Beavan, b 1950, UK; lives in Cornwall; Education: Manchester Metropolitan University.
'Water saturates, shifts, seeps, explores, exploits, distracts, destroys, manoeuvers, penetrates, mixes, grades, attacks, finds a way, a path, a passage, dislodges, surrounds, circulates, gravitates, yet can be drawn upwards to form clouds.'

Sofia Beça, b 1972, Oporto; lives in Portugal; Education: The Soares dos Reis School of Decorative Arts.
Beça's themes are nature, the human presence, interpersonal relationships and the dehumanizing globalization.

Susan Beiner, b 1962, USA; lives in Arizona; Education: University of Michigan, Ann Arbor; Rutgers, the State University of New Jersey.
'The most recent concerns in my work deal with making what is organic synthetic. In today's world, almost everything is manufactured of artificial materials. As a viewer we are challenged by our own perceptions of what is authentic and what is not.'
susanbeinerceramics.com

Tony Bennett, b 1949, Evesham, Worcestershire; lives in the UK; Education: Stourbridge College of Art; University of Wolverhampton (formerly Wolverhampton Polytechnic); Royal College of Art, London.
'For me the history and tradition of ceramics offer the most profound understanding. Working with clay is a sensuous experience and I have always wanted to retain a strong tactile quality in my work.'

Karen Bennicke, b 1943, Copenhagen; lives in Bregentved; Education: apprenticeships in different potter's studios, Denmark.
'My works are spatial visions. Constructions – reminiscent of architecture – that constitute a kind of form-bearing membrane between the exterior and the interior. I try to eliminate the distance between the logical/concrete world of form, that we know from everyday life, and the illogical, unknown and absurd.'

Belinda Berger; lives in Westerstede, Germany; Education: Falmouth College of Arts.
The material is tasteful elegance. The unusual handles and feet of the items give this unique collection an extraordinary and humorous character. *Country Life* are creative, funny, slightly whimsical and definitively unusual.
www.belindaberger.de

Rob Bernard, b 1949, Lexington, Kentucky; lives in Timberville, Virginia; Education: University of Kentucky; research student, Kyoto University of Fine Arts in Japan under the late Kazuo Yagi.
In Japan Bernard showed in numerous juried exhibitions and had five solo exhibitions. In 1978 he returned to the United States and was awarded a National Endowments for the Arts Fellowship. He has returned to Japan numerous times for solo exhibitions in Tokyo, Nagoya and Osaka.

Bertozzi & Casoni, Giampaolo Bertozzi, b 1957, Borgo Tossignano, Bologna; Stefano Dal Monte Casoni, b 1961, Lugo di Romagna, Ravenna, 1961; Education: Ceramic Art College, Faenza.
After meeting as art students, Bertozzi & Casoni have worked together in a collaborative partnership, handling different ceramic materials. They 'always start with the idea of decay, because it is a very intense vision of the world...the true essence of things can be found in decay, in everything that has been rejected.'

Robin Best, b 1953, Perth, Australia; lives in Western Australia; Education: South Australian School of Art, University of South Australia.
Best's work is informed by patterns from nature and, more recently, by cultures other than her own including the Pitjantjatjara artists of Ernabella in the far north-west of South Australia and the porcelain artists of Jingdezhen in China.
www.jamfactory.com.au

Jurgen Bey, b 1965, the Netherlands; lives in the Netherlands; Education: Design Academy Eindhoven.
'If you want to circumnavigate the earth, you can go right or left. If the majority of the people go right, I go left. My strength rests in viewing the world from an unorthodox perspective.'

David Binns, b 1959, UK; lives in Wales; Education: Manchester Metropolitan University.
'My work is inspired by a complex mix of emotions and experiences, with pieces inspired by architectural form and mathematical repetition and the rich surfaces found in rock formations and polished beach pebbles.'
www.davidbinnsceramics.com

Stephen Bird, b 1964, Stoke-on-Trent; lives in Sydney, Australia and Dundee; Education: Duncan of Jordanstone College of Art & Design, Dundee; Cyprus College of Art, Lemba, Paphos;. Angus College of Further Education.
An Australian citizen, Bird was brought up in the Potteries district of England. His collaged ceramic platters and figures combine ready-made and modelled elements to create highly complex compositions rich in imagery.

Les Blakebrough, b 1930, UK; lives in Australia; Education: National Art School, Sydney; apprenticeship at Sturt Pottery, Mittagong with Ivan McMeekin.
www.lesblakebrough.com.au

Matthew Blakely, b 1963, UK; lives in the UK; Education: University of Southampton; National Art School, Sydney.
'My work is wheel-thrown: the energy of the process and the qualities of plastic clay showing in the final piece. The soft forms are often distorted to add tension and movement.'
www.matthewblakely.co.uk

Ruth Borgenicht, b 1967, USA; lives in the USA; Education: Rutgers, the State University of New Jersey.
'Like ancient armour, my pieces are made of a fabric of moveable interlocking rings. Using clay to make a protective mesh is contradictory; for how can it defend anything, much less itself?'

Wim Borst, b 1946, Gouda, the Netherlands; lives in Delft, the Netherlands.
Borst's ceramics have their roots in the Dutch geometrical abstract tradition. Within the boundaries of the self-chosen restrictions of the geometric abstraction, he takes liberties with colours, materials and themes.
www.wimborst-ceramics.nl

Lidia Bosevski, b 1959; lives in Croatia; Education: High School of Applied Arts, Zagreb; Technology Faculty Department of Textile and Clothes Design, Zagreb.
Bosevski exhibited drawings and fashion designs at various collective and fashion shows. In 1986, she had her first solo exhibition of drawings.
www.owl97.com

Charles Bound, b 1939, New York City; lives in Wales; Education: Union University, Jackson, Tennessee.
Bound came to ceramics in 1983, setting up a studio while working as a college technician and teaching. In 1994 he was gifted the use of space on a farm where he could build his own wood-fired kiln, which he has been working with since.
www.charlesbound.com/about/index.html

Clive Bowen, b 1943, Wales; lives in the UK; Education: Cardiff College of Art.
'For me the taste, the look and the presentation of food are so important. I really enjoy good food and get great pleasure from making pots with that end in mind.'

Dylan Bowen, b 1967, UK; lives in the UK; Education: Shebbear Pottery, Devon; Camberwell College of Arts, London.
'I make wheel-thrown and hand-built slip-decorated earthenware, fired in an electric kiln. Working with slip is for me all about the moment, everything else is preparation for that.'
www.dylanbowen.co.uk

Stephen Bowers, b 1954, Australia; lives in Australia; Education: Alexander Mackie College of Advanced Education, Sydney.
Bowers brings many of the traditions from the history of ceramics. Traces of many familiar styles and decorations, witty collages that betray thoughtful research and intelligent observation may be found in any one piece.
www.jamfactory.com.au

Alison Britton, b 1948, London; lives in London; Education: Central Saint Martins College of Art and Design, London; Royal College of Art, London.
'The pot is an ordinary object, a vehicle for making images of disparity and connection, sculpture and painting, or *form and fiction*. This jolting pair of words suits my work, where I look for a clearer sense of ambiguity.'
www.bmgallery.co.uk

Alexander Brodsky, b 1955, Moscow, Russia; lives in Moscow; Education: The Moscow Institute of Architecture.
Almost everything that Brodsky does is a memorial or a monument to people, things, events, and cities. The strange iconography of the heads, pocked and etched with age, alludes to a collective subconscious memory of unrecorded civilizations.

Christie Brown, b 1946, UK; lives in London; Education: Camberwell College of Arts, London.
'My figurative sculpture is largely inspired by ancient artefacts and archaic figures, and a response to their incomplete narrative and

fragmented state to reflect the world of the imagination and the struggle to comprehend mortality and loss.'
www.christiebrown.co.uk

Sandy Brown, b 1946, Tichborne, Hampshire, UK; lives in the UK; Education: Daisei Pottery, Mashiko, Japan.
Brown is famed for her spontaneous, passionate use of clay and colours. Her almost provokingly simple use of form and her strong, energetic brush decorations feed from direct emotion and from confidence in her own intuition.
www.sandybrownarts.com

Neil Brownsword, b 1970, Stoke-on-Trent, UK; lives in England; Education: School of Art and Design, University of Wales Institute, Cardiff; Royal College of Art, London.
'The metaphoric exploration of absence, fragmentation and the discarded signifies the inevitable effects of globalization which continue to disrupt a heritage economy which has supported a local population for almost five hundred years.'

Andrew Burton, b 1961, Bromley, Kent, UK; lives in the UK; Education: Newcastle University.
Burton uses thousands of tiny handmade ceramic bricks to construct sculptures, often resembling vessels or architectural structures, celebrating bricks as a common denominator across much human experience.

Kyra Cane, b 1962, Southwell, UK; lives in the UK; Education: West Nottinghamshire College; Camberwell College of Arts, London and Crafts; Goldsmiths, University of London.
'My pots explore simple formats, working in series to gradually extend the boundaries of the ceramic structures. There are remnants in these vessels of the vast landscapes, which have always been my inspiration.'

Simon Carroll, 1964–2009, UK; lived in England; Education: University of the West of England, Bristol (formerly Bristol Polytechnic).
Carroll was inspired by the red, slip-decorated earthenwares of seventeenth- and eighteenth-century Staffordshire. 'Tableware feels right, function adds to the richness of making and drawing and painting. Everything that function feeds, it enriches.'

Claudi Casanovas, b 1956, Barcelona, Spain; lives in Spain.
'I have forgotten what the wheel looks like with its hypnotic movements, making perfect revolutions around the centre, listening only to the rhythm and its cadence. I no longer know whether the models need to be made on a small scale or the size of the final result.'
www.galeriebesson.co.uk

Fernando Casasempere, b 1958, Chile; lives in London.
Casasempere, like other artists who have worked with a fierce dedication to chart new technical areas, is concerned not to let the techniques rule him and not to be trapped by a formulaic style.

Halima Cassell, b 1975, Pakistan; lives in the UK; Education: City College Manchester; University of Central Lancashire.
'I create a mood and feeling of dynamic tension by playfully manipulating the planes and facets of the patterns against each other. My work is influenced by an emphasis on the balance between masculine and feminine forms.'
www.halimacassell.co.uk

Marek Cecula, b 1944, Poland; lives in the USA and Poland.
'AIR, WATER & FIRE provides conditions in which the meanings and values of ceramics aesthetics are being reevaluated and repositioned. Industrial mass-produced forms are transformed by fire, water and air – *beauty of imperfection.*'
www.marekcecula.com

Sun Chao, b Taiwan; lives in Taiwan.
Recently Sun Chao has moved from making decorative crystal patterns on vases and bowls to large, flat glaze 'paintings' that combine Chinese ink landscapes with abstract expressionism.

Nick Chapman, b 1954, South Wales; lives in the UK; Education: Harrow School of Art.
'I have always made tableware. I love the intimacy that grows with a favorite mug or bowl, our kitchen is full of such favourites.'

Nicole Cherubini, b 1970, Boston, USA; lives in New York; Education: Skowhegan School of Painting and Sculpture, Skowhegan; New York University, New York; Rhode Island School of Design, Providence.
www.nicolecherubini.net

Lubna Chowdhary, b 1964, UK; lives in the UK.
'A key project over the last ten years has been *Metropolis* of over 1,000 clay sculptures based on the urban environment. The obsession with gathering, grouping and ordering is now applied to groups of tiles to create large-scale compositions.'
www.lubnachowdhary.co.uk

Linda Christianson, b USA; lives in Minnesota; Education: Hamline University (apprenticeship program), Saint Paul, Minnesota; School of Fine Arts Ceramic Residency Program, Banff Center, Alberta, Canada.
'The pots we use in our home are like stage sets. At rest on a table, dish drainer, or in a

cupboard, they are visually engaging. This daily relationship with the pots offers up both utility and continual visual inquiry.'

Ying-Yueh Chuang, b Taiwan; lives in Eastern Canada; Education: Emily Carr Institute of Art and Design, Vancouver; The Nova Scotia College of Art and Design, Halifax.
Through her sculptural installations, Chuang creates environments inhabited by ceramic creatures. The works will be suspended from the ceiling while others are displayed on pedestals.

Carina Ciscato, b 1970, Brazil; lives in London.
'Spontaneous and fluid pots that are the result of thoughtful deliberation. Carefully conceived, the subtle and delicate marks gently applied, the pots distorted and altered. They are content to be perfectly imperfect.'

Claudia Clare, b 1962, UK; lives in London; Education: University of Westminster, London.
'I use an interdisciplinary approach, combining established social research methodologies with ceramic practices to commit to "material memory" the narratives of social research.'

Michael Cleff, b 1961, Bochum, Germany; lives in Germany.
Cleff's sculptures impress with their concentrated power, a power drawn from their simplicity, from their compactness and from the stringency with which he pursues and powers forward his intention.

Bruce Cochrane, b Vancouver, Canada; lives in Canada; Education: Alfred University, New York; The Nova Scotia College of Art and Design, Halifax; John Abbott College, Montreal, Quebec.
'After 25 years of working in clay, utility continues to serve as the foundation for my ideas. The pots I make, no matter how simple or complex, are meant to be experienced on a physical and visual level.'

Kirsten Coelho, b 1966, Australia; lives in Australia; Education: South Australian School of Art, University of South Australia.
'A juncture between stark simplicity of form and subtle abstracted surfaces and the potential beauty that can exist in the breakdown of the industrial are possibilities that are explored through the making.'

Susan Collett, b 1961, Toronto; lives in Toronto; Education: Central Technical School of Art, Toronto; The Cleveland Institute of Art, Ohio; Lacoste School of Art, France.
'In contrast to the vessel as a traditional marker of containment, the Moiré series is pierced to release its interior space with a positive and light filled shadow. I am interested in the

dichotomy of strength versus fragility and the movement of the light with the clay.'
www.susancollett.ca

Nic Collins, b 1958, UK; lives in the UK; Education: Derby College of Art.
All of Collins's work is made on a momentum kick wheel, using local clay. The work is then wood-fired in an *anagama*-type kiln for four days to temperatures in excess of 1300°C. New work includes large sculptural pieces fired using wet clay.
www.nic-collins.co.uk

Fiamma Colonna Montagu, b 1971; lives in London; Education: Oxford University.
Colonna Montagu is best known for making large-scale ceramic forms and installations that create a strange, dream-like mood when placed in the landscape, inviting the viewer to walk around it as if in a reverie or on a stage.
www.fiammamontagu.com/biog.html

Cynthia Consentino, b USA; lives in Northampton, Massachusetts; Education: The Cooper Union for the Advancement of Science and Arts, New York; University of Massachusetts, Amherst.
'My sculptures utilize the human figure to explore gender, familial and societal roles, religious and cultural mores, and human perception, incorporating the universal within the personal.'
www.umass.edu/art271/spring95/consenti/home.html

Emmanuel Cooper, b 1938, Derbyshire, UK; lives in London; Education: Bournemouth School of Art; Hornsey School of Art.
'My work is influenced by the urban city environment, by such things as hard, textured surfaces, street lighting, endless movement and sense of urgency. Colours are those of roads, pavements and buildings, textures those of the metropolis.'

James Coquia, b 1972, Oakland, California; lives in Arizona.
'The current direction of my work leans toward the figure. The timeless quality of the human form has always been a perfect platform from which the concepts for my work begin their development. My work is a celebration of the aberrant.'
www.jamescoquia.com

Annette Corcoran, b 1930, USA; lives in California.
'My teapots at this time are the result of the interplay between observation, fantasy, imagination, and technical skill. The teapot form offers a structural challenge, the clay on the other hand is often pushed to the limits of stability and instability.'

Daphné Corregan, b 1954, France; lives in France; Education: Ecole des beaux-arts de Toulon; Ecole supérieure des beaux arts de Marseille; Ecole supérieure d'arts d'Aix-en-Provence.
Corregan is more inclined to work on the representation of the piece than on the piece itself. She wants to show that a pot taken out of context can be just as important and impressive as a piece of sculpture or a painting.

Phoebe Cummings, b 1981, UK; lives in the UK; Education: University of Brighton; Royal College of Art, London.
Cummings's work explores the psychological spaces of objects and landscapes of the interior, directing the attention of the viewer towards a shifted sense of the familiar.

Claire Curneen, b 1968, Ireland; lives in Wales UK; Education: Crawford College of Art and Design, Cork, Ireland; University of Ulster, Belfast; School of Art and Design, University of Wales Institute, Cardiff.
Curneen's interpretation shows the porcelain figure in a state of change, the branches engulf and are topped with gold suggesting the delight in her fate. They serve as a reminder of our mortality with a comforting presence.

Bernadette Curran, b 1974, USA; lives in Ardmore, Pennsylvania.
'The animal has been drawn to make and made to draw – the sum of which remains vaguely superimposed. What is captured are the bleary bits and fragments, the chance events and partly registered perceptions of a story.'

Natasha Daintry, b 1966, UK; lives in the UK; Education: West Surrey College of Art and Design; Royal College of Art, London.
Inspired by the stepped, architectural structures of Ancient Mesopotamia, recent work uses lines, steps and discs of colour to explore how colour and form interconnect.

Wouter Dam, b 1957, Utrecht, the Netherlands; lives in the Netherlands; Education: Gerrit Rietveld Academie, Amsterdam.
Dam throws forms that he later cuts. From the parts thus obtained he puts together new forms. The colours are woven into the skin, a technique that gives his objects a 'dry' impression.
www.franklloyd.com

Malcolm Davis, b 1944; lives in Upshur County, West Virginia.
'For me the making of pots is a way to celebrate the mundane rituals of daily life and to make them holy.'

Robert Dawson, b 1953, UK; lives in the UK; Education: Royal College of Art, London; Camberwell College of Arts, London.

'You play with perception and distortion in your work quite a lot. What is this manipulation trying to achieve? Maybe it's a sense of uncertainty about everything. One's self included, there being no centre of consciousness.'

Richard Deacon, b 1949, Bangor UK; lives in the UK; Education: Somerset College of Arts and Technology; Central Saint Martins College of Art and Design, London; Royal College of Art, London; Chelsea College of Art & Design, London.
Materials are of vital concern to Deacon, who is known for sculptures in which 'a powerful impression of over-the-top craftsmanship is a keynote of his poetic.'

Janet DeBoos, b 1948, Australia; lives in Australia; Education: East Sydney Technical College, Darlinghurst.
'My practice has always been focused on domestic ceramics, the processes by which it comes into being and the performative aspects of use by which it gets "remade".'

Mieke de Groot, b 1953, the Netherlands; lives in the Netherlands; Education: Gerrit Rietveld Academie, Amsterdam.
'A step-by-step development has always been an essential factor in my work. My oeuvre is a logical, linear history of forms, which proceed one another in small variations. For me, the logic behind the sculptures contributes to their beauty.'
www.miekedegroot.nl

Redo Del Olmo, b 1961, Bayamón, Puerto Rico; lives in Hato Rey, Puerto Rico.
Creates organically derived forms.

Edmund de Waal, b 1967, UK; lives in the UK; Education: Cambridge University (apprenticeship with Geoffrey Whiting).
'I have tried to create new interpretative frameworks for understanding the relationship between contemporary studio ceramic practice and the historical canon, becoming increasingly interested in site-specificity.'

Lola Dimova, b 1981, Bulgaria; lives in Bulgaria.
'I am interested in both ceramic design and expressive conceptual works. Visually I am searching for simplicity and stillness, inspired by the whole meaning of the word "life".'

Susan Disley, b 1951, Lancashire UK; lives in the UK; Education: Bolton College of Art and Design; University of Wolverhampton (formerly Wolverhampton Polytechnic).
'The measured, repetitive process of making by hand releases recollections of hidden thoughts and feelings; memories – irreversible lost time. My work references those contained emotions: anger, sadness, joy.'
www.susandisley.co.uk

Stephen Dixon, b 1957, County Durham; lives in the UK; Education: Manchester Metropolitan University; Royal College of Art, London.
Dixon's work is a personal response to the social and political issues which surround our everyday lives, questioning the moral and ethical conditions of our times.

Jack Doherty, b 1948, Northern Ireland; lives in the UK; Education: Ulster College of Art and Design.
'Mostly, working with porcelain is a joy. It is soft and sensual, a pleasure to touch and use. At other times, lack of concentration and distractions can mean that it is easy to miss the subtle changes in the condition of the clay as it dries.'
www.dohertyporcelain.com

Karen Downing, b 1958; lives in the UK.
'At the heart of my work are resonances of the landscape that helped to form my aesthetic and my approach to the work. Wide, white sandy beaches with far horizons, tidal rivers and estuarine reed beds.'

Pippin Drysdale, b 1943, Australia; lives in Australia; Education: Curtin University of Technology, Western Australia.
Drysdale's memory of a trip to Ayres Rock, now named Uluru – its original aboriginal title – is not of a triumphal climb along its ancient folded crest, but of the infinite intimate sensations and colours to be found on the long trek round its base.
www.pippindrysdale.com

Ruth Duckworth, b 1919, Hamburg, Germany; lives in the USA; Education: Hammersmith School of Art, London; Liverpool School of Art and Design; Central School of Arts and Crafts, London.
Duckworth creates new and unexpected forms and objects, demonstrating deep connections to nature, culture and the human figure with groundbreaking minimalist sculptures and major currents in twentieth-century modernism.

Ken Eastman, b 1960, Hereford UK; lives in the UK; Education: Edinburgh School of Art; Royal College of Art, London.
Eastman uses the vessel as a subject to give form and meaning to an expression. The content is, literally, the space within, defining emptiness as presence. The constant dialogue between form and surface is at the heart of his work.
www.bmgallery.co.uk

Michael Eden, b UK; lives in the UK; Education: Royal College of Art, London.
Eden together with his wife Victoria produce slip-decorated earthenware with bold, simple, thrown forms and restrained decoration. Eden has now

become involved with computer-aided design and new ceramic materials.
www.edenceramics.co.uk

Victoria Eden, b UK; lives in the UK.
'*February 5th 2004* is a ceramic installation that commemorates the deaths of 23 cockle pickers in the sands of Morecambe Bay, intended as a metaphorical pathway to the families and communities in China that lost people in the tragedy.'

Isobel Egan, b 1976, Ireland; lives in Ireland; Education: The National College of Art and Design, Dublin.
'I explore Fragility, Personal Space and Memory. The linear structures lead you across the horizontal and through the vertical encapsulating the notion of travelling through space and time.'

Osamma Eman, b 1974, Cairo, Egypt; lives in Egypt; Education: Helwan University, Cairo.

Tanya Engelstein, b 1950, Jerusalem, Israel; lives in Yavneh, Israel; Education: Bezalel Academy of Arts and Design, Jerusalem.

Antje Ernestus, b Germany; lives in North Norfolk, UK; Education: Camberwell College of Arts, London.
'I work mainly in porcelain chosen for its whiteness and colour response at high firing temperatures. Pots are made through a combination of throwing and hand-building techniques.'

James Evans, b 1964, Essex UK; lives in London; Education: Central Saint Martins College of Art and Design, London; University of Colorado at Boulder.
'It is my intention to make the form as economic in line and texture as possible while offering an infinite number of references. With their humanistic imperfections and mimicry I strive to convey an ample softness that is suggestively tactile.'

Simcha Even-Chen, b 1958, Israel; lives in Rehovot, Israel.
'I investigate the elements of ambiguity and dynamic of opposites. Ambiguity is expressed by exploration of the ratio between mass, volume and balance, using simple precise shapes that give the expression of a solid and massive body.'

Christine Fabre, b 1951, France; lives in France.
'Now I am rediscovering the skin of the clay. No longer wishing to cover its surface with glaze, I have stripped it bare. Naked, it sends me back to a rupturing, fissuring world. Accompanied by only, perhaps, a few obstinate guardians.'

Dorothy Feibleman, b 1951, Indianapolis; lives in the UK; Education: Rochester Institute of Technology, New York.
'I use translucent, non-translucent, textured laminated ceramic imaging handmade or reverse technology. Similar imaging for industry such as coloured graduations of naturally white porcelains and translucent porcelains that I have formulated.'

László Fekete, b 1949, Hungary; lives in Hungary; Education: Academy of Applied Arts, Budapest (under Imre Schrammel).
Fekete makes intricate stoneware and porcelain sculpture with social commentary, sometimes decorating with ready-made industrial decals. He also creates works by assembling seconds from the Herend Porcelain Manufactory.

Michael Flynn, b 1947, Cork, Ireland; lives in Cardiff, Wales; Education: Cardiff College of Art and Design; Birmingham College of Art.
'Juggling elements to fashion ideas expressed in purely visual form, trying to embrace nebulous concepts, pushing my thinking further towards a goal which I cannot fully define.'

Jean-François Fouilhoux, b 1947, France; lives in Loir-et-Cher, France.
The court is filled by the voice of the bell in the wind (from Wang Shizeng, *Fullness, emptiness*) 'To work otherwise, emptiness as a container. I pull a flexible blade, folding it at will, through a mass of clay, the clay keeping the memory of the body movement.'

Léopold L. Foulem, b 1945, Canada; lives in Canada.
'The sources that nourish and stimulate my artistic output emanate primarily from the ceramic lexicon. The conscientious use of exact and pre-established parameters enables me to arrive at a synthesis that is unquestionably ceramic in origin.'

Debra Fritts; lives in the USA.
'As time and experience embraces me as a sculptor in clay, I feel free of art trends and fashionable art. My expression is basic yet intrigues me daily to continue this exploration of clay and the female figure.'

Lie Fung; lives and works in Korea.

Alessandro Gallo, b 1974, Genoa; lives in Italy; Education: University of Genoa; Central Saint Martins College of Art and Design, London; Chelsea College of Art & Design, London.
His work was included in the Monoprint Show at Jill George Gallery, London and in art fairs in Britain and USA.

David Garland, b 1941, UK; lives in the UK.
Garland worked as a painter, sculptor and designer before becoming a potter at the age

of thirty. His pots are thrown on the wheel using earthenware clay, and often slipped with white or coloured slips.
www.davidgarland.co.uk

Angel Garraza, b 1950, Navarra, Spain; lives in Spain; Education: School of Arts and Crafts in Pamplona, Fine Arts in Bilbao.
Garraza explores the concepts of duality and balance through a variety of forms including black and white clays.

Michael Geertsen, b 1966, Denmark; lives in Denmark.
Geertsen produces assemblages made up of recognizable fragments of cups, cylinders and everyday tableware glazed in shiny bright colours that refer to the early modernists and Russian Constructivists.

Gert Germeraad, b 1959, Utrecht; lives in the Netherlands; Education: Academy of Fine Arts, Rotterdam; Free Academy of Arts, The Hague.
'I am fascinated by thoughts and theories about character and personality and how people through time have tried to read and interpret the faces of other people.'

Maggi Giles, b 1938, England; lives in Amsterdam; Education: Bromley Art College. Giles came to the Netherlands in 1965, later working in Delft at the Delft Blue Factory designing wall reliefs for public buildings. All her work is colourful and makes use of little raised 'walls' to keep the colours with black 'line drawings'.
www.maggigiles.com

Shannon Goff, b 1974, USA; lives in the USA; Education: Cranbrook Academy of Art, Bloomfield Hills.
'My work seesaws between complexities and freedoms, two steps mr. ordinary with maam extraordinary, do-si-dos familiar and foreign. What results is a humanization of the mundane. My objects become accessories to relationships and responses to the subtleties and nuances of daily life.'

Tanya Gomez, b 1974, UK; lives in the UK; Education: University of Brighton; Camberwell College of Arts, London; Bournemouth and Poole College of Further Education; Royal College of Art, London.
'I have developed an affinity with the sea as I have learnt to appreciate it for its different states and levels – its vast, endless, openness; the feeling of buoyancy and its power, from the pulls and tugs of the waves to make objects that incorporate and reflect this.'
www.tgceramics.co.uk

Morgen Hall, b 1960, Roseville California; lives in Wales; Education: Gray's School of Art, Aberdeen; School of Art and Design, University of Wales Institute, Cardiff.

Hall is totally committed to the idea of functional handmade pottery. She wants her pots 'to be comfortable to use, and at the same time delicious to the eye so that they might be able to push a mere tea break into a tea party'.

Sam Hall, b 1967, Yorkshire UK; lives in the UK; Education: Loughborough College of Art.
Hall creates pots without practical function and uses ceramic surfaces as canvas, attacking them in a painterly and intuitive way.
In many senses it defies definition, fluidly approaching the boundaries between art and craft.

Susan Halls, b 1966, Kent, UK; lives in the USA; Education: Medway College of Art and Design, Rochester; Royal College of Art, London.
'I've always been overwhelmed by the diversity and energy of Nature. My obsession with animals is at the centre of this fascination. I've never doubted the sense of integration between myself and animals, which are the dominant subject of my work.'
www.susanhalls.com

Jane Hamlyn, b 1940, London; lives in the UK; Education: Harrow College of Art.
'My functional pots have always been made to celebrate the rituals of daily life – serving, receiving and sharing. I still believe in the eloquent usefulness of function but am discovering a wider interpretation of its meaning.'
www.saltglaze.fsnet.co.uk

Lisa Hammond, b 1956, UK; lives in the UK.
'For the last 28 years I have been making vapour glaze functional, high-temperature soda glaze pots for the preparation, cooking and serving of food, in the broadest sense of the word.'
www.greenwichgateway.com/mazehill

Jeong Yong Han; lives in Seoul, South Korea; Education: Kookmin University, Seoul; Seoul National University.
'I've got a lot of influences from the aesthetic of the Yi Dynasty porcelain. I'm always looking for a happy accident, even though my work is very controlled.'

Ashraf Hanna, b 1967, Egypt; lives in Wales; Education: El-Minya College of Fine Art; Central Saint Martins College of Art and Design, London.
'As a maker I am excited by the endless possibilities which exist within the simple form of the vessel. One key component is to develop one's capacity for observation.'

Ineke Hans, b the Netherlands; lives in the Netherlands; Education: Hogeschool voor de Kunsten, Arnhem; Royal College of Art, London.

Hans's work has acquired the identity most clearly of a designer, with the impulses of a sculptor, and the industrial experience needed to define products with a commercial life.
www.inekehans.com

Gwyn Hanssen Pigott, b 1935, Ballaray, Australia; lives in Australia; Education: University of Melbourne; apprenticeship with Ivan McMeekin, Mittagong.
'Still lifes, trails, parades. The contradictions implicit in the titles are the works' concern, and the clue to their reading. Approach and hesitation: seduction and *noli me tangere*. Bottles, cups, bowls, beakers mirror (perhaps) our own fragile substantiality.'

Zahara Harel, b 1957, Jerusalem; lives in Israel; Education: Tel Aviv University; Bezalel Academy of Arts and Design, Jerusalem.

Kerry Harker, b 1971, UK; lives in Leeds, UK; Education: University of Leeds.
'My one-off ceramic pieces employ a range of decorative techniques, such as in-glaze and on-glaze ground colours, hand-painting, typography, ceramic transfers, stencilling, rubber stamping and gilding, usually on bone china plates and vases.'

Keith Harrison, b 1967, West Bromwich, UK; lives in England; Education: School of Art and Design, University of Wales Institute, Cardiff; Royal College of Art, London.
'The direct transformation of clay from a raw state using industrial and domestic electrical heating systems as an intrinsic part of the viewing experience is a continuing enquiry.'

Steve Harrison, b 1952, Australia; lives in Australia.
'All of my work is made from raw materials that I dig up in my immediate locality. I am trying to make work that represents me, my locality and my self-reliant philosophy.'

Barbara Hashimoto, b 1955, New Jersey; lives in Indiana; Education: apprenticeship at Junko Yamada Studio, Saitama, Japan; Yale University, New Haven; Baruch College, New York.
Hashimoto works in sculpture, installation and performance and is best known for her ceramic work in which she fires clay with books addressing women's societal roles, cross-cultural identity and the structures and strategies of power.
www.barbarahashimoto.com

Makoto Hatori, b 1947, Japan; lives in Ibaraki, Japan; Education: apprenticeship with master potter Ken Fujiwara; Nihon University; College of Arts, Gifu Prefectural Institute of Ceramics.
'Creativity requires some preconditions. To make/create things does not necessarily mean creativity. I would like to sketch a few

restrictive conditions that can be observed in the world of Japanese work describing the spirituality in Japanese work.'

Kathryn Hearn, b 1953, UK; lives in London.
'My work has included the development and production of decorative vessels using cast porcelain in a range of colours in combination. This work is a celebration of material informed by techniques, processes and by the natural and built environment.'

Regina Heinz, b 1957, Austria; lives in the UK; Education: Wimbledon College of Art, London; Goldsmiths, University of London; London Guildhall Univeristy (formerly City of London Polytechnic); Sir John Cass Faculty of Art, Ecole Supérieure d'Arts Appliqués, Geneva; University of Vienna.
Heinz's 'pillow' forms are individual abstract sculptures or part of a wall panel series. Inspired by nature and hand-built from soft slabs of clay, they display an organic and sensual quality but are essentially abstract.
www.ceramart.net

Elisa Helland-Hansen; lives in Norway.
'Why use glazes in a wood-fired kiln? Why not? What really *matters* is the individual artist's ability to investigate and take advantage of the possibilities offered by the specific kind of kiln you have chosen to work with.'

Eduard Hermans, b 1959, the Netherlands; lives in the Netherlands.
'I am an artist and theatre designer. It really is a great combination. The creative challenge in both fields is surprisingly equally demanding.'
eja-man@dds.nl

André Hess, b South Africa; lives in the UK.
'I make simple shapes that are both familiar and fugitive. Shapes that require the viewer to question what the pieces mean rather than what they resemble or represent.'

Annie Hewett, b 1950, UK; lives in the UK; Education: Central Saint Martins College of Art and Design, London; University of Bristol.
'My work is, for the most part, inspired by natural forms. Plants play a large part in my life, whether by observation or cultivation, both of which I enjoy immensely. The influences of illustrators, textile designers and painters are always present.'

Marian Heyerdahl, b 1957, Oslo, Norway; lives in Norway, Italy, China; Education: National Academy of Art and Design, Oslo, Norway.
The sculptures of Heyerdahl are influenced by her travels around the world. *The Terracotta Woman Project* is a unique project linking the cultural heritage of China to the contemporary art scene.
www.mheyerdahl.com

Wayne Higby, b 1943, Colorado Springs, Colorado; lives in the USA.
'For many years I have worked in earthenware, raku technique. My current efforts in porcelain are in response to travel and work in the People's Republic of China and to an ongoing commitment to keeping the adventure in the studio alive.'

John Higgins; lives in the UK; Education: Wolverhampton College of Art.
'In order to retain a freshness the constructions are made quite intuitively, allowing the forms to have as much say as the maker. The forms tend toward the architectural and the surfaces are mostly dry but with the use of colour.'
www.studiopottery.co.uk

Louise Hindsgavl, b 1973, Denmark; lives in Denmark; Education: The School of Arts and Crafts, Kolding, Denmark; School of Ceramics, Caldas da Rainha, Portugal.
'The porcelain figurine belongs to a ceramic genre that boasts many virtues and the figurines are pretty. However, the classic figurines seem toothless and represent an idealized and romanticized world.'

Sin-Ying Ho, b 1963, Hong Kong; lives in the USA; Education: The Nova Scotia College of Art and Design, Halifax; Louisiana State University, Baton Rouge.
'The exploration of the idea of technology and our place in society in the twenty-first century is a continuing concern. My interest and expertise derive from living in three countries and speaking two languages.'

Charlotte Hodes; lives in London; Education: Slade School of Fine Art, London; Brighton School of Art.
Hodes is a painter, her most recent work consisting of large-scale papercuts and ceramics. In her practice she combines both 'hands on' processes in the studio such as drawing and collage alongside digital imagery.

Nina Hole; lives in Denmark.
'I build site specific, part sculpture – part performance. The peak moment is when we let the curtain fall and the sculpture is revealed in its glowing stage. A short moment, never to be repeated.'
www.ninahole.com

Niek Hoogland, b 1953, the Netherlands; lives in the Netherlands.
'I am a slipware potter, I like to work as directly as possible, the enjoyment is in the action of the making, the gestures of wedging, throwing and pulling handles, of slipping, painting and slip-trailing. It's like telling stories.'

Satoru Hoshino, b 1945, Niigata Prefecture, Japan; lives in Japan; Education: Ritsumeikan University, Kyoto.

Ashley Howard, b 1963, UK; lives in the UK; Education: Kent Institute of Art and Design, Rochester; Royal College of Art, London.
'Howard's approach has always been one of physical expansion and openness. He is the broadest, most gestural kind of thrower, leaving instilled in the finished form the richly, but too rarely explored, expressive power of the wheel.' (David Whiting)

Joanna Howells, b 1960, UK; lives in Wales.
'My work concentrates on form and texture. I make pieces which are simple yet have a softness, a freedom and a sculptural quality. Inspiration ranges from Cycladic sculpture to the South Wales coastline, to modern industrial artefacts.'
www.joannahowells.co.uk

Sang-Wook Huh, b Korea; lives in Kyoungi-Do, South Korea; Education: Kookmin University.
Huh works in stoneware producing thrown and hand-built forms such as trays, bottlers, lidded boxes and teapots. Although reflecting the long Korean tradition, the honed down simplicity gives the work a modern feel.

Sylvia Hyman, b USA; lives in Nashville; Education: George Peabody College, Nashville; Buffalo State College, Buffalo; Albright Art School, Buffalo.
Hyman's works inhabit a 'desert of the real'. Seen through a postmodern lens, these objects are simulacra, a world where middle class life is understood through vestiges of its material culture, painstakingly portrayed in clay.

Steve Irvine, b 1952, Canada; lives in Ontario, Canada; Education: Sheridan College, School of Crafts and Design.
'Pottery has always been more to me than just a way to earn a living. Clay is an instrument of understanding – a way to look for meaning, truth and harmony in my life, which helps me to find my place in the world.'
www.steveirvine.com

Sergei Isupov, b 1963, Stavrapole, Russia; lives in Massachusetts; Education: Ukrainian State Academy of Art; Estonian State Art Institute of Tallinn.
'Art is a life-style for me. Everything that surrounds and excites me is automatically processed and transformed into the final result: an artwork. The dreamlike, surreal narratives are self-portraits exploring male and female relationships through graphic sexual images.'

Hwang Jeng-daw, b 1962, China; lives in Taiwan.
Jeng-daw is an internationally acclaimed teapot maker. 'Teapots show us different ways and we also give teapots different appearances. Drinking tea is not only a way of life.'

Ole Jensen, b 1950; lives in Denmark; Education: The Design School, Kolding, Denmark.
In work for Royal Copenhagen Jensen has created a range of sculptural, innovative designs – a large and varied dinnerware series called 'Ole', created around a common idea: to unite form and function and turn work into play.

Liu Jianhua, b 1962, Ji'an, Jiangxi Province, China; lives in Kunming and Jingdezhen.
Since the early 1990s Jianhua has used Chinese style apparel as a leitmotif, from Sun Yat-Sen jackets and double-breasted suits to cheongsam, with Chinese male dress being the main symbolic element used in his cryptic compositions.

Christin Johansson; lives in Copenhagen, Denmark; Education: Glass and Ceramics School, Nexø; The Danish Design School, Copenhagen (exchange student); Kunsthøjskolen Thorstedlund, Frederikssund.
'My works emanate from a fascination with sterile, clinical environments and industrial sanitary designs. The shapes indicate functions and perfect, shiny surfaces of my objects provide clear references to such environments and designs.'
www.christin.dk

Hella Jongerius, b 1963, the Netherlands; lives in the Netherlands; Education: Academie voor Industriële Vormgeving, Eindhoven.
Works as a designer for industrial production and also makes individual pieces.
www.jongeriuslab.com

Tavs Jørgensen, b 1969, Demark; lives in the UK; Education: School of Art and Design, University of Wales Institute, Cardiff.
'I believe in the free movement of creativity across traditional disciplines and boundaries. My work, which includes commercial designs, craft practice and concept-based pieces, also focuses on research into the creative use of digital development tools.'

Debbie Joy; lives in London.
'All my work is thrown on the wheel aiming to retain echoes of the pleasure I take in this tactile and dynamic experience. My domestic ware combines the human warmth of the traditional hand-thrown pot with the pretty yumminess of contemporary sugared-almond colours.'

Nina Jun, b 1953, Seoul, South Korea; lives in the USA; Education: California State University, Long Beach (Phi Beta Kappa).
'Things that are perishable or impermanent, like a fleeting sunset or fresh flowers, are beautiful. Projecting light images on heavy ceramic surfaces gives me an opportunity to address these issues of impermanence and perishables.'

Gitte Jungersen, b 1967, Denmark; lives in Denmark; Education: The Danish School, Copenhagen.
'I feel a childish need to seduce the eyes with material. Let myself be absorbed, like a tiny insect finding its way deep into the middle (centre) of the flower. Shiny glossiness, clear colours, seething and bubbling. Ceramics can make all this.'

Mo Jupp, b 1938, UK; lives in London; Education: Camberwell College of Arts, London; Royal College of Art, London.
'Jupp's work has become increasingly calm. His intense and loving explorations of the female nude reveal an artist at peace with the world. His images have become less fractured and more whole – in essence if not in structure – more celebratory.' (David Whiting)

Michael Kalmbach; lives in the USA; Education: University of Delaware; Virginia Commonwealth University; Bloomsburg University of Pennsylvania.
'For some years during the nineties I was in charge of a ceramic factory located in a remand prison. I portrayed the men with whom I collaborated. Later I continued by making portraits of friends. The figures represent the depicted persons.'

Maciej Kasperski, b 1969; lives in Poland; Education: The Academy of Fine Arts, Wrocław, Poland.
'My recent ceramics belong to a collection Ctrl C, Ctrl V, which refer directly to two popular keyboard abbreviations used by most computer programs. There are three groups of ceramic objects *Triplex System*, *SVC*/ *SHC* and *Useless Forms*. Each refers to the issue of repetition (shape, idea or gesture).'

Margaret Keelan; lives in San Francisco; Education: University of Utah, Salt Lake City; University of Saskatchewan, Saskatoon, Canada.
'My figurative sculptures confront issues of mortality, innocence, love, good and evil, hinting at a narrative of natural and magical forces.'
www.margaretkeelan.com

Walter Keeler, b 1942, UK; lives in Wales; Education: Harrow School of Art.
'I see the role of the potter as "academic" – to be provocative within one's own sphere, to generate ideas or combine ideas in ways that encourage others to develop new ideas. I wish to create a sense of mystery and adventure in tableware.'

Chris Keenan, b 1960, UK; lives in London; Education: apprenticeship with Edmund de Waal.
'The first pots I saw that provoked more than a passing interest in me were functional studio pots. They are the pots I wanted to learn to

make when I made the change from working as an actor. I want them to give pleasure and do the job well.'

Jonathan Keep, b 1958, South Africa; lives in the UK; Education: Royal College of Art, London.
'Approaching my pots as sculptural objects that have an inside and an outside offers me the opportunity to explore the idea of internal self and external persona while using the fragile shell of earthy clay.'
www.keep-art.co.uk

Bonnie Kemske, b 1954, USA; lives in the UK; Education: Royal College of Art, London; London Metropolitan University; Goucher College, Baltimore.
Kemske makes curved and textured forms by 'casting hugs' with her own body, sculptural artworks made *from* the embrace and *for* the embrace, works that invite viewers to become touchers, an engagement of the 'thoughtful body'.

Gail Kendall, b 1944, USA; lives in Nebraska; Education: Eastern Michigan University, Ypsilanti; University of Michigan, Ann Arbor.
'My work is influenced by various European pottery traditions since the 13th century. Both "peasant" and "palace" pots inspire me. Early English slipware, Delftware and Renaissance Maiolica are sources I refer to routinely.'

Rob Kesseler, b 1951, Solihull, UK; lives in the UK; Education: Central Saint Martins College of Art and Design, London.
Kesseler uses craft skills and design methods to explore a range of subjects and ideas. The thread that holds these strands together is his fascination with the plant world and the way its image has adorned clothes, furniture, walls and floors.

Sun Kim, b 1977, lives in London; Education: Alfred University, New York; Fundacao Armando Alvares Penteado, São Paulo (assistantship with Edmund de Waal).
'My work is focused on functional wares and I use the throwing wheel as my major tool to produce them. I enjoy the quality of the clay that is genuine and shows the spirit of the maker. My aim is to find a balance among all these elements: volume, shape, proportion, form; and be able to give each piece its own sense of presence and stability.'

Cindy Kolodziejski, b 1962, Augsburg, Germany; lives in the USA; Education: California State University, Long Beach; Otis Art Institute of Parsons School of Design, New York.
Kolodziejski combines her knowledge of ceramics and painting. The familiar domestic vessel (vase, tureen or teapot) is transformed by the addition of unusual narrative imagery,

frequently juxtaposed, overlayed or presented in continuous panorama.

Charles Krafft, b 1949, USA; lives in Seattle. From porcelain machine guns to plates commemorating hideous disasters, Krafft's grimly satirical work sheds strange light on an age when terror is rattling our teacups.

Anne Kraus, 1956–2003; lived Short Hills, New Jersey; Education: University of Pennsylvania; New York State College of Ceramics at Alfred University, New York. Kraus first practised as a painter before discovering ceramics. 'One thing that distinguishes ceramics for me – and which never happened with painting – is that I tumbled head over heels into it. It was like being swept up by a great wave.'

Mervi Kurvinen, b 1974, Finland; lives in Finland; Education: South Carelia Polytechnic; Gerrit Rietveld Academie, Amsterdam; Lappeenranta College of Arts and Crafts, University of Joensuu.
Kurvinen makes contemporary jewelry, jewelry-like objects and installations. Her aim is to work conceptually with an open mind with no need to classify herself into any categories. She thinks humour is very close to spirituality. www.norsu.info/eng_artists.html

Eva Kwong, b 1954, Hong Kong; lives in New York City; Education: Rhode Island School of Design, Providence; Tyler School of Art, Philadelphia.
The ceramics of Kwong sparkle and dance. Her sense of energy – from work in the traditions of vases and platters to sculptural forms that reach towards human proportion – balance contemplative order and the necessities of motion.

Lut Laleman, b 1958, Belgium; lives in Belgium.
The work of Laleman is built up from thin coils of porcelain. The object is thin and fragile, simple form and minimum in use of colour. In Laleman's work 'light' preserves both its meanings: translucence and light in weight.

Anne-Marie Laureys, b 1962, Beveren, Belgium; lives in Belgium; Education: Institute for Higher Education in the Science and the Arts, Saint Lucas, Ghent, Belgium.
'I like my ceramics to have a sense of excitement and a freshness, and they must be tactile. I aim to develop a great variety of senses, to show the results of a very physical and palpable human gesture which is mysterious like the sexual experience.'
www.centrumgoedwerk.be

John Leach, b 1939, UK; lives in England; Education: apprenticeship with David Leach and Bernard Leach.

'The extraordinary plastic qualities of clay make it so tempting to the human touch… I love it. It is a huge privilege to create useful pottery by hand from such a humble raw material.'
www.johnleachpottery.co.uk/gallery.asp

Cheon-Soo Lee, b Korea; lives in Korea. Thrown and press-moulded tableware in stoneware that celebrates a free, almost casual approach. Even so, the plates, vases, bowls and dishes have a powerful sense of history with a contemporary understanding.

Eun-Bum Lee; lives in ChungChongBuk-Do, South Korea.
'Most of my works are tableware. I am inspired by traditional Korean celadon that I interpret in contemporary ways.'

Jennifer Lee, b 1956, Scotland; lives in London; Education: Edinburgh College of Art; Royal College of Art, London.
Lee's sculptural stoneware pots are subdued, the surfaces mottled and speckled. They address the formal issues of fine art.
www.galeriebesson.co.uk

Yong Phill Lee; lives in Korea; Education: Hongik University, Seoul, South Korea; Keramic skolan Industerial technical, Linköping, Sweden; Ceramic Studio, Fiskars, Finland.
'I build the ceramics using the casting method among many ways. Each shape of the movable small structures, the ceramic works, is decided by its masses that were "inter-mixed" independently.'

Young-Ho Lee, b 1958, Manager, Yusan Pottery; Education: BS College of Fine Arts, Seoul National University.

Zhu Legeng, b 1952, Jingdezhen, China; lives in China.
Legeng has produced ceramics for the inner and outside walls of the Wheat Music Hall in Seoul, South Korea. He developed clay bricks that give a visionary effect of a coloured picture featuring traditional Chinese ink painting style.

Shirley Leslyn Sheppard, b 1953, UK; lives in the UK; Education: University of Brighton.
'I have been exploring my interest in people and their characteristics using various media. My work tends to be ornamental, having no functional use, and therefore must evoke something, by way of a reaction, from the observer or I have failed.'

Pamela Leung, b 1962, Hong Kong; lives in London; Education: Middlesex University, London (formerly Middlesex Polytechnic); Goldsmiths, University of London.
'My work has been primarily formed by my dual cultural background. I was brought up in

both Hong Kong and Britain. Originally my subject matter came from Chinese mythology, but as time passed I have created my own mythology.'

Natasha Lewer, b 1967, Sri Lanka; lives in London; Education: City Lit, London.
'I make groups of large-scale sculptural, semi-abstract and playful work. Texture, tactility and colour are vital elements, and synthetic materials, such as flock, contrast with the clay. Sources range from microbiology to toys.'
www.natashalewerceramics.co.uk

Sonia Lewis, b 1946, UK; lives in the UK.
'My elegant and functional porcelain begin on the wheel. Decoration is minimal. I live in the Fens in England and aim to reflect the quality of light – cool blue/greens and misty yellows where definition is uncertain and horizons are hazy.'

Chun Liao, b 1969, Taiwan; lives in London; Education: Royal College of Art, London.
'The emotions, simple but overwhelmingly strong, have inspired me. Through my work I am expressing a range of emotional extremes and jumbled feelings, mixed with personal struggles.'
www.bmgallery.co.uk

Claire Lindner, b 1982, Perpignan, France; lives in London; Education: Camberwell College of Arts, London; Ecole supérieure des arts décoratifs de Strasbourg; Norwich School of Art and Design.
'When you take a mass of soft clay and stretch it from inside, it enlarges and metamorphoses while all the interventions engendered by the hand remain imperceptible. The form appears to transform itself, giving the impression of being alive.'
www.clairelindner.com

Ole Lislerud, b 1950, Greytown, South Africa; lives in Italy, Norway, China; Education: Rorkes Drift Art Centre, South Africa; University of Oslo (Law School); Oslo National Academy of the Arts, Norway.
'Ceramic tile can be seen as a skin on architecture. It can also be regarded as a metaphor for interpretation and visual perception. I etch calligraphy, writings and marks into the surface of porcelain tiles to create symbols and metaphors.'
www.olelislerud.com

Nicole Lister, b 1966, Sydney; lives in Sydney; Education: National Art School, Sydney; City Art Institute, Sydney.
'Food and consumerism, trade and cultural exchange, memory and identity are themes that underpin and unite my seemingly diverse body of work. Porcelain, with its historically high symbolic value, provides a vehicle for my conceptual interests.'
www.nicolelister.com.au

Andrew Livingstone, b 1967, Birmingham; lives in the UK; Education: Camberwell College of Arts, London; University of Ulster, Belfast.
Livingstone uses ceramic and varied media to examine the interface between traditional practice and contemporary expansion. His investigation challenges and reconfigures preconceptions within an acknowledged ceramic vernacular.
www.andrewlivingstone.com

Morten Løbner Espersen, b 1965, Aalborg, Denmark; lives in Copenhagen and Gothenburg; Education: Ecole supérieure des arts appliqués, Duperré, Paris; The Danish Design School, Copenhagen.
'I make proud, arrogantly pure shapes, a hand-built cylindrical vessel, cut straight at the top. The shape is calm and decisive, a form to be destroyed or brought alive, fusing shape, surface and colour.'
www.espersen.nu

Uwe Löllmann, b 1955, Germany; lives in Germany; Education: with Horst Kerstan. Löllmann has learned how to make visible the clay's inherent beauties. The artist thus appeals to that yearning for the natural, which is a deep innate quality of our humanity.

Richard Long, b 1945, Bristol; lives in Bristol; Education: West of England College of Art, Bristol; Central Saint Martins College of Art and Design, London.
Long's thought-provoking and influential work expresses humankind's relationship with the landscape, using photographs, maps, drawings and sculptures, constructed from natural materials that he gathers on his walks.
www.richardlong.org

Tyler Lotz, b 1975, Ketchikan, Alaska; lives in Bloomington; Education: New York State College of Ceramics at Alfred University, New York; Pennsylvania State University.
'I create ceramic sculpture informed by the human inclination to imitate, interpret and manipulate aspects of the physical universe. I am inspired by the "architecture of nature" and its inventive aptitude for survival and perpetuation.'
www.tylerlotz.com

Martin Lungley, b 1967, UK; lives in the UK; Education: Kent Institute of Art and Design, Rochester; Royal College of Art, London.
'I produce a range of thrown porcelain tableware and larger, more individual pieces. Larger individual pieces explore material qualities and the narrative of process. Fluidity, movement and softness are qualities I aim to explore in all my work.'

Ivar Mackay, b 1950; lives in France; Education: Harrow College of Art.
'I work within the classic tradition of wheel-thrown ceramics. Whilst I aim for control in my forms, I induce elemental or spontaneous qualities in my glazes. My work is a continuing process of study and experiment.'

Firth MacMillan, b 1964, USA; lives in the USA.
MacMillan's large-scale sculptural installations reflect her concern with society's state of malaise and fear as people struggle to navigate urban life.

Carol McNicholl, b 1943, Birmingham UK; lives in London; Education: Leeds Metropolitan University (formerly Leeds Polytechnic); Royal College of Art, London.
'In an age of information technology, making things by hand is supremely anachronistic. The capacity for making things has always seemed to be a defining human characteristic.'
www.bmgallery.co.uk

Sheryl McRoberts, b 1950, USA; lives in Plymouth, USA.
'My work is moving toward a less serious sensibility, appropriating imagery from still life painters and placing their paintings into a three-dimensional context. The still life painter creates the illusion of reality on a two-dimensional surface.'

Martin McWilliam, b 1957, Cape Town, South Africa; lives in Germany; Education: The Art Institute at Bournemouth; Dartington Pottery Training Workshop.
'What I am looking for with "clay and fire" lies in their own essential beauty and the play between them – a beauty subjective, difficult to define, control or repeat – something to do with chance coincidence.'

Heather Mae Erickson, b 1977, USA; lives in Philadelphia; Education: Cranbrook Academy of Art, Bloomfield Hills; The University of the Arts, Philadelphia.
'My work discusses the coupling of ideas of mass-produced industrial design with traditional craft techniques. I am interested in the implications found not only in the utilization of the ware, but also in the various methods of storing each piece.'
http://homepage.mac.com/heathermaeerickson/ceramicdesign/menu92.html

Jim Malone, b 1946, Sheffield; lives in the UK; Education: Camberwell College of Arts, London.
Malone's high-fired wheel-thrown stoneware is influenced by Korean, early Chinese and medieval English ceramics, which is not meant to shock or make radical statements. 'The work represents my own personal search for beauty which, in my opinion, is the only justification of any art.'

Kate Malone, b UK; lives in England/France; Education: University of the West of England, Bristol (formerly Bristol Polytechnic); Royal College of Art, London.
'I work with ceramics on large-scale projects for the public sector and on making "one of kind" pieces for collectors and collections. My work is inspired by the natural world and the magic of growth'
www.kmaloneceramics.clara.net

Janet Mansfield, b 1934, Sydney, Australia; Education: National Art School, Sydney.
'The ceramics I make are wood-fired and I specialise in salt and natural ash deposit glazing. My work is not the safe option, but there are others who understand the boundaries of the potter's art.'

Bodil Manz, b 1943, Copenhagen, Denmark; lives in North Seeland, Denmark; Education: School of Arts & Crafts, Copenhagen; Escuela de Diseno y Artesanias, Mexico; University of California, Berkeley.
Manz's egg-shell porcelain cylinders are slip-cast and decorated with geometrical patterns on both sides, applied with plain decals. Interior and exterior play off one another and merge to form a complex whole.

Alice Mara, b 1972, UK; lives in London; Education: University of Westminster, London; Royal College of Art, London.
'Using a process of photography and digital technology I produce images that depict the urban landscape. I often create scenes that are fantastical and I am drawn to buildings that have a nostalgic familiarity about them.'

Tony Marsh, b 1954, New York City; lives in California; Education: California State University, Long Beach; apprenticeship with Japanese potter Shimaoka, Mashiko, Japan; New York State College of Ceramics at Alfred University, New York.
'Working at pottery seems now to have served as a vehicle for great lessons that have stayed with me. I painfully taught myself to speak another language, which in turn allowed me to begin to see the world through the lens of another culture.'

Justin Marshall, b 1962, UK; lives in the UK. Marshall's research has involved investigating the integration of a range of digital technologies into 'traditional' art and craft practices to facilitate innovative work that challenges the relationship between maker and consumer.
www.autonomatic.org.uk

Gareth Mason, b 1965, Wales; lives in the UK; Education: Farnham School of Art.
'Some objects, works of literature, music, painting, or simply moments in time can be charged with life and significance. My work springs from a child-like relish of the stuff of

earth, an evolving well of experience and a love of mystery.'
www.garethmason.net

John Mason, b 1927, Madrid, Nebraska; lives in the USA; Education: Otis Art Institute, Los Angeles; Chouinard Art Institute, Los Angeles.
Mason is a pioneer in the revolution of clay from craft to fine art. In *ARTnews*, Suzanne Muchnic wrote, 'Mason has proved himself a master builder and sculptor who knows how to get the most out of a relatively simple three dimensional form.'

Naomi Mathews, b 1977; lives in the UK; Education: Royal College of Art, London.
'My work stems from an interest in the relationship between humans and the non-human animal, how we regard other species in relation to ourselves and whether this links to how humans judge and treat each other.'

Paul Mathieu, b 1954, Canada; lives in Canada; Education: University of California, Los Angeles; San Francisco State University, San Francisco; Banff Center, Alberta, Canada; L'Université du Québec à Montréal; North Staffordshire Polytechnic, Stoke-on-Trent; Alberta College of Art and Design, Calgary; Cégep du Vieux Montréal.

Ken Matsuzaki, b 1950, Japan; lives in Mashiko, Japan.
'Thinking about the pottery making, I begin with what and how I want to fire. I need suitable clay for that; high-refractory clay or low-refractory clay, plastic clay or non-plastic clay. I look for a clay of forceful personality.'

Angela Mellor, b Cheshire, England; lives in England; Education: Manchester University; University of East Anglia; University of Tasmania, Hobart.
'My work investigates the translucency of bone china and its potential for the transmission of light, reflecting landscapes, light and coastal environments. Textures of organic forms – rocks, driftwood, coral and shells – are recreated using bone china paper-slip.'
www.angelamellorgallery.com

Richard Milette, b 1960, Canada; lives in Canada.
'Most of the shapes and surfaces that I use are stereotypical or historical: I borrow them, I do not invent them. My works are ceramic representations of various ceramic containers. They are ceramic sculptures, not pots.'

Eva Mileusnic, b 1959; lives in Yorkshire, UK; Education: Bradford School of Art; Leeds College of Art & Design.
'My art practice is concerned with social and political issues related to the dispersion and movement of people within Europe and the

resulting consequences of loss of national identity and the construction of new identities and familial estrangement.'

Seung-Ki Min; lives Icheon, South Korea; Education: Kookmin University, Seoul.
Buncheong wares are not known for being especially innovative in form. It may be that the basic requirements for an ewer are that it should be functional and small. The ware can have unique elements that are in harmony and modern.
www.minseungki.com

Craig Mitchell, b 1967; lives in Edinburgh; Education: University of Sunderland; Royal College of Art, London; Bolton Institute of Higher Education.
'My work is informed by the constant unravelling of events in contemporary culture and universal themes such as love, loss and our roles in society. Nothing in my life escapes close scrutiny is collaged along with other collected imagery into my work.'
www.craigmitchellceramics.com

Mariana Monteagudo, b 1976, Caracas; lives in the USA; Education: Cranbrook Academy of Art, Bloomfield Hills; Emily Carr Institute of Art and Design, Vancouver.
'I aim to create a race of hybrid characters that represent combinations of different cultural manifestations, from the ancestral and mysterious to the most current and derivative of mass popular culture.'
www.marianamonteagudo.net

Tony Moore, b 1948, USA; lives in the USA; Education: Yale University, New Haven; University of South Wales, Wales; School of Art and Design, University of Wales Institute, Cardiff.
'My work is concerned with the relationship of humanity and nature. I conceive of an expanded concept of "Nature" as embodying all existence, both the seen and unseen, socio-political events, daily occurrences, as well as private intuitions.'
www.TonyMooreArt.com

Kristen Morgin, b 1968, Brunswick, Georgia; lives in Los Angeles, California; Education: California State University; New York State College of Ceramics at Alfred University, New York.
Working with unfired clay, Morgin can, as if by magic, create facsimiles of objects found in both nature and culture. Whether they are teacups or carousel horses, her works have the patina of great age and are fractured into many pieces.

Anne Helen Mydland, b 1971, Norway; lives in Bergen, Norway.
In Mydland's work many themes conjoin. In *Still Life*, which consists of a staged setting – a heap of cups and plates from diverse sets of

china – a series of eighty slides is projected, each showing scenes from family gatherings.

Ron Nagle, b 1939, San Francisco; lives in the USA.
Nagle's diminutive sculptural work is colourful, ironic, and layered with texture and detail. This seminal Californian artist continues his fascination with intimately scaled, finely crafted objects.
www.franklloyd.com

Márta Nagy, b 1954, Hungary; Education: Hungarian Academy of Craft and Design, Pécs University.
The poetic credibility of Nagy's recent works results from a modest self-appraisal based on self-knowledge. Nagy believes that humanity is moving in one direction, and that it is moving towards something.

Barbara Nanning, b 1957, The Hague; lives in Amsterdam.
Nanning has developed ways of working in which wheel-thrown pieces serve as starting point to create complex pieces. She works in groups or families, her work in constant revolution, one set of forms giving way to the next one.

Hylton Nel, b 1941, N'Kana, Zambia; lives in South Africa; Education: Rhodes University, Grahamstown South Africa; Koninklijke Academie voor Schone Kunsten en de Hogere Instituten, Antwerp.
Nel describes himself as an 'artist-potter' which aptly refers to his interest in painted imagery as well as with form and function. His imagery ranges from penises to Madonnas, and from cats through to angels.

Anna Noel, b 1958, Swansea; lives in Wales; Education: Bath Academy of Art; Royal College of Art, London.
Noel's work is inspired by the mystery and dream world quality of myths and legends and the role animals play in them. She is interested in the way animals are used to symbolize human qualities and emotions.

Richard Notkin, b 1948, USA; lives in the USA; Education: Kansas City Art Institute; University of California, Los Angeles.
'We have stumbled into the 21st century with the technologies of "Star Wars" and the emotional maturity of cavemen. As André Malraux observed, "Art is a revolt against man's fate".'

Justin Novak, b 1962, Canada; lives in the USA.
'Because the tradition is rooted primarily in lyricism, cuteness, and nostalgia, the ceramic figurine has a remarkable potential to disorient or disrupt when it deviates from the established norm.'

Kati Nulpponen, b 1974, Finland; lives in Finland.
Nulpponen works primarily as a jeweller/sculptor using a wide variety of materials including ceramics.

John Nuttgens, b 1948, UK; lives in Somerset, UK; Education: Harrow Studio Pottery Course.
'My abiding interest as a potter has always been with the traditional elements of earth, fire, air and water, the elements by which we have traditionally measured and felt our world throughout the ages.'

Maria Nuutinen, b 1975, Lappeenranta, Finland; lives in Finland.
'I enjoy myself around objects. I prefer old and ordinary things rather than modern and new. I love flea markets – toothmarks, broken pieces, missing parts and fading colours are part of my life that keep my mind open and clear.'
www.norsu.info/eng_artists.html

Magdalene Odundo, b 1951, Kenya; lives in England; Education: Farnham School of Art; Royal College of Art, London.
'I know that clay has delighted and enchanted me so far, but I am also aware of the many occasions when this material has frustrated and angered me. I continue to try to create that ultimate elusive simple vessel that will hold magic for me.'

Virgil Ortiz, b 1969, Santa Fe, New Mexico; lives in the USA.
'Not to get pigeon-holed in my craft and to refrain from staying within the American Indian galleries and only doing American Indian Art shows is a priority. My main focus is to pave the road for the younger generation and show them they can break out of the norm.'

Matthias Ostermann, 1950–2009, Germany; lived in Montreal, Canada.
'My desire to combine drawing with clay surface led me to explore the brighter colour palette of low-fire maiolica (tin glaze), which is largely narrative and figurative, drawing on mythology, dreams, human relationships and dilemmas.'
www.matthiasostermann.com

Damian O'Sullivan, b 1969, England; lives in Rotterdam; Education: Royal College of Art, London.
'The design of medical prosthetics today has more in common with the hospital than the home. With this in mind I redesigned medical prosthesis using porcelain in the hope of arriving at more dignified solutions.'

Lawson Oyekan, b 1961, London; lives in the UK; Education: Central Saint Martins College of Art and Design, London; Royal College of Art, London.

Oyekan grew up in his parents' native Nigeria. In 1983 he returned to England. Whether in clay or in stone, Oyekan's sculptures link past to present and pulse with an animistic energy – 'fruitage, colouration, and dispersal of seeds as notable points of transformation'.

Pekka Paikkari, b 1960, Somero, Finland; lives in Finland; Education: Oriveden Opisto, Orivesi Institute; Craft and Design Academy, Kuopio, Finland; Turku Polytechnic, Finland; worked at Arabia Factory, Finland.
'For me human presence is the starting point of art. Clay is a flexible material for expression and as such contains the history of time. As an artist I construct a never-ending story.'
www.artarabia.fi

Satyendra Pakhalé, b India; lives in Amsterdam.
'I am interested in craftsmanship, citing the Japanese designer Issey Miyake. His unique creations, such as "pleats please" and "a-poc", have universal appeal. My aim is to create contemporary objects blending the old and the new.'
www.satyendra-pakhale.com

Abhay Pandit, b 1978, India; lives in India.
'Clay is the only material so plastic in nature that almost anything can be formed out of your hand. The sculptures are based on the fossils that I have seen in museums of leaves, tree trunks, fish skeletons and the pattern of water currents left by the sea.'

B. R. Pandit, b 1949, India; lives in India.
Pandit's mastery over the medium is just not about his creative depths, but more about his unending exploitation of the elements, the subtle play of hues. His unpretentious pots are informed by an enthusiasm to embrace universal ideas.

Sue Paraskeva, b 1971, UK; lives in England; Education: Middlesex University, London.
'I throw porcelain on a stick-driven momentum wheel, creating fine cylindrical forms. I cut some of these, removing the base and rejoining to form sculptures. Decorative marks are applied using wood ash slips, oxides and inlays.'
www.sueparaskeva.co.uk

Greg Payce, b 1956, USA; lives in the USA.
'The realm between the virtual and the real contains unique narrative possibility. The negative spaces between ceramic albarelli become strange, non-dimensional, yet oddly three-dimensional images. Archetypal relationships between human and vessel form cannot help but manifest themselves.'

Kaye Pemberton, b Australia; lives in Canberra, Australia; Education: Australian National University.

'In China I researched Chinese porcelain, which has influenced my current work in which enclosed forms are used as pillows for domestic tea ware. The process of throwing leads one further into investigating each form.'

Gustavo Pérez, b 1950, Mexico City; Education: School of Design and Art, Mexico.
Pérez makes vessels that are simple and symmetrical. Their elegance is due to the precision of the incised lines and other markings on the pots. Pure in form, they have significant structure and definition.

Rafa Perézi, b 1957, Spain; lives in Spain.

Grayson Perry, b 1962, Essex, UK; lives in London; Education: Braintree College of Further Education, Portsmouth University (formerly Portsmouth Polytechnic).
A Turner Prize winner, Perry is as well known as a transvestite as an artist. His ceramics are coiled built in classical vase/bottle forms and decorated with painted/incised/printed decoration addressing modern, often controversial themes.

William Plumptre, b Kent UK; lives in the UK; Education: Chelsea College of Art & Design, London (apprenticeship in Japan).
Plumptre's reduction-fired works use glazes created from local woods and stones. The muted colours and organic forms show the influence of the area in which he lives, while retaining their Japanese influence.

David Pottinger, b Dalby, Queensland; lives in Melbourne, Australia; Education: RMIT University, Melbourne.
Pottinger produces cylindrical or bowl-like forms with a patterned web of rhythmic line 'weavings' in muted tones that reveal a peppering of colour under close inspection and come alive under the spell of light.

Ken Price, b 1935, Los Angeles, California; lives in Venice, California and Taos, New Mexico; Education: New York State College of Ceramics at Alfred University, New York; Art Institute of California, Los Angeles; University of Southern California.

Sue Pryke, b 1966, Suffolk, UK; lives in the UK; Education: De Montfort University (formerly Leicester Polytechnic), Leicester; Royal College of Art, London.
Pryke, a designer of tableware and homeware products, works with a range of materials to create functional, balanced and desirable objects. She currently works with major manufacturers and retailers to design successful everyday products.

Jeanne Quinn; lives in the USA; Education: Oberlin College, Ohio; University of Washington, Seattle.

'The words decoration and decorum are rooted in the same Latin word, *decorus*: handsome and seemly. From this, decoration constructs the beautiful world in which we behave well. Graceful ornament calms me, making me realize the order of the world.'
www.jeannequinnstudio.com

Peder Rasmussen, b 1948, Naestved, Denmark; lives in Denmark; Education: apprenticeship with Herman A. Kähler, Istituto Statale per la Porcellana, Sesto Fiorentino; Accademia di Belle Arti, Florence.
'The vessel will probably be there for ever – the classic vase with engobe decoration under a transparent lead glaze. Although form is important, it is the multitude of insisting figurations that are my ever rummaging reason for starting off yet another vessel.'
www.pederrasmussen.dk

David Regan, b 1964, USA; lives in Missoula, Montana; Education: Rochester Institute of Technology, New York; New York State College of Ceramics at Alfred University, New York.
'Pottery interests me because it nourishes both body and spirit. It has a connection to everyday sustenance and can be a powerful reminder of simple, yet vital necessities.'

Aneta Regel Deleu, b 1976, Poland; lives in London; Education: University of Westminster, London; Royal College of Art, London.
'I create objects that exist neither in the natural nor in the manufactured world, but which, once brought into being, can reflect and transmit information and feelings about nature and my own existence.'
www.anetaregel.com

Nicholas Rena, b 1963, UK; lives in the UK; Education: Cambridge University; Royal College of Art, London.
Rena's austere and imposing vessels are underpinned by a modernist rationality. In his exploration of the formal possibilities of the vessel, he creates fine tensions between outer mass and inner volume.
www.bmgallery.co.uk

Lee Renninger, b 1951; lives in the USA; Education: University of Florida, Gainesville, Florida.
'Much of my work has evolved from a fascination with repeated patterns and multiple units. It is primarily ceramic based but often incorporates other media in an installation format – an alchemy that challenges some of the traditional uses of clay.'
www.leerenninger.com

Nick Renshaw, b 1967, Driffield, Yorkshire; lives in Amsterdam; Education: Sandberg Instituut, Amsterdam.
Renshaw's work generally includes large- and small-scale sculptures, each use techniques

from coil building to casting, a process he sees as one that creates 'tensions brought about by combining and contrasting organic and industrial ways of making.'

Petra Reynolds, b 1972, UK; lives in the UK; Education: School of Art and Design, University of Wales Institute, Cardiff.
Reynolds uses paper templates, deftly cut clay slabs bent and joined to form a wide range of domestic pots that include serving dishes, drinking beakers, jugs, vases and teapots once-fired with soda in wood-firing kilns.

Lucie Rie, 1902–1995, Austria; lived UK; Education: School of Applied Art, Vienna.
Worked with earthenware in Vienna, making decorative vases, beakers and bowls as well as teasets in a style greatly influenced by modernist architecture. In the UK she developed and refined her ideas in stoneware and porcelain, producing work that was part of the European modernist movement.

Patricia Rieger, b 1952, USA; lives in Portland, USA; Education: Goddard College, Vermont; New York State College of Ceramics at Alfred University, New York; University of North Carolina at Chapel Hill, North Carolina.
'There is an intentional poetic attitude in my art that allows me to work and to imagine with a sense of purpose. There is an attempt towards precision. Meaning is always ambiguous and metaphorical.'

Kristina Riska, b 1960, Helsinki, Finland; lives in Finland; Education: The University of Art and Design, Helsinki (apprenticeship at Arabia Factory, Helsinki).
'One of my very first memories is a shadow moving on a white wall. How the light comes into the material fascinates me. By cutting holes into the walls I can make the object transparent. I wish this silent concentration could be sensed in the object.'
www.norsu.info/eng_calendar.html

David Roberts, b 1947, Sheffield, UK; lives in the UK; Education: Bretton Hall College, Yorkshire.
'My vessel-orientated forms exhibit a concern with the volumetric qualities of hand-wrought pots together with a fascination for, and control over, surface markings arising from the firing processes to express meaning and define form.'
www.davidroberts-ceramics.com

Phil Rogers, b 1951, Newport, South Wales; lives in Wales; Education: Newport School of Art, Media and Design, Swansea College of Art, Swansea College of Education.
'My pieces are inspired by pots from different cultures – Korea, Germany and England and China, the magnificent wood-fired jars from Shigaraki and Bizen and early settler pottery from the east coast of the United States.'

Diego Romero, b 1964, USA; lives in the USA; Education: Institute of American Indian Arts (IAIA), Santa Fe; Otis College of Art and Design, Los Angeles.
Born into a family of traditional Cochiti painters, but raised in Berkeley, California, Romero's work is truly cross-cultural. His imagery has a distinct narrative and voice, a 'master satirist in fired clay'.

Duncan Ross, b 1943, UK; lives in the UK.
'My work is thrown and burnished using many layers of a fine terra-sigillata slip with resist and inlay decoration to develop a rich surface with a combination of form and pattern that would be integral to the clay. The challenge is in the relationship of form and pattern.'

Fritz Rossmann, b 1958, Cologne, Germany; lives in Germany; Education: apprenticeship at National School of Ceramics, Höhr-Grenzhausen.
'Tableware offers the opportunity to play with the possibilities and to exploit the characteristics that evolve as I work with clay. There will be always a future for craft-made tableware.'
www.keramikgruppe.de

Gunhild Rudjord, b 1961, Trondheim, Norway; lives in Denmark; Education: The Design School, Kolding, Denmark.
Rudjord moved to Denmark to train as a potter at Kunsthåndværkerskolen in Kanpur. Her ceramic works – large pots and drums – are carriers of a unique and personal expression, revealing a unique handling of material and process.

Anders Ruhwald, b 1974, Denmark; lives in London; Education: Bornholm, Denmark; Royal College of Art, London; University Center Rochester, Minnesota.
'I am interested in working with the "thingness" of the ceramic object. My sculptures mediate the domestic sphere – existing as an actual everyday item, and a commentary on that item.'

Karen Ryan, b UK; lives in England.
'I find it almost impossible to reconcile my love for design and making with the ever-increasing sense of greed, violence and suffering that confronts me daily. Love, fate, autobiography and politics are the starting point of my working process.'
www.bykarenryan.co.uk

Bretton Sage Binford, b 1980, Puerto Rico; lives in Portland, Oregon; Education: Alfred University, New York; Oregon College of Art and Craft, Portland.
'My creative investigations focus on the practice of human emotional growth. They encompass the broad spectrum of safety and risk presented to us through both internal and external stimuli.'
www.mudsharkstudios.org/brett.php

Antonia Salmon, b 1959, UK; lives in the UK; Education: Sheffield University; Harrow School of Art.
Salmon's works speak of a quiet dynamism. They draw the viewer into an abstract world that has visual references to ancient hand tools, sacred sites, small organic objects, rock formations and large landscapes.
www.antoniasalmon-ceramics.co.uk

Jane Sawyer, b 1959 Australia; lives in Australia.
Sawyer has created a language of form and colour that makes a virtue of humility. She trained at a traditional Japanese pottery and maintains a Japanese rigour in her work while breaking certain traditions attached to materials.
www.janesawyer.com.au

Adrian Saxe, b 1943, Glendale, California; lives in the USA; Education: California Institute of the Arts; Chouinard Art Institute, Los Angeles.
Peter Schjeldahl, critic for *The New Yorker*, has written 'Saxe is a virtuoso in sharp focus and at a screaming pitch, nothing if not overbearing. [He] makes of the collectibles trade an improbable site of reflection on civilization and its discontents.'
www.franklloyd.com

Dorothee Schellhorn, b 1947, Schaffhausen, Switzerland; Education: Kunstgewerbeschule, Zurich; Central Saint Martins College of Art and Design, London.
'My fascination with clay began in Barcelona with the mosaics of Antoni Gaudí in Park Güell and visits to the Museuo de Ceràmica. My assemblage-like vessels and plates became more colourful. Paul Cézanne: "Colour is the place where the mind and the universe meet."'

Jeff Schmuki, b 1969, USA; lives in the USA.
'I consider what may lie beyond the horizon in regard to landscape. My latest works are inspired by the interrelationships between cartography, the documentary, memory, geologic time and the natural/manmade environment.'
www.jeffschmuki.com

Paul Scott, b 1953, UK; lives in the UK; Education: St Martins College, Lancaster.
'Images have long been disseminated on ceramic forms commemorating celebrating and democratising. My work makes particular reference to that most English of traditions the printed blue and white genre.'
www.cumbrianblues.com

Zeita Scott, b 1974, Northern Ireland; lives in London; Education: University of Ulster, Belfast; Royal College of Art, London.
'The pieces are made to engage people. Through innovative and passionate use of both material and colour the work conveys a sense of robust playfulness; souvenirs of the repeatable and the unrepeatable.'
www.zeitascott.co.uk

Bonnie Seeman, b 1969; lives in the USA; Education: University of Miami, University of Massachusetts Dartmouth.
'I am interested in the utilitarian object and how it can be used as a means of narration. My work blends the macabre with the beautiful, which acts as a metaphor for the fragility and resiliency of life.'
www.bonnieseeman.com

Sarah-Jane Selwood, b 1969, UK; lives in Scotland; Education: Edinburgh College of Art.
'My work has an alchemy through both its physical transformation and its design concept; a perfect thrown form, the fluidity of the soft clay controlled and the proportions and ultimate character of the piece are defined.'

Mark Shapiro, b 1955, USA; lives in Worthington, USA; Education: Amherst College, Massachusetts.
'The town is sacked. Silver and gold, even bronze, are beaten into crude billets to be hauled off and melted. Houses burned; prisoners taken, or not. And in the wreckage: bones, stones, and pot-sherds.'
www.stonepoolpottery.com

Richard Shaw, b 1941, Hollywood, California; lives in the USA; Education: University of California, Davis; San Francisco Art Institute.
Shaw, a master of trompe-l'oeil sculpture, has used clay to re-create the mundane objects of everyday life, gathering them together into ceramic sculpture that has the power both to amuse and amaze.
www.franklloyd.com

Julie Shepherd, b 1956, Rockhampton, Australia; lives in Australia.
Shepherd specializes in fine polished porcelain with pierced or translucent decoration using bowl and sculptural forms. The outward appearance of the porcelain is of fragility, however the work has immense inner strength and durability.
www.julie.shepherd.weby.com.au

Alev Siesbye, b 1938, Turkey; lives in France.
Siesbye is a master of the reductive vessel. Her pots have an immediacy and a clarity of statement so it is easy to overlook that these are the result of an exacting process of evolution, converting a vessel to a work of art.

Linda Sikora, b 1960, USA; lives in the USA; Education: The Nova Scotia College of Art and Design, Halifax; University of Minnesota, Minneapolis.
'Jars and teapots are at the front of my recent inquiry. The teapot, more demanding of specific engineering particular to its function, and the jar, a generous canvas, its criteria of containment more permissive.'

Kim Simonsson, b 1974, Finland; lives in Finland; Education: University of Art and Design, Helsinki.
'I combine traditional ceramic art with popular culture phenomenon in my large ceramic sculptures. For me the unusual is interesting. Therefore I create my own strange world of characters that comment on everyday life and its weirdness.'
www.norsu.info/eng_artists.html

Bente Skjøttgaard, b 1961, Denmark; lives in Denmark.
In much the same manner as a runner or an existential philosopher, Skjøttgaard cultivates her material, which is clay overcoated with an application of glaze. She is 'inside' the clay in the sense that she is challenging herself every time she creates new work.

Richard Slee, b 1946, UK; lives in London; Education: Central Saint Martins College of Art and Design, London; Royal College of Art, London.
Slee finds inspiration in the diversity of ornamental ceramic traditions, from eighteenth-century Sèvres porcelain and nineteenth-century curios to more recent pottery knick-knacks. The works are frequently wry comments on social issues, either political or more broadly cultural.
www.bmgallery.co.uk

Olav Slingerland; lives in the Netherlands; Education: Design Academy Eindhoven.
At college Slingerland became interested in the possibilities of moulding in the ceramics production process. His pieces are intensely personal and reflect his cheerful character.

Caroline Slotte, b 1975, Helsinki, Finland; lives in Finland; Education: Bergen National Academy of the Arts, Norway; The Design School, Kolding, Denmark.
'Objects from the private sphere intrigue me. Second-hand items have a way of directing our gaze to the past, symbols of the life stories of those who used them. I explore the links and tensions between individuals, objects and the memories they evoke.'
www.norsu.info/eng_artists.html

Carolein Smit, b the Netherlands; lives in the Netherlands; Education: St Joost Academy, Breda.
Through her predisposition for experiment together with her own ingenuousness and uninhibitedness has led Smit to original, surprising ceramic animals, which emote a rare vulnerability.

Martin Smith, b 1950, UK; lives in London; Education: Ipswich School of Art; University of the West of England, Bristol (formerly Bristol Polytechnic); Royal College of Art, London.
Smith was described by Chris Dercon, the Director of the Museum Boijmans van Beunigen in Rotterdam, as 'the most abstract and geometrically orientated ceramist in England and possibly of our times'. Smith uses the formal limitations of the vessel to investigate different conditions of space.
www.bmgallery.co.uk

Inger Södergren, b 1941, Zambia; lives in Sweden; Education: Linköping University.
'By combining the slow, controlled hand-building and rapid smoke-fire, where the fire leaves its traces, I load the objects with energy. I explore the contrasts between tranquility and motion, uncertainty and security, boredom and total chaos.'
www.ingersodergren.com

Bodo Sperlein, b 1966, UK; lives in London; Education: Camberwell College of Arts, London.
Sperlein is concerned with the detrimental effects that dispensable, mass-produced items have on both design culture and the environment, his interest in luxury and collectable items ensures that ideas and functional items are available to future generations.
www.bodosperlein.com

Rupert Spira, b 1960, London; lives in the UK; Education: West Surrey College of Art and Design (apprenticeship with Michael Cardew).
Spira's fascination with ceramics was initially stimulated by a Michael Cardew retrospective exhibition. That led him to study historic ceramics – Song, Tang, Jomon, Shino, Oribe. 'What was it that made these pots so good, he asked himself, wherein lay their beauty?' (Kenji Kaneke)
www.rupertspira.com

Vipoo Srivilasa, b 1969, Bangkok, Thailand; lives in Australia; Education: University of Tasmania, Hobart; Monash University, Melbourne, Rangsit University, Thailand.
www.vipoo.com

Julian Stair, b 1955, UK; lives in London; Education: Camberwell College of Arts, London; Royal College of Art, London.
'Whereas much of my work is concerned with the manner of art's engagement with human activity and pottery's haptic qualities, the funerary ware that I am currently engaged in has a different relationship with the body.'

Jeremy Steward, b 1972, UK; lives in the UK; Education: Falmouth School of Art; School

of Art and Design, University of Wales Institute, Cardiff.
'I make kitchen, table and oven ware which fits comfortably into everyday use in the home. The pots, thrown on a momentum wheel, are decorated to provide movement. They are once-fired with soda in wood-firing kilns.'

Piet Stockmans, b 1940, Leopoldsburg, Belgium; lives in Belgium.
'Creation is the result of activity and not of thinking. It is activity that generates ideas which, themselves, give rise to other ones. It is a quest for simplicity, peace and physical well-being.'
www.pietstockmans.be/home.php

Jenny Stolzenberg, b 1953, USA; lives in London; Education: University of Westminster (formerly the Polytechnic of Central London).
'My interest as a ceramic artist is about translating humanitarian issues into clay. *Forgive and Do not Forget* is a series of installations consisting of many pairs of individually hand-built ceramic shoes inspired by my family history, a journey to Auschwitz and the writings of Primo Levi.'
www.jennystolzenbergceramics.com

Madhvi Subrahmanian, b 1962, Singapore; lives in Singapore; Education: Southern Methodist University, Dallas.
Subrahmanian trained as a functional potter in Pondicherry with Ray Meeker and Debora Smith. 'Most of my recent work is built by layering coil over coil, with the form spiraling upward in a meditative rhythm, which is quiet and slow.'

Goro Suzuki, b 1941, Toyota City, Aichi Prefecture, Japan; lives in the USA.
Suzuki has revitalized the aesthetics of classical Oribe ware. His most innovative technique, *yobitsugi* (patchwork), demonstrates his playful nature, and enables him to produce pieces larger than his kiln might otherwise accommodate.
www.franklloyd.com

Toshiko Takaezu, b 1922, Hawaii; lives in the USA; Education: University of Hawaii; Cranbrook Academy of Arts, Bloomfield Hills.
Takaezu absorbed a philosophy of irregularity and asymmetry drawing upon diverse artistic influences from Europe, Asia and the natural world, bridging her American, Hawaiian and Japanese background.

Akio Takamori, b 1950, Miyazaki, Japan; lives in the USA; Education: Musashino Art School; Kansas City Art Institute; Alfred University, New York.
'I like to draw. I construct figurative clay forms to draw on the surface, enjoying the correlation of the form, gravity and texture of the surface. Working with the clay gives me

the opportunity to build in two and three-dimensional images.'

Kaori Tatebayashi, b Japan 1972; lives in the UK.
'I make both functional and sculptural ceramics. For my sculpture, I use clay as a device to make fragments of time visible. I want to preserve the intimate and transient recollections of our lives and seal them in the clay.'
www.kaoriceramics.com

Louisa Taylor, b 1980, UK; lives in the UK; Education: Bath Spa University; Royal College of Art, London.
'My tableware can adapt and "multifunction" to suit contemporary living. The cup has been integrated with the saucer and therefore can stack on top of another. The small cream jug can function as a lid to the sugar pot to become a tidy set.'

Janice Tchalenko, b 1942, Rugby, Warwickshire, UK; lives in London; Education: Putney School of Art and Design; Harrow College of Art.
Tchalenko is best known for her success in translating decorative studio pottery into designs for batch and large-scale production. Influences range from the Bernard Palissy to the rich decorative traditions of Russia and Iran.

Yo Thom, b 1973, Tokyo, Japan; lives in London.
Thom started her studies in the UK. After the apprenticeship at Maze Hill Pottery, London, she established her own studio producing functional tableware with Gosu (indigo) glaze in an electric kiln, and one-off vessels with *shino* glaze in a wood-fired kiln.

Jim Thomson, b 1953, USA; lives in Canada.
'My current ceramics involve only a few visual elements. The incongruity of surface, shape and pattern may persuade the viewer to reconcile these objects as the expression of an active element of art and of craft.'
www.jimthomson.ca

Peter Ting, b 1959, Hong Kong; lives in the UK; Education: Farnham School of Art.
Ting set up his own company, Tingware, and worked for companies such as Thomas Goode and Asprey in the 1980s and 1990s. Ting is currently exploring porcelain in Jingdezhen and Blanc de Chine from Dehua injecting them with a contemporary twist.

Marit Tingleff, b 1954, Norway; lives in Norway; Education: College of Art and Design, Bergen, Norway.
'My first encounter with clay – the smell, the sensual, moist clay sliding pliantly between the fingers of the potter – was the reason for my choice of profession. It filled me with a deep

feeling of something fantastic, a feeling that is still with me.'

Anne Tophøj, b 1960, Århus, Denmark; lives in Denmark; Education: College of Applied Arts (Skolen for Brugskunst), Copenhagen; Pratt Institute, New York.
Tophøj examines concepts and offers alternative solutions such as in the Souvenix project which she did with Jobim Jochimsen. They created a series of souvenirs – often with humorous undertones – with obvious local connections.

Marie Torbensdatter Hermann, b 1979, Denmark; lives in London; Education: Royal College of Art, London.
'I explore the relationship between us and the object. The relationship between the singular and the multiple, how they chance when we move around them and how we place them in relation to ourselves.'

Xavier Toubes, b 1947, Coruña, Spain; lives in the USA; Education: Goldsmiths, University of London; Winchcombe Pottery; Alfred University, New York.
Toubes's constant and insistent search for a new language for ceramics does not stop him from incorporating elements of pop culture and, especially, cognitive and educational values into his pieces.

Jack Troy, b 1938, USA; lives in Huntingdon, Pennsylvania.
'Since 1962, when I made my first pot, working with clay has afforded me a way of life in which challenges and fulfillment are in good proportion. I have a sense of gaining on the unknowns of my art and craft.'

Vladimir Tsivin, b 1949, Leningrad; lives in St Petersburg; Education: V. Muchina Higher School of Arts and Crafts, St Petersburg.
Tsivin uses either porcelain or china clay for his simple sculptural pieces based upon a reinterpretation of figurative forms. The shape of the body is subtlety rather than explicitly expressed.

Ruthanne Tudball, b 1948, USA; lives in Norfolk, England. Education: University of Reading; Goldsmiths, University of London.
'Rhythms expressed as patterns in the landscape and seascape, the human form and the organic quality of clay inspire me. All my work is thrown and manipulated wet on the wheel to try to capture those rhythms.'

Annie Turner, b 1958, Kent, UK; lives in London; Education: University of the West of England, Bristol (formerly Bristol Polytechnic); Royal College of Art, London.
Turner's sculpture is imprinted with the river Deben's past and present, the cycles of nature and the interaction of

man – 'objects that trigger the memory', as much collective memory as personal recollection.

Clare Twomey, b 1968, UK; lives in London; Education: Edinburgh College of Art; Royal College of Art, London.
Twomey works with clay in large-scale installations, sculpture and site-specific works. The themes are influenced by observations of human interaction and political behaviour.
www.claretwomey.com

Kenji Uranishi, b 1973, Nara Prefecture, Japan; lives in Australia; Education: Nara College of Fine Arts.
'Delicately small teacups, lidded sugar boxes and milk jugs. Smooth surfaces interrupted by sparse incisions filled with soft colours. Collectively, they form a *tea ceremony* of a distinct kind, inspired by simple insights into everyday life.'
www.kamenendo.blogspot.com

Catherine Vanier, b 1943, Paris, France; lives in Bissy-sur-Fley, Saône-et-Loire, France; Education: Ecole des Arts Décoratifs, Geneva, Switzerland.
'In 1963, when visiting the Victoria and Albert Museum, I realized how important Islamic mediaeval ceramics were to me. Since then I have developed a real passion for drawing. My work has remained within the field of slipware for a long time.'

Kukuli Velarde, b 1962, Lima, Peru; lives in the USA; Education: Hunter College, New York.
'As a Peruvian artist with American citizenship I left Peru aware of its racial, social, cultural and economic climate. My cultural background is the sum of a continuous hybridization defined, redefined and tormented by the simultaneous influences of pre-Columbian, post-Colonial, and Republican eras.'

Prue Venables, b 1954, Australia; lives in Australia; Education: Royal College of Art, London.
'Making tableware presents the opportunity to make objects for use…that will be held in close contact with people. The hope of bringing some stillness and simple pleasure…to make an object that becomes important in the lives of others.'

Kathy Venter, b 1951, USA; lives in Canada; Education: Port Elizabeth School of Art and Design, Cape Province, South Africa.
'In the Immersion Series traditional material is combined with complete freedom of composition, altered viewing points, diminished force of gravity and an alternate elemental influence – that of water. Suspended by cables frees the

work from its traditional pedestal, form, mass and weight.'

Angela Verdon, b 1949, UK; lives in England; Education: Royal College of Art, London.
'My work – burnished bone china and porcelain – is concerned with exploring the passage of light through carved surface marks, creating images which are illuminated by glowing lines of light.'
www.angelaverdon.com

Tina Vlassopulos, b 1954, UK; lives in London.
Vlassopulos builds her containers by coiling, exploring the relationship between form, volume and contained space, seeking a constantly reinvented equilibrium. The forms are organic in nature, reminiscent of her Mediterranean homeland.
www.tinavlassopulos.com

Patricia Volk, b 1951, Belfast, Northern Ireland; lives in the UK; Education: Middlesex University, London (formerly Middlesex Polytechnic); Bath College of Higher Education.
'Heads have become an obsession in the search to create modern icons: whether flawed Heroes, outwardly noble and courageous but nevertheless a victim; or ambiguous Virgins, the symbol of perfection but also of female repression – of history and of now.'
www.patriciavolk.co.uk

Ane-Katrine von Bülow, b 1952, Denmark; lives in Denmark; Education: The Danish Design School, Copenhagen.
A feature in the work of von Bülow is the exploration of repeated pattern on subtly defined and geometrical porcelain vessels. The black-and-white graphic ornamentation makes a playful contrast to any organic shapes and colour.'

Wendy Walgate; lives in Toronto; Education: University of Manitoba, Winnipeg; Cranbrook Academy of Art, Bloomfield Hills; University of Toronto; George Brown College. Toronto.
Walgate's life-long love of colour reflects her Ukrainian heritage, where painted Easter eggs, colourful embroidery and the colour red are manifestations of a reverence for ornament.
www.walgate.com

Josie Walter, b 1954, UK; lives in England; Education: University College London, Leicester University, Chesterfield College; Staffordshire University.
'Qualities inherent in the materials are explored by pouring slips thinly to let the colour of the body through. The slip is also used very thickly and applied with a brush whilst the pot is rotating on the wheel to give a "wrapped" look.'
www.josiewalter.co.uk

Patti Warashina, b Washington, USA; lives in Seattle; Education: University of Washington, Seattle.
'These ceramic containers (or vase heads) were made in response to my personal passion for flowering plants. I am reminded also of an extended trip to Rome, and some of the warm impressions of women at the flower market in the Campo de Fiori.'
www.warashina.com

Sasha Wardell, b 1946, Negombo, Sri Lanka; lives in the UK; Education: Bath Academy of Art, Corsham; Ecole Nationale des Arts Décoratifs, Limoges; North Staffordshire Polytechnic, Stoke-on-Trent; Royal Doulton, Stoke-on-Trent.
'Bone china is a seductive material, possessing qualities of intense whiteness, translucency and strength. It is a "single-minded" clay, which forces the maker to work with clarity and precision.'

Rebecca Warren, b 1965, UK; lives in London; Education: Goldsmiths, University of London; Chelsea College of Art.
Warren's unfired clay sculptures, roughly two thirds life size 'project a sense of unleashed creativity, appearing to explode out of and merge back into the amorphous properties of the material.'

Thomas Weber, b 1958, Baden, Germany; lives in Ludwigsburg, Germany.
'My work has to do with people and so it has to do with me. They are metaphors for the interplay of proximity and distance between people. Allegories for the yearning for security and protection.'
www.skulptur-thomas-weber.de

Katy West, b 1977, Dublin, Ireland; lives in Glasgow, Scotland; Education: Glasgow School of Art, Royal College of Art, London.
'My practice is concerned with the re-contextualisation of existing generic objects, reinterpreting their form, and reinventing their function, devoid of nostalgia and workable within our culture today.'
www.katywest.co.uk

Andrew Wicks, b 1973, Harare, Zimbabwe; lives in England; Education: University of Brighton; Royal College of Art, London.
Wicks designs and hand makes porcelain ceramics. He produces a slip-cast range of functional tableware and, more recently, thrown pieces including large vessels and mugs with subtly tinted glazes in watery colours.

Pauline Wiertz, b 1955, Amsterdam; lives in France; Education: Rietveld Academie, Amsterdam.
Inspired by the passionate traveller/collector from previous centuries who would bring home exotic treasures and jewels, shells, rocks,

corals as animals, Wiertz combines such elements to create fantastical sculptural still-lifes.

Betsy Williams, b USA; lives in the USA; Education: apprenticeship at Karatsu, Saga Prefecture, Japan.
'An object is a time machine, a stasis engine, fusing past, present and potential futures. My objects are born out of my need to express myself through making, my practice rooted in the physical experience of my body in the world.'

Conor Wilson, b 1964, UK; lives in Bristol, UK; Education: School of Art and Design, University of Wales Institute, Cardiff; University of the West of England; South Nottingham College of Further Education.
Wilson makes objects for domestic spaces – to be lived with, handled, enjoyed and, perhaps, to disturb. Preoccupied with sex, religion, maleness and the tension between group and individual identities, his work is sensual and ambiguous.
www.conorwilson.co.uk

Carole Windham, b 1949, UK; lives in the UK; Education: Royal College of Art, London; Stoke-on-Trent College of Art; Manchester Metropolitan University.
'My work is rooted in the Pop Art movement of the 60s, and is inspired by the figurative mantelpiece ornaments, or flatbacks of the nineteenth-century Staffordshire potters. The sculptures comment on contemporary events and celebrities.'

Robert Winokur, b 1933, Brooklyn; lives in the USA; Education: Tyler School of Fine Art of Temple University, Philadelphia; New York State College of Ceramics at Alfred University, New York.
'Having been a potter for a long time it occurred to me that a house was a unique kind of container. To a child a house represents warmth, family, love, security and identity. For me it is a symbol of choice.'
www.robertwinokur.com

Petra Wolf, b 1957, Germany; lives in Germany; Education: Krefeld, Fachhochschule Niederrhein-Fachbereich, Design, Studiengang.
www.neuewolfkeramik.de

Henk Wolvers, b 1953, the Netherlands; lives in the Netherlands; Education: Academy of Arts, Enschede; Royal Academy of Art and Design, 's-Hertogenbosch.
Wolvers transforms porcelain into exceptional pieces of art. Important aspects are movement and transparency in combination with structures and variety of colours, continuously reinvented and reshaped to generate mystic pieces of art.
www.henkwolvers.com

Betty Woodman, b 1930, USA; lives in the USA and Italy; Education: Alfred University, New York.
'It makes good sense to use clay for pots, vases, pitchers, and platters, but I like to have things both ways. I make things that could be functional, but I really want them to be considered works of art.'

Takeshi Yasuda, b 1943, Tokyo, Japan; lives in the UK and China; Education: apprenticeship with Daisei-Gama Pottery, Mashiko.
'I like making functional pottery, not for moral or aesthetic reasons but because I love eating. I like cooking eating and making pots and they all go together.'

Kato Yasukage, b 1964, Japan; Education: Studied under Yamamoto Tôshû, Nagoya Arts University, Aichi Prefecture.
Yasukage represents the 14th generation in a historic lineage. Yasukage *chawan* (tea bowls) have great character and dignity, working in the Japanese Mino tradition.

Yuk Kan Yeung, b 1959, Hong Kong; lives in the Netherlands.
'My work is about a moment in time, memories from the past and the present living experiences. Different fragments and elements are often composed into one work. While poets use words to express their feelings, I use my colours and forms.'

Masamichi Yoshikawa, b 1946, Chigasaki City, Japan; lives in Japan; Education: The Japanese Design Academy.
'The Water of Life though ceramic art requires technical, scientific methods, the act of creation is for me an act of prayer. Throughout history, in literature, music, and philosophy, humanity has sought new ways to deepen the joy of living.'

Paul Young, b UK; lives in the UK; Education: Chesterfield Art College.
Young produces slip-glazed earthenware, either decorated dishes of modelled groups of figures. Much of the inspiration for his figure groups comes from the Pew Groups produced in the mid-eighteenth century in and around the Potteries, Stoke-on-Trent.

SELECTED ART GALLERIES AND MUSEUMS WITH COLLECTIONS OF CONTEMPORARY CERAMICS

AUSTRALIA
Powerhouse Museum
500 Harris Street Ultimo
Haymarket, Sydney, NSW 1238
Tel +61 2 9217 0111
www.phm.gov.au

Shepparton Art Gallery
Locked Bag 1000
Shepparton, Victoria 3632
Tel 03 5832 9861
www.sheppartonartgallery.com.au

AUSTRIA
Hafnerhaus
www.hafnerhaus.at

Kunsthistorisches Museum
Main Building
Maria Theresien-Platz
A-1010 Vienna
Tel. +43 1 525 24 0
www.khm.at

MAK
Österreichisches Museum für
angewandte Kunst/Gegenwartskunst
Stubenring 5, A-1010 Vienna
Tel +43 1 711 36 0
www.mak.at

CANADA
Burlington Art Centre
1333 Lakeshore Road at Brock
Burlington, Ontario L7S 1A9
Tel 905 632 7796
www.burlingtonartcentre.on.ca

George R. Gardiner Museum
of Ceramic Art
111 Queen's Park (at Museum
Subway Station)
Toronto, Ontario M5S 2C7
Tel 416 586 8080
www.gardinermuseum.on.ca

CHINA
FuLe International Ceramic
Art Museums
Fuping Pottery Art Village
Shaanxi
Tel 138 0913 6827
www.flicam.com

DENMARK
Museum of International Ceramic
Art – Denmark
Kongebrovej 42, 5500 Middelfart
Tel 6441 4798
www.grimmerhus.dk

The Royal Copenhagen Collection
Amagertory 6, 1160 Cophenhagen K.
Tel +45 381 4 9697
www.royalcopenhagen.com/service/
Museum.aspx

FRANCE
Musée des Arts Décoratifs
107 rue de Rivoli, 75001 Paris
Tel +33 (0) 1 44 55 57 50
www.lesartsdecoratifs.fr

Musée National Adrien Dubouché
8bis, place Winston Churchill
87000 Limoges
Tel +33 (0)556 33 08 50
www.musee-adriendubouche.fr/

Musée National de Céramique Sèvres
Place de la manufacture, 92310 Sèvres
Tel +33 (0)1 41 14 04 20
www.musee-ceramique-sevres.fr

GERMANY
Altonaer Museum für Kunst und
Kulturgeschichte
Museumstrasse 23 (Altona)
22765 Hamburg
Tel 040 428 135 3582
www.altonaermuseum.de

Deutsches Historisches Museum
Unter den Linden 2, 10117 Berlin
Tel +49 (0)30 20304 0
www.dhm.de

Deutsches Museum München
Museumsinsel 1, 80538 München
Tel 089 2179 1
www.deutsches-museum.de

Deutsches PorzellanMuseum
Freundschaft 2
95691 Hohenberg an der Eger
Tel +49 (0)9233 7722
www.porzellanikon.org

Grassi Museum für Angewandte
Kunst
Johannisplatz 5–11, 04103 Leipzig
Tel +49 (0)341 22 29 100
www.grassimuseum.de

Grossherzoglich-Hessische
Porzellansammlung
Prinz-George-Palais, Schlossgardenstr.
10, 64289 Darmstadt
Tel 06151 71 32 33
www.porzellanmuseum-darmstadt.de

Hetjens-Museum
Schulstrasse 4
40213 Düsseldorf
Tel +49 (0)211 89 94210
www.duesseldorf.de/hetjens

Internationales Keramik-museum
Waldsassener Kasten
Luitpoldstrasse 25, 92637 Weiden
Tel +49 (0)9 61 3 20 30
www.die-neue-sammlung.de/z/
weiden/blick/deindex.htm

Keramik-Museum Berlin (KMB)
Schustehrusstr. 13
10585 Berlin-Charlottenburg
Tel +49 30 9029 12 948
www.keramik-museum-berlin.de

Keramikmuseum Westerwald
Deutsche Sammlung für Historische
und Zeitgenössische Keramik
Lindenstraße 13
56203 Höhr-Grenzhausen
Tel 049 (0)26 24/94 60 10
www.keramikmuseum.de

Kunstgewerbemuseum
Herbert-von-Karajan-Str. 10
10785 Berlin-Tiergarten
Tel +49 (0)30 266
www.smb.museum

Münchner Stadtmuseum
St.-Jakobs-Platz 1, 80331 München
Tel 089 233 22370
www.stadtmuseum-online.de

Museum Burg Frankenberg
Bismarckstrasse 68, 52066 Aachen
Tel 0241 432 4410
www.burgfrankenberg.de

Museum Folkwang
Kahrstrasse 16, 45128 Essen
Tel. +49 (0)201 88 45 301
www.museum-folkwang.de/
wirkun.htm

Museum für Angewandte Kunst
An der Rechtschule, 50667 Cologne
Tel +49/221/221 23860 and 26714
www.museenkoeln.de/mak

Museum für Kunst und Gewerbe
Hamburg
Steintorplatz, 20099 Hamburg
Tel (040) 428 134 27 32
www.mkg-hamburg.de

Ofen-und Keramikmuseum Velten
Wilhelmstr. 32, 16727 Velten
Tel 03304 31 76 0
www.ofenmuseum-velten.de

Porzellansammlung
Zwinger, Sophienstrasse
01067 Dresden
Tel +49 (0)3 51/49 14 66 12
www.skd-dresden.de/en/museen/
porzellansammlung

Rheinische Keramik
Stiftung Keramion – Zentrum für
moderne + historische Keramik
Frechen, Bonnstraße 12
50226 Frechen
Tel 02234 69 76 90
www.rheinische-keramik.de

Schlossmuseum
9867 Gotha
Tel 03621 8234 14
www.stiftungfriedenstein.de

Tonbergbaumuseum Westerwald
Poststraße, Postfach 1132
56427 Siershahn
Tel 02623 951363
www.tonbergbaumuseum.de

Vitra Design Museum
Charles-Eames-Str. 1
79576 Weil am Rhein
Tel +49 (0)7621 702 3200/3590
www.design-museum.de

INDIA
Sanskriti Museum of Indian Terracotta
Anandgram, Mehrauli Gurgaon Road
New Delhi 110001
Tel 011 26501125

IRELAND
National Museum of Ireland
Collins Barracks
Benburb Street, Dublin 7
Tel +353 1 6777444
www.museum.ie

ITALY
International Museum of Ceramics
in Faenza
Via Campidori 2, 48018 Faenza
www.micfaenza.org

Museo della Ceramica
Palazzo De Fabris, 36055 Nove (VI)
Tel 0424 829807
www.ceramics.it/museo.nove

Museo Montelupo
Piazza Vittorio Veneto 8–10
50056 Montelupo, Fiorentino
Tel +39 0571 51352/51087
www.museomontelupo.it

JAPAN
The Japan Folk Crafts Museum
4–3–33 Komaba Meguro-ku
Tokyo 153–0041
Tel (81) 3 3467 4537
www.mingeikan.or.jp

Mashiko Museum of Ceramic Art
3021 Mashiko, Mashiko City
Haga-gun, Tochigi 321–4217
Tel 0285 72 7555
www.art-mashiko.jp

Museum of Modern Ceramic Art,
Gifu
4–2–5, Higashi-machi
Tajimi-city, Gifu, 507–0801
Tel +81 572 28 3100
www.cpm-gifu.jp

The National Museum of Modern Art
1–1 Kitanomaru-koen
Chiyoda-ku
Tokyo 102–8322
Tel 102 0091
www.momat.go.jp

Raku Museum
Aburanokoji Nakadachiuri Agaru
Kyoto 602–0923
Tel +81 (0)75 414 0304
www.raku-yaki.or.jp

KOREA
Incheon World Ceramic Center
World Ceramic Exposition
Foundation San 69–1
Gwan-go-dong
Icheon-shi, Gyeonggi-do 467–020
Tel +82 31 631 6513
www.wocef.com

National Museum of Contemporary
Art, Korea
427–701, San 58–4 (Gwangmyeong-
gil 209)
Makgye-dong, Gwacheon-si,
Gyeonggi-do
Tel +82 2 2188 6000
www.moca.go.kr

THE NETHERLANDS
Museums Boijmans Van Beuningen
Museumpark 18–20
3015 CX Rotterdam
Tel +31 (0)10 44 19 400
www.boijmans.nl/en

Rijksmuseum
The Masterpieces and Infocentre
(The New Rijksmuseum)
Jan Luijkenstraat 1, 1070 Amsterdam
Tel +31 (0)20 67 47 000
www.rijksmuseum.nl

SM's - Stedelijk Museum
's-Hertogenbosch
Magistratenlaan 100
5223 MB 's-Hertogenbosch
Tel. +31 73 6273680
www.museumhetkruithuis.nl

NORWAY
Nordenfjeldske
KunstindustriMuseum
Munkegaten 3–7
7013 Trondheim
Tel 73 80 89 50
www.nkim.museum.no

POLAND
Muzeum Ceramiki w Bolesławiec
ul. Mickiewicza 13ł
59–700 Bolesławiec
Tel +48 75 644 47 00
www.muzeum.boleslawiec.net

SPAIN
Museo de Cerámica Popular
Ctra. Nacional
43860 L'Ametlla de Mar
Tel 977 486 810
www.museuceramica-ametlla.com

Museu de Ceràmica
Palau Reial de Pedralbes
Av. Diagonal, 686, 08034 Barcelona
Tel 34 93 256 34 65
www.museuceramica.bcn.es

Museu del Càntir Argentona
Pl. de l'Esglesia, 9
08310 Argentona (Barcelona)
Tel +34 93 797 21 52
www.museucantir.org

SWEDEN
Rörstrand Museum
Fabriksgatan 4, 531 30 Lidköping
Tel +46 510 25080
www.rorstrand-museum.se

SWITZERLAND
Gewerbemuseum Winterthur
Kirchplatz 14,CH - 8400 Winterthur
Tel. +41 (0)52 267 51 36
www.gewerbemuseum.ch

UNITED KINGDOM
The Ashmolean Museum of Art and
Archaeology
Beaumont Street, Oxford OX1 2PH
Tel 01865 278000
www.ashmolean.org

Birmingham Museum & Art Gallery
Chamberlain Square
Birmingham B3 3DH
Tel 0121 303 2834
www.bmag.org.uk

The British Museum
Great Russell Street
London WC1B 3DG
Tel 020 7323 8299
www.britishmuseum.org

Fitzwilliam Museum
Trumpington Street
Cambridge CB2 1RB
Tel 01223 332900
www.fitzmuseum.cam.ac.uk

Manchester Art Gallery
Mosley Street, Manchester M2 3JL
Tel 0161 235 8888
www.manchestergalleries.org

National Museums of Scotland
(Royal Museum Craft Gallery and
National Museum of Scotland)
Chambers Street
Edinburgh EH1 1JF
Tel 0131 247 4422
www.nms.ac.uk

The Potteries Museum & Art Gallery
Bethesda Street
Hanley
Stoke-on-Trent ST1 3DW
Tel 01782 232323
www.stoke.gov.uk

Sainsbury Centre for Visual Arts
University of East Anglia
Norwich NR4 7TJ
Tel 0160 359 3199
www.scva.org.uk

University of Wales Aberystwyth
The Ceramic Collection and Archive
School of Art
Buarth
Aberystwyth SY23 1NG
www.aber.ac.uk/ceramics/index.htm

Victoria and Albert Museum
Cromwell Road
London SW7 2RL
Tel 020 7942 2000
www.vam.ac.uk

UNITED STATES OF AMERICA
American Museum of Ceramic Art
(AMOCA)
340 S. Garey Avenue
Pomona, CA 91766
Tel 909 865 3146 or 3147
www.ceramicmuseum.org

Buchsbaum Gallery of Southwestern
Pottery
Museum of Indian Arts &
Culture
710 Camino Lejo off Old Santa
Fe Trail
Santa Fe, NM 87504
Tel 505 476 1250
www.indianartsandculture.org

Crocker Art Museum
216 O Street
Sacramento, CA 95814
Tel 916 808 7000
www.crockerartmuseum.org

Everson Museum of Art
401 Harrison Street
Syracuse, NY 13202
Tel 315 474 6064
www.everson.org

The Metropolitan Museum of Art
1000 Fifth Avenue at 82nd Street
New York, NY 10028–0198
Tel 212 535 7710
www.metmuseum.org

Mint Museum of Craft and Design
220 North Tryon Street
Charlotte, NC 28202
Tel 704 337 2000
www.mintmuseum.org

Museum of Contemporary Craft
724 Northwest Davis Street
Portland, OR 97209
Tel 503 223 2654
www.contemporarycrafts.org

The Museum of Modern Art
11 West 53 Street
between Fifth and Sixth avenues
New York, NY 10019–5497
Tel 212 708 9400
www.moma.org

National Ceramic Museum &
Heritage Center
7327 Ceramic Road NE
Roseville, OH 43777
Tel 740 697 7021
www.ceramiccenter.info

National Czech & Slovak Museum
& Library
30 16th Avenue SW
Cedar Rapids, IA 52404
Tel 319 362 8500
www.ncsml.org

Penn Museum
University of Pennsylvania Museum
of Archaeology and Anthropology
3260 South Street
Philadelphia, PA 19104
Tel 215 898 4000
www.upenn.edu/museum

The Schein-Joseph International
Museum of Ceramic Art
Alfred University Campus
Binns-Merrill Hall
Pine Street
Alfred, NY 14802
Tel 607 871 2421
ceramicsmuseum.alfred.edu

The following website lists many
museums with collections of
contemporary ceramics:
www.ceramic-link.de/Seiten/ICD-
Museums.htm

BIBLIOGRAPHY

Adamson, Glenn, *Thinking Through Craft*, Berg, Oxford and New York, 2007
Alfoldy, Sandra (ed.), *NeoCraft: Modernity and the Crafts*, The Nova Scotia College of Art and Design Press, Halifax, 2007
Britton, Alison and Martina Margetts (eds), *The Raw and the Cooked: New Work in Clay in Britain*, The Museum of Modern Art, Oxford, 1993
Cecula, Marek with Dagmara Kopala, *Object Factory: The Art of Industrial Ceramics*, Gardiner Museum, Toronto, 2008
Cho, Chung Hyun, curator, *Tradition Transformed: Contemporary Korean Ceramics*, exhibition catalogue, International Arts and Artists/The Korea Foundation, Seoul, 2006
Clark, Garth (ed.), *Ceramic Millennium: Critical Writings on Ceramic History, Theory, and Art*, The Nova Scotia College of Art and Design Press, Halifax, 2006
Cochrane, Grace (ed.), *Smart Works: Design and the Handmade*, Powerhouse Publishing, Sydney, Australia, 2007
Cooper, Emmanuel, *Ten Thousand Years of Pottery*, British Museum Press, London, 2000

Danius, Sara and Patrik Johansson, *Voices/Röster: Contemporary Ceramic Art from Sweden*, Carlssons Bokförlag, Stockholm 2007
de Waal, Edmund, *Twentieth Century Ceramics*, Thames and Hudson, London and New York, 2003
Dietz, Ulysses Grant, *Great Pots: Contemporary Ceramics from Function to Fantasy*, The Newark Museum and Guild Publishing, Madison, Wisconsin, 2003
Gaspar, Monica and Love Jönsson, *Place(s): Papers and Exhibition 2006*, Think Tank, 2006
Groom, Simon (ed.), *A Secret History of Clay: From Gauguin to Gormley*, Tate Publishing, London, 2004
Hanaor, Cigalle, *Breaking the Mould: New Approaches to Ceramics*, Black Dog Publishing, London 2007
Joris, Yvonne (ed.), *Functional Glamour: Utility in Contemporary American Ceramics*, Museum Het Kruithuis, 's-Hertogenbosch, 1987
Klanten, Robert, Sven Ehmann and Sabrina Grill (eds), *Fragiles: Porcelain, Glass and Ceramics*, Gestalten, Berlin, 2008
Miller, Tressa R. and Trevor Norris, *Material Affinities: To Clay and Back*,

USC Fisher Gallery, University of Southern California, 2007
Naturel, Michele, *Céramique Contemporaine: Un Autre Regard*, Châteauroux 14e Biennale Internationale, Musées de Châteauroux, Châteauroux, 2007
NCECA 40th Annual Conference, *Explorations and Navigations: The Resonance of Place*, National Council on Education for the Ceramic Arts, NCECA Journal, vol. XXVII
Peltier, Yves (ed.), *Céramique Contemporaine Biennale Internationale*, Somogy Editions d'Art, Vallauris, 2006
Reijnders, Anton, *The Ceramic Process: A Manual and Source of Inspiration for Ceramic Art and Design*, European Ceramic Workcentre, A & C Black, London and University of Pennsylvania Press, Philadelphia, 2005
Risatti, Howard, *A Theory of Craft: Function and Aesthetic Expression*, University of North Carolina Press, Chapel Hill, 2007
Tarkasis, Kostas, *Clay in Art International Yearbook 06*, Athens, Greece, 2006
——, *Clay Art International Yearbook 06/07*, Athens, Greece, 2007

——, *Clay in Art International Yearbook 07*, Athens, Greece, 2007
Ting, Peter (curator), *To Hold*, exhibition catalogue, Brantwood Publishing, London, 2006

Magazines and Journals
Ceramic Art, Taiwan
Ceramic Review: The International Magazine of Ceramic Art and Craft, www.ceramicreview.com
Ceramics Art Monthly, Seoul, Korea
Ceramics: Art and Perception, www.ceramicart.com.au
Ceramics Monthly, www.ceramicsmonthly.org
Keramik Magazin, www.keramikmagazin.de
Keramik Magazin Europa, www.kunstwelt-online.de
Neue Keramik, www.neue-keramik.de
Norske Kunsthåndverkere, www.kunsthandverk.no
Revista Internacional Ceramica, www.revistaceramica.com
La Révue de la Céramique et du Verre, www.revue-ceramique-verre.com

ACKNOWLEDGMENTS

Assembling the images and biographical information for a book of this size has relied on the generosity and help of many individuals. Artists and galleries have often gone far beyond the realm of duty to help and I am forever in their debt. I should like to mention in particular Yo Thom, who patiently and diligently helped with the extensive research required for a book of this size. Also to David Horbury, who read the text and made helpful suggestions.

Thanks to Arario Gallery Beijing; Ben Eldridge; Barrett Marsden Gallery, UK; Contemporary Ceramics, UK; Ferrin Gallery, USA; Frank Lloyd Gallery, USA; Galerie Besson, UK; Jam Factory, Australia; Natasha Crawley; Prime Gallery, USA; Tae-Lim Rea; and to all the individual artists and galleries who contributed information and images.

PHOTOGRAPHIC CREDITS

The following abbreviations have been used: a above; b below; c centre; l left; r right; t top

8 Courtesy Lisson Gallery and the artists; 9 © Y Mayer/CSC 2004; 16b Photo Terence Bogue; 17l photo Grant Hancock Associates Pty Ltd; 19 Courtesy Michael Stevenson, Cape Town, South Africa; 20a photo Sara Morris; 26l photo Erik and Petra Hesmerg, Sneek; 26r Michael Harvey Photography; 27a, 27b photo Grant Hancock Associates Pty Ltd; 28a, 28b Michael Harvey Photography; 29 Howard McAlpine Photography; 35ar, 35b photo Yo Thom; 36a Courtesy Galerie Besson (photo Terence Bogue); 42l, 42ar, 42br Courtesy of Michael Stevenson, Cape Town, South Africa; 46b photo Fotostudio Articus and Röttgen; 49a photo Terence Bogue; 50a photo ANU Photography; 51 photo Julie Shepherd; 55b Courtesy Galleri Nørby (photo Ole Akhøj); 56–57 photo Ole Alchøj; 58l photo Abbas Nazari; 59r Copyright Mike Abrahams; 64l Copyright of Jonathan Keenan Photography; 65b photo Shannon Tofts; 66l, 66r Peer van der Kruis; 67ar photo JFF; 68 Private collection, courtesy Garth Clark Gallery (photo John White); 69l Collection of Sonny and Gloria Kamm, courtesy Garth Clark Gallery (photo Anthony Cunha); 69r Private collection, courtesy Garth Clark Gallery (photo John White); 73br photo Sussie Ahlbury; 77 Copyright of Jonathan Keenan Photography; 75a, 75b photo Peer van der Kruis; 79l, 79r Courtesy Barrett Marsden Gallery; 81al, 81ar photo Lars Henrik Mardahl; 82l, 82r Courtesy Barrett Marsden Gallery; 83ar photo copyright Adrian Lambert, Acorn Photography

Agency; 83l photo Robert Frith, Acorn Photos Perth; 84al Courtesy Galerie Besson (photo Alan Tabor); 84ar photo Patrick Muller; 84bl Courtesy of Galerie Besson (photo Alan Tabor); 84br photo Patrick Muller; 86l, 86br Courtesy Galerie Besson (photo Alan Tabor); 90l, 90r Courtesy Clare Beck at Adrian Sassoon; 94l photo Ilan Amichay; 96a, 96b photo Grant Hancock Associates Pty Ltd; 98bl photo Stephen Dee; 99 all Courtesy Gadfly Gallery (photo Grant Hancock Associates Pty Ltd); 100 all photo Sin-Ying Ho; 102a photo Mark Lawrence; 103l photo Andrew Barcham; 103r photo Agnieszka Kolman; 104al photo Matthew Collins; 104bl photo Abbas Nazari; 105a photo Ole Alchøj; 106b photo Tsuyoshi Inui; 109 both photo Ilan Amihai; 111l Collection of artist, courtesy Anthony Slayter-Ralph Fine Art; 111ar Collection Hugh J Freud, courtesy Anthony Slayter-Ralph Fine Art; 111br Collection Frankel Foundation for Art, courtesy Anthony Slayter-Ralph Fine Art; 115al Courtesy Galleria Norsu (photo © Rauno Träskelin, 2007); 115ar, 115b photo Joachim Riches, Copyright Riches Photographie & Werberg Bremen; 116al Courtesy Galleria Norsu (photo © Rauno Träskelin, 2007); 117bl and 117r Courtesy Frank Lloyd Gallery (photo Anthony Cuñha); 118al photo Shannon Tofts; 119l Courtesy Barrett Marsden Gallery; 121al photo Ben Ramos, 2006, All rights reserved; 122, 123ar, 123bl photo copyright Roger de la Harpe; 126 photo Jin Xiang Dong; 127a, 127l photo Sebastian Zimmer; 128l photo Patrick Tergenza Photography; 129 Courtesy Lisson Gallery; 130 photo Richard Ansett;

131l Courtesy Barrett Marsden Gallery; 131r photo Michael Harvey; 132 photo Richard Milette; 135b Courtesy Frank Lloyd Gallery (photo Tony Cuñha); 138a photo Sebastian Zimmer; 138b photo Michael Harvey; 139br photo Adrian Lambert, Acorn Photo Agency, 2007; 139bl Courtesy Barrett Marsden Gallery; 140br photo David Binns; 142l, 142r photo Matthew Donaldson; 145l photo Sussie Ahlburg; 146r Courtesy Galerie Besson (photo Alan Tabor); 147al, 147bl Courtesy Galerie Besson (photo Cece Ariman); 149al photo Jin Xiang Dong; 152l Courtesy Lisson Gallery; 154a, 154b Courtesy Frank Lloyd Gallery (photo Tony Cuñha); 155l, 155r photo Sylvain Deleu; 156al, 156bl photo Patrick Tergenza Photography; 157a The Egyptian Academy of Arts, Rome, Italy; 159al, 159bl Courtesy Barrett Marsden (photo Peter Cattrell); 160br photo Richard Milette; 164l photo Gert Germeraad; 173bl Private Collection; 179b Courtesy Frank Lloyd Gallery (photo Tony Cuñha); 181l, 181r photo Shannon Tofts; 182bl, 182r photo Richard Milette; 183al Courtesy Gallery Norsu; 183bl, 183r Courtesy Frank Lloyd Gallery (photo Tony Cuñha); 187al photo Terhi Korhonen; 189l photo Paul Tucker; 195l, 195r Courtesy Barrett Marsden (photo Phil Sayer); 196a Courtesy Koppe Gallery, Copenhagen, Denmark; 198l, 198r Courtesy Frank Lloyd Gallery (photo Tony Cuñha); 202l photo Kalle Kataila; 202r photo Kim Simonsson; 203l, 203r Courtesy Barrett Marsden Gallery; 204r photo Carolein Smit; 205a photo Andrew Barcham; 205b photo Terence Bogue; 206a, 206br Courtesy Frank Lloyd Gallery (photo Tony Cuñha);

207b, 208a, 208b Courtesy Barrett Marsden Gallery; 209 photo Akio Takamori; 210b photo Siri Berrefjord; 211l, 211r Courtesy Frank Lloyd Gallery. (photo Tony Cuñha); 218a, 218b photo Carlos Azevedo; 221l, 221r Courtesy of LA Louver, Venice, CA; 225l photo Andy Paradise; 226l Permanent Collection, Center for Disease Control and Prevention, Atlanta, GA (photo Jim Gathamy); 227l Galerie De Witte Voet, Amsterdam; 230l photo S. Wagstaff; 233l Courtesy Madame Lillies, London; 235l photo Dan Prince; 235r photo Jason Ingram; 236bl Courtesy Galleria Norsu; 237 Garth Clark Gallery; 238a Installation at Kenyon College, Gambier, OH (photo Dan Younger); 242a, 242b Courtesy Ronald Feldman Fine Arts, New York (photo John Lamka); 251bl Conor L photo; 253 Architecture-based ceramic work, Miral Concert Hall, Seoul, Korea; 254r photo Red Mansion Foundation; 258l photo Adrian Newman; 258r photo Steve Yates; 262b Nymphenburg Porcelain Factory; 264a Arabia Ceramic Factory; 265a photo Michel Brouet; 269 photo Peter Abrahams; 270l Nymphenburg Porcelain Factory; 271c Arabia Ceramic Factory; 272al photo courtesy of Habitat; 272bl photo *Ceramic Review*; 274br photo Terence Bogue; 282bl (c) Collection Brighton Museum and Art Gallery; 283l photo Michel Brouet

INDEX